On the Margins of Modernism

T0386737

Edinburgh East Asian Studies Series
Series Editors: Natascha Gentz, Urs Matthias Zachmann and
David Der-Wei Wang

Covering language, literature, history and society, this series of academic
monographs and reference volumes brings together scholars of East Asia to
address crucial topics in East Asian Studies. The series embraces a broad
scope of approaches and welcomes volumes that address topics such as
regional patterns of cooperation and social, political, cultural implications of
interregional collaborations, as well as volumes on individual regional themes
across the spectrum of East Asian Studies. With its critical analysis of central
issues in East Asia, and its remit of contributing to a wider understanding
of East Asian countries' international impact, the series will be crucial
to understand the shifting patterns in this region within an increasingly
globalised world.

Series Editors
Professor Natascha Gentz is Chair of Chinese Studies, Director of the
   Confucius Institute for Scotland and Dean International (China) at the
   University of Edinburgh.
Professor Urs Matthias Zachmann is Professor of History and Culture
   of Modern Japan at the Institute of East Asian Studies, Freie Universität
   Berlin.
Professor David Der-Wei Wang is the Edward C. Henderson Professor of
   Chinese Literature at the Fairbank Center for Chinese Studies at Harvard
   University.

Editorial Board
Professor Marion Eggert, Bochum University
Professor Joshua A. Fogel, York University, Toronto
Professor Andrew Gordon, Harvard University
Professor Rikki Kersten, Murdoch University
Dr Seung-Young Kim, University of Sheffield
Dr Hui Wang, Tsinghua University, Beijing

Titles available in the series:
*Asia after Versailles: Asian Perspectives on the Paris Peace Conference and the
   Interwar Order 1919–1933*
Urs Matthias Zachmann (Editor)

*On the Margins of Modernism: Xu Xu, Wumingshi and Popular Chinese
   Literature in the 1940s*
Christopher Rosenmeier

On the Margins of Modernism

Xu Xu, Wumingshi and Popular Chinese
Literature in the 1940s

Christopher Rosenmeier

EDINBURGH
University Press

Edinburgh University Press is one of the leading university presses in the UK. We publish academic books and journals in our selected subject areas across the humanities and social sciences, combining cutting-edge scholarship with high editorial and production values to produce academic works of lasting importance. For more information visit our website: edinburghuniversitypress.com

© Christopher Rosenmeier, 2017, 2019

Edinburgh University Press Ltd
The Tun – Holyrood Road
12(2f) Jackson's Entry
Edinburgh EH8 8PJ

First published in hardback by Edinburgh University Press 2017

Typeset in 10/12 Ehrhardt by
Servis Filmsetting Ltd, Stockport, Cheshire
and printed and bound in Great Britain by
CPI Group (UK) Ltd, Croydon CR0 4YY

A CIP record for this book is available from the British Library

ISBN 978 0 7486 9636 9 (hardback)
ISBN 978 1 4744 4447 7 (paperback)
ISBN 978 0 7486 9637 6 (webready PDF)
ISBN 978 1 4744 2646 6 (epub)

The right of Christopher Rosenmeier to be identified as the author of this work has been asserted in accordance with the Copyright, Designs and Patents Act 1988, and the Copyright and Related Rights Regulations 2003 (SI No. 2498).

Contents

Acknowledgements

This book has taken me far too long to complete, and innumerable debts of gratitude – too many to list in a reasonable manner – have been incurred over the years. My greatest debt is to Michel Hockx, who supervised the doctoral thesis at SOAS upon which this book builds. In addition to his invaluable guidance, he helped to secure financial support without which I would not have been able to embark on a career studying Chinese literature. Margaret Hillenbrand, Henry Zhao, Vibeke Børdahl and Susan Daruvala were all very helpful in providing useful suggestions early on. I am also grateful to the exceedingly competent and patient staff of Edinburgh University Press, my anonymous readers, the Edinburgh East Asian Studies series editors – Natascha Gentz, Urs Matthias Zachmann and David Der-Wei Wang – who, along with my colleagues at the University of Edinburgh, have helped me in many ways over the years, and, finally, my students, a source of inspiration and knowledge more often than I let them know.

Chapter 1

Introduction

The Japanese invasion of China proper on 7 July 1937 heralded yet another period in a long chain of devastation, suffering and internal displacement. Viewed from the perspective of literary history, however, the widespread mayhem and chaos of war became a catalyst for important developments as the established Chinese cultural field was broken up and fragmented. Old hierarchies were challenged and overthrown, and some authors and intellectuals took advantage of the upheaval to experiment with novel ways to cross what had formerly been sharp boundaries – between the elite and the popular, romanticism and modernism, tradition and modernity. With a focus on popular Chinese literature of the Second Sino-Japanese War (1937–1945), the present study is an examination of some of these experiments.

Xu Xu 徐訏 (1908–1980) and Wumingshi 無名氏 (1917–2002) were among the most widely read authors throughout the period, and they remained popular for many years afterwards. Both of them wrote short stories and novels that counted among the bestselling works of the time, which at first glance appear to be simple love stories and romances. Closer reading nonetheless makes it clear that these writings defy such easy categorisation, touching upon numerous more complex issues, including utopian fantasies, nationalism, sexuality and questions of identity. Some of these short stories and novels use distinctive narrative techniques bordering on modernist experimentation, echoing the Shanghai modernist writers of the early 1930s, most notably Shi Zhecun 施蟄存 (1905–2003) and Mu Shiying 穆時英 (1912–1940). On the whole, while Xu Xu's and Wumingshi's works remain melodramatic tales of passionate love and exotic adventure, at the same time they also demonstrate the diversity and sophistication that flourished in the popular wartime literature of the 1940s.

Many of China's literary experiments and new developments during this period stem from what Edward M. Gunn calls the 'literature of disengagement', works produced by authors who refrained from engaging in resistance and national or social activism.[1] A few of these writers remain widely known today, in particular Zhang Ailing 張愛玲 (or Eileen Chang, 1920–1995) and Qian Zhongshu 錢鐘書 (1910–1998), who both worked in occupied Shanghai. The continued popularity of their fiction may be attributable to some extent to its not being overly concerned with the details of the political ideology and the national events of the time. Other popular Chinese authors of the 1940s have been less fortunate, and most of them are no longer remembered today.

Xu Xu and Wumingshi similarly stayed outside politics, emerging in the late 1930s as two of the most widely popular authors of the wartime period. Regrettably, they have now been largely forgotten, and this study attempts to remedy that situation. Both writers played important roles in China's wartime literary field, publishing works in Chongqing and elsewhere in the early 1940s. Much like the better-known authors who worked in Shanghai, Xu Xu and Wumingshi sought new ways to straddle the divide between the elite and the popular in their fiction, and succeeded in producing material with wide appeal that managed to offer some literary depth as well.

After the fall of Shanghai to the Japanese in 1937, a great number of Chinese authors and intellectuals left the city for the free areas in the hinterland, Wumingshi and Xu Xu among them. Wumingshi first moved to Hankou and later relocated to Chongqing to take up journalism.[2] Xu Xu 徐訏 remained in Shanghai until 1941 before moving inland. After a stint as a university lecturer in Chongqing, he took up journalism as well, including a period as a foreign correspondent in the United States.[3]

Both writers produced hugely successful bestsellers. Xu Xu's novella *Ghostly Love* (*Gui lian* 鬼戀) from 1937 was a roaring success, and his novel *The Rustling Wind* (*Feng xiaoxiao* 風蕭蕭), a love story-cum-spy thriller, sold so well in 1943 that some publishers called it 'the year of Xu Xu' ('*Xu Xu nian*' 徐訏年).[4] His novels feature a full panoply of popular stereotypes, including pirates, prostitutes, corrupt officials, female assassins and passionate lovers. Wumingshi's two novels, *North Pole Landscape Painting* (*Beiji fengqing hua* 北極風情畫) and *The Woman in the Tower* (*Tali de nüren* 塔裡的女人), from 1943 and 1944, respectively, were also among the bestselling works of the wartime period. Yet despite their fiction containing a good deal of narrative experimentation, they are still principally romantic tales of love, jealousy and escapist fantasy.

The works of these two authors are notable in terms of style, navigating the border between romanticism and modernism. Aspects of both are found in their writings, exemplifying the fluidity of such classifications in the literature of the day. While Xu and Wumingshi stayed outside the political factions and groups that engulfed many other intellectuals and writers at the time, the echoes of earlier modernist styles and tropes marked their political independence and served to lend their novels and short stories an air of sophistication. In this study, their fiction will be analysed in some detail, partly to shed overdue light on these authors in their own right and partly to illustrate a broader pattern in Chinese literature of the 1940s.

More specifically, three recurrent themes will be traced in this study: the role of tradition and the supernatural, the reaction against realism, and the use of psychology. Readers will recognise these themes as the hallmarks of Chinese modernist writing from the 1930s, particularly that of the New Sensationists (*xinganjuepai* 新感覺派), including Shi Zhecun and Mu Shiying.[5] One of the main points that will be argued is that much of the Chinese popular literature of the 1940s was indebted to the modernist Shanghai authors of the 1930s in various ways. New Sensationist writings are rarely seen as having much impact on later Chinese literature, but I believe that their style was an important influence on the popular wartime literature of the following decade: the latter was partly built upon aspects of Shanghai modernism, appropriating both content and narrative style. In order to outline this development, I will also be dealing with a few works by Shi Zhecun and Mu Shiying.

This next section presents a brief discussion of what constitutes popular literature in 1940s wartime China, as well as an overview of the several ways in which Xu Xu and Wumingshi have been classified and evaluated. In Chinese literary scholarship they are often discussed together and represented as relating to certain other categories and groupings in Chinese literature. Some of these categories merit further discussion and critique, particularly the notion of *haipai* 海派, Shanghai School fiction, which incorporates practically all literature of the late Republican period not deliberately engaging with social or national issues.

Chapter 2 is intended to provide context through discussion of several works by Shi Zhecun and Mu Shiying, two of the most prominent modernist writers of the early 1930s. A few works are analysed to highlight the hybrid nature of their writings, showing how they frequently rely on cultural tradition, legend and tropes from popular literature. The main purpose of this section is to put down some markers for later comparison.

Chapter 3 discusses wartime popular literature more generally, touching upon the works of a few other authors. This section also sets out some context for the literary field and the changes within it happening at the time. In addition to showing the diversity of popular literature during the war, some background is provided for the more specific analyses of works in subsequent chapters.

Chapters 4 and 5 focus on Xu Xu and Wumingshi, respectively. I analyse their works in roughly chronological order and argue two more general points: first, that both authors incorporated elements of modernism into their highly romantic popular novels and short stories, thereby crossing such categories in new ways; and, second, that they were indebted to the 1930s modernists, echoing their works in both style and content. The two authors also show an interesting trajectory, starting with more modernist works and eventually writing popular romances.

Functioning largely as a conclusion, Chapter 6 is more comparative, mapping out characteristics of the principal authors presented here. This section also expands upon and highlights some of the more general points or themes that as mentioned above recur throughout this study:

1. *The use of cultural tradition and the supernatural in popular literature.* The wartime years have been seen as a period during which Chinese tradition was re-appropriated and revitalised, mainly in drama.[6] Yet apart from promoting nationalism, this aspect of Chinese writing has rarely been explored

to see to what other ends tradition was used. Xu Xu's writings frequently feature mystical, otherworldly women. In these pieces, the female characters appear as exotic and unattainable supernatural beauties steeped in tradition, legend and myth. This is tradition as a source of storytelling material and entertainment, rather than as a source of pride, nationalism or exhorting the masses to action. Xu Xu's allusions to history and otherworldly tradition become specific story elements that play a specific role within the unfolding plot. Wumingshi's works rarely make reference to Chinese legends and myth. Nevertheless, Huashan Mountain 華山 features frequently in his writing, representing something primordial, majestic and ultimately Chinese. It is the retreat of Buddhist monks and loners who are seeking a space beyond their personal tragedies in love, representing the diametrical opposite of the protagonists' previously international and extroverted lives. On the whole, however, Chinese history and tradition play a minor role in Wumingshi's stories.

2. *The reaction against realism.* Several modernist narrative innovations from the 1930s spread to popular literature. Writers like Wumingshi consciously departed from realism, both in narrative style and story content. Such modernist approaches presented a challenge to the nationalist discourse promoted by the war writers of the 1940s. Wumingshi developed a highly distinctive narrative style characterised by continuous streams of metaphors. In some of his early short stories, this technique resembles the fragmented Expressionist style used by Mu Shiying. But in later works the narrative style assumes a more expansive form adapted to convey pathos, drama, vistas of history and high emotion, becoming an integral part of the flow of the text. Xu Xu similarly experimented with unreliable narrators, flashbacks, starting in medias res, etc. While his works are less experimental in terms of narrative technique, they do again demonstrate certain parallels with earlier Chinese modernist writing. In Xu Xu's writings, it is the settings rather than the language that mark a departure from realism. His romances are mostly set in exotic and alluring locales, from cruise yachts and opulent mansions to secret island hideouts. Many of his stories take place in Europe, although the foreign settings are rarely developed and mostly serve as abstract, fantastic backgrounds highlighting the cosmopolitan nature of the male Chinese protagonist.

3. *The use of psychology.* Among Chinese writers who continued publishing during the war, the works of Zhang Ailing have become known for their psychological depth. Other Shanghai writers, such as Su Qing 苏青 (1914–1982), also produced studies of urban psychology that were unparalleled in this respect since the short stories by Shi Zhecun a decade earlier. But it was not only in occupied Shanghai that writers turned towards explorations of inner emotions while war raged in the background. For some, the use of psychology, madness and nervous conditions was a marker of difference from the more stereotyped characters found in war literature. Most of Xu Xu's short stories are set in the city and feature protagonists facing challenges to

their modern rational outlook. Psychology becomes an important factor in the protagonist's relationship with two women in the novel *The Lament of the Mental Patient* (*Jingshenbing huanzhe de beige* 精神病患者的悲歌). In the works of the New Sensationist writers, irrationality and madness constituted an attack on modern rationality and the belief in progress. By the 1940s, psychological portrayals and explanations had entered into more mainstream depictions of the character's vicissitudes.

On literary categories and other scholarship

Various labels and categorisations have been applied to the works of Xu Xu and Wumingshi, as well as to popular Chinese literature of the Republican period more broadly. These attempts to classify this kind of literature inherently indicate certain assessments of their works, usually dismissive. This section presents an overview of such classifications, and briefly discusses the notion of popular literature in a Chinese context. Specifically, I want to critique the notion in Chinese literary studies of a 'Shanghai School' ('*haipai*' 海派). The New Sensationist writers, as well as both Xu Xu and Wumingshi, are often subsumed under this label, and I do not wish to validate this classification by comparing them here. Despite some surface similarities between their works, I think that this term does more harm than good in trying to see how these authors positioned themselves on the cultural scene at the time. The following section debates such terms and provides an overview of literature in the field.

While scholarship on Xu Xu and Wumingshi has recently begun to appear in Western languages, both authors still remain little known. Looking at studies in Chinese, the situation is a bit better, but not by much. Academics in the West looking at Chinese literature from the 1940s have tended to focus on individual authors, such as the more famous Ding Ling 丁玲 (1904–1986).[7] Many of the influential wartime writers had, of course, made their names in the previous decades and continued to be quite prominent.

Broader studies of Chinese wartime literature have to a large extent been concerned with the impact of the war and the cultural developments in Yan'an, including Mao Zedong's influential 'Talks at the Yan'an Forum on Literature and Art' ('*Zai Yan'an wenyi zuotanhuishang de jianghua*' 在延安文藝座談會上的講話) in 1942 and the injunctions that came to inform creative writing in the People's Republic in the following years.[8] A few important studies look at how the war affected the literary milieu in Shanghai. Poshek Fu examines the difficult choices facing writers who remained after the occupation in 1941: joining the resistance, collaborating with the Japanese or retreating from the literary field altogether.[9]

In a recent relevant study, Carolyn FitzGerald demonstrates that modernism remained a prevalent influence on Chinese art and literature during the war years.[10] She does not focus on popular literature, but she does incorporate widely different types of material, including poetry, film and cartoons. As for fiction, she discusses works by Wang Zengqi 汪曾祺 (1920–1997) and Fei Ming 廢名 (1901–1967), finding that their creative writing incorporated aspects of traditional forms of literature and Daoist philosophy. Such literature illustrates a continuation of Chinese modernist influence from before the war and shows new aspects within Chinese modernism.

> Wartime culture should thus be understood as a maturation of, rather than an end to, the Westernized cosmopolitanism of the previous decades. By reinventing modernism in the context of native traditions and writing on the theme of rural return, wartime writers and artists followed in the footsteps of their predecessors. However, they achieved a new level of aesthetic looseness when they intermixed modernist forms with a wide array of traditional forms, many drawn from regional popular culture.[11]

While confirming the revival of tradition during this period, one of FitzGerald's main findings is that even modernist modes of art were put to use in promoting Chinese nationalism and supporting resistance against the Japanese. Her study provides important examples of modernist art continuing as an influential style in China into the 1940s.

There have been some studies focusing on popular literature during the wartime period in English. Edward Gunn's excellent *Unwelcome Muse* looks at the literary field in Japanese-occupied areas, mostly Shanghai and Beijing, including Zhang Ailing's short stories and Qian Zhongshu's famous satirical novel *Fortress Besieged* (*Weicheng* 圍城, 1947).[12] One of the most important studies of popular literature in the Republican era, Perry Link's *Mandarin Ducks and Butterflies*, remains a classic. Link focuses mostly on works from the 1920s and early 1930s, such as Zhang Henshui's 張恨水 (1895–1967) hugely popular *Fate in Tears and Laughter* (*Tixiao yinyuan* 啼笑因緣, 1929–30).[13] Nicole Huang's *Women, War, and Domesticity* explores how a number of women's journals and female writers, including Zhang Ailing and Su Qing, emerged in Shanghai during the Japanese occupation.[14] With the old guard having departed for the interior and nationalist topics being banned, the war opened up new avenues for publishing for some writers, particularly women, and new, perhaps more introspective, topics were explored, including relationships and gender issues.

Focusing on wartime developments in the Nationalist-controlled hinterland, Chang-tai Hung presents a different aspect of popular culture during this period. In *War and Popular Culture*, he studies how popular art forms were adapted for propaganda in both Nationalist and Communist areas to promote the anti-Japanese resistance movement, including a wealth of historical drama, cartoons and newspaper dispatches.[15] These efforts were accompanied by a discussion of popular national forms and how artists might use such forms to have the greatest impact with their writings.

Studies of individual popular writers include those on Zhang Ailing, Qian Zhongshu and Zhang Henshui.[16] Most of Zhang Henshui's popular literature was written in the 1930s, but there has been some analysis of his more serious wartime work as well.[17] There are also occasional studies of individual novels, for example, Qin Shou'ou's 秦瘦鷗 (1908–1994) incredibly popular *Begonia* (*Qiuhaitang* 秋海棠), serialised in 1941, which a great many readers found deeply moving.[18]

While only touching upon a few works of relevant scholarship here, this short section shows that contemporary scholars have looked into what they consider 'popular Chinese literature' in a number of remarkably different ways, focusing on quite diverse material. Tellingly, there is little agreement on what constitutes popular literature in a Chinese context, and the concept thus remains open to interpretation. Various studies have appropriated the term to mean a number of different things. As Chang-tai Hung notes, this has been an issue for Chinese intellectuals as well, and even during the course of the war, many intellectuals used the term 'popular literature and art' ('*tongsu wenyi*' 通俗文藝) interchangeably with 'folk literature' ('*minjian wenyi*' 民間文藝).[19] Given the intersecting historical, political and pejorative connotations, it is worth discussing the terminology a bit further.

Some thoughts on popular literature: terms and limitations

Any attempt to categorise literature according to epithets such as 'elite' or 'popular', or to apply any other such labels that imply class, quality or sophistication, invites suspicion. Who are the arbiters of such distinctions, what are the principles of demarcation, and is it even possible to draw lines between such arbitrary groups? What would be the point in doing so? Much like 'lowbrow', that which is seen as 'popular' is given little credit as literature worth spending any time on. Popular literature is considered primarily commercial, thereby situating it as the diametric opposite of that which is elite, highbrow or avant-garde. The terms thereby discursively circumscribe and define each other with little reference to intrinsic literary qualities, and they seem to impose a binary view of cultural production and appreciation with no space for a middle ground.[20]

Nevertheless, notions of elite and popular art persist and the distinction remains useful in categorising all sorts of cultural products and practices, from poetry, films and music to sculpture, dance, painting and drama. Arguably, it is exactly the interrelational aspect of these terms that makes them useful, showing how art is perceived in different ways on a spectrum that relates to class and varying degrees of social and cultural recognition.

Pierre Bourdieu's well-known theories about the 'field of cultural production' map out how such systems are established and maintained – creating hierarchies of art and cultural prestige ('symbolic capital') that become second nature ('habitus') to the people operating within the system.[21] Bourdieu's analysis focuses on the distinction between the elite and the popular in the world of art in nineteenth-century France, and he proceeds from this to show how it operated as an 'autonomous field', separate from economic and political concerns.

More useful from the perspective of Chinese literature, Bourdieu establishes these structures of taste and distinction without tying them to the intrinsic nature of the art itself, for example, through evaluations of quality or style. The hierarchies of recognition in cultural circles were regulated by unspoken rules and strategies, including the aspiring artist professing a disinterest in financial gain. The author of popular literature was thus one who 'sold out' in terms of artistic vision.

As Michel Hockx demonstrates, Bourdieu's theories are also highly useful in analysing Chinese literature of the Republican period.[22] Conceiving of the literary field as a set of positions in which various intellectuals and writers form groups, denounce each other and seek symbolic capital fits the Chinese situation well during the New Culture Movement (1917–1925). Yet Hockx shows that important differences need to be addressed as well. Unlike nineteenth-century France, the Chinese literary field in the 1920s was not fully autonomous since political capital was as important as cultural or symbolic capital in determining a writer's position in the literary field. The New Culture Movement intellectuals were interested in social issues, including progress, modernity and the fate of the nation. The corollary of this is that authors who professed no interest in such issues were dismissed or looked down upon, regardless of the quality of their writing. This intersecting relationship between culture and politics in Republican China makes mapping out different views on what constitutes elite and popular literature quite complex.

Before returning to Hockx and Bourdieu, a few examples might illustrate this point. Several Chinese authors who made their names in the 1940s, including Zhang Ailing and Qian Zhongshu, have been seen as popular writers since they largely remained outside the political fray of the time.[23] Judging these works today from a perspective of literary merit or complexity, this trivialising classification seems dubious. Their writings contain some of the most subtle character portraits of the time, depicting urban intellectuals facing complex psychological and social issues. Su Qing might be included in this list as well.[24] Qian Zhongshu was certainly academically accomplished, and he was well known for his extensive knowledge of both Chinese and Western literature.[25] The main reason these writers are considered 'popular' is due to the way in which this term has been defined according to the New Literature (*xin wenxue* 新文學) position that writing of any worth should engage with nation, modernity and social issues.

At the opposite end of the spectrum, a socialist author like Zhao Shuli 趙樹理 (1906–1970) attempted to produce proletarian literature in Yan'an using a colloquial, local style, later called the 'Potato School' ('*shanyaodanpai*' 山藥蛋派). While Zhao deliberately sought mass appeal with his down-to-earth and frequently humorous short stories, he is usually not considered a writer of popular literature, largely because his works were principally guided by political considerations and served as Communist propaganda. So this confirms the notion that what is considered popular or elite seems to depend more on political and social concerns than literary depth or quality.

A different and less subjective yardstick with which to determine whether lit-erature is popular or elite would be to simply look at sales volume. In Bourdieu's framework, popular art is more concerned with mass audience, and thus com-mercial success, than intellectual recognition. Zhang Ailing's short stories and Qian Zhongshu's *Fortress Besieged* are enjoyed by millions of readers in China today, so by that standard their works should perhaps indeed be seen as popular literature. Conversely, Zhao Shuli's works are no longer widely read today except by those interested in literary history. Sales numbers are, of course, rel-evant, but the popularity of an author today says nothing about how their works were perceived at the time. We cannot label literature 'popular' retrospectively. More importantly, Bourdieu points out that respected authors who eventually gain high 'symbolic capital' become widely read through canonisation, literary prizes, anthologies, etc. Thus, high sales volume alone cannot be used to consign an author's works to 'popular literature'. Similarly one could easily imagine an author aiming to write a simple romance or 'potboiler' crime story, but failing to reach the desired mass audience with it. Such literature could still justifiably be considered 'popular literature' despite poor sales.

There are various Chinese terms for popular literature in the Republican period, the main ones being 'Mandarin Ducks and Butterflies' ('*yuanyang hud-iepai*' 鴛鴦蝴蝶派) or 'Saturday School' ('*libailiu pai*' 禮拜六派). Through the 1920s, various May Fourth intellectuals voiced sharp critiques of popular fiction, dismissing a number of works as sentimental drivel featuring superficial symbols of love, for example, 'mandarin ducks' and 'butterflies'. Already in 1918, Zhou Zuoren 周作人 (1885–1967) denounced traditional literature, arguing that it hindered the development of the nation.[26] Other May Fourth intellectuals such as Zheng Zhenduo 鄭振鐸 (1898–1958), Mao Dun 茅盾 (1896–1981) and Ye Shengtao 葉聖陶 (1894–1988) also voiced similar critiques of traditional fiction through the 1920s. According to Zheng, traditional-style writers who wrote for money were 'literary prostitutes' ('*wenchang*' 文娼) who corrupted the minds of innocent readers.[27]

These terms have influenced the understanding of what constitutes popular Chinese literature in Western academia. 'Mandarin Ducks and Butterflies' and 'Saturday School' have both been adopted by literary studies.[28] So while the labels originated as slurs, they have since been expanded to characterise popular literature more broadly in the Republican period. Yet, due to the origin of the term and the diversity of the literature covered by it, Denise Gimpel cautions against using it in academic studies.[29] The scope of the literature included under the epithet is simply too broad and often masks greater sophistication than the derogatory labels imply. In addition, the critics of popular fiction at the time largely overlooked that such literature often did deal with modern life and social changes in China, rather than ignoring or overlooking it.

As Perry Link notes, popular fiction helped many readers to grapple with the changes of modernity by presenting clear-cut cases of good and evil, and demon-strating the continued validity of frugality, filial piety and other such traditional values in a rapidly changing world.[30] Similarly, Ng Mau-sang argues that the serialised texts of popular writers like Zhang Henshui and Bao Tianxiao 包天笑 (1875–1973) achieved their popularity by being 'a composite of commonly held sets of beliefs and values which not only signify a continuity with the past, but also fix certain aspects of the shifting landscape of modernity into a dialectic relationship with this symbolic past'.[31] In addition to being entertaining, popular literature helped its readers to deal with modernity and social change.

Despite such reservations in using terms like 'Mandarin Ducks and Butterflies', I am not proposing to redefine the term 'popular literature' when applied to Chinese literature in the Republican period. There is now an established convention that most writers outside the New Literature canon, such as Zhang Ailing and Su Qing, are considered popular writers, and I suspect that a challenge to this usage would serve only to muddle the terms further.

These examples help to confirm Hockx's ideas about the literary field, and they offer a way of looking at popular literature that is in accordance with the New Literature view, yet still frees us from evaluating intrinsic qualities of literary works or adopting 'Mandarin Ducks and Butterflies', even with suitable caveats. If, as Hockx proposes, literary recognition needs to be measured along both symbolic and political axes, then popular art would naturally situate itself at the bottom of both scales while still seeking a mass market. This seems to fit, as popular literature in China on the whole does not engage directly with politics and social movements, or seek intellectual recognition.

Adopting this approach also allows one more readily to reference Bourdieu's notions of the literary field and symbolic capital on occasion. Despite the splintering of the literary field during the war, the framework still has merit as it helps us to see how authors and intellectuals took different cultural positions in relation to each other. It is perhaps also worth noting from the outset that folk literature will not be included under the umbrella of 'popular literature' here.

As shown in the following section, Xu Xu and Wumingshi are more often than not classified as popular writers and I do not intend to challenge that view. While their writings do contain modernist elements, making them arguably more sophisticated than many others, their novels and short stories from the wartime period are nevertheless principally romantic escapist melodrama. Perhaps more importantly, I would like to stress that this study is not about the application of a label. Their works are often hybrid, crossing boundaries between the popular and the elite, as well as between modernism and romanticism, so there is no need to place them categorically in one group or the other. Showing how such fluid positions were possible in the wartime literary field is one of the main arguments of this study.

The Shanghai School: a critique

A common term in Chinese literary studies is the 'Shanghai School' ('*haipai*'). Several studies categorise Xu Xu and Wumingshi as writers of this type of literature alongside Shi Zhecun and Mu Shiying. The label refers to popular literature targeting middle-class Shanghai readers with some spare income and leisure time to read for pleasure.[32] Much like 'Mandarin Ducks and Butterflies', the label originated as a pejorative term. It was used by some New Culture Movement writers like Zhou Zuoren and Shen Congwen 沈從文 (1902–1988) in the 1930s as a derogatory epithet for the cheap commercial literature produced in Shanghai.[33] They argued that such literature was useless if not downright damaging, given its lack of political and social vision. It did not serve the proper function of good literature: to enlighten the people.[34] A good deal has been written elsewhere about this historical debate, so there is no further need to delve into its details.[35] The following briefly describes how the term is used by present-day scholars to represent a variety of authors as belonging to a single literary group or trend.

In a monograph on the Shanghai School, Wu Fuhui 吳福輝 uses the term to denote authors from the late 1920s to 1940s who wrote about Shanghai in a modern style, including the New Sensationists of the 1930s as well as Xu Xu.[36] Wu distinguishes Shanghai School writers from the authors of 'Mandarin Duck and Butterfly' fiction whose works he considers more traditional and anchored within premodern genres of Chinese fiction, including martial arts stories and court romances. Shanghai School literature was mostly fast-paced with an emphasis on plot, and the authors strove for sophistication while aiming for broad popular readership at the same time.[37] Their writings adopted elements of modern narrative styles from New Literature sources and foreign literature in order to remain fresh and chic. On the other hand, Shanghai School literature also borrowed many elements from popular literature so as to maintain the interest of readers. In an earlier study, Wu Fuhui divides the Shanghai School into three main subcategories: the so-called 'Mandarin Duck and Butterfly' literature, 'New Sensationism' and 'Late Romanticism'.[38] In this scheme, the Shanghai modernists belong to the second subgroup and Xu Xu and Wumingshi to the third. Each of the three groupings are seen as reflecting the interests of mass readership in certain periods or as being connected with specific popular Shanghai journals of the time. A few other studies propose similar tripartite divisions of Shanghai School literature, for example, those by Yan Jiayan 嚴家炎 and Yang Yi 楊義.[39]

The understanding that such literature is fairly similar or homogeneous seems to be widely accepted. Although several Chinese scholars attempt to differentiate between subgroups or periods of Shanghai School writers, the validity of the category itself is rarely contested and it has been adopted by some scholars in the West as well.[40] Taken as an academic term, the 'Shanghai School' presents a number of problems. Apart from the negative connotation due to its origin, it is extremely broad as it crosses the boundaries of literary groups and societies and overlaps with other categorisations, such as modernist fiction. Considering the Shanghai School as an undifferentiated whole is an oversimplification of their work, and the endeavour to portray these authors as a coherent group that spanned three decades leads to overly broad generalisations and a neglect of the real differences among them. Even the so-called 'Mandarin Duck and Butterfly' authors of the 1910s were interested in modernity and social progress and cannot sensibly be seen as forming a coherent whole.[41] Subsuming these writers under an umbrella term like 'Shanghai School' makes even less sense given the differences between, say, supposed 'Saturday School' martial arts novels and the psychologically intricate works by Shi Zhecun and Zhang Ailing. Even the commercial interest aspect does not sensibly apply to all of the authors categorised as 'Shanghai School' writers. Several Shanghai School authors wrote works that were highly contentious and poorly received at the time, both by the cultural elite and the public at large. The jagged, disruptive style of the New Sensationist writers was novel, and many readers took it as an affront.[42] Claiming that they were merely pandering to popular tastes is a misrepresentation of their works.

One of the causes for the persistence of the Shanghai School as a category is that subsequent literary historiography has been written from the perspective of the cultural elite of the time. The views of prominent intellectuals such as Lu Xun 魯迅 (1881–1936), Zhou Zuoren and Shen Congwen have come to define the image of the Shanghai School and their writing. Thus, rather than being constituted in a constructive manner as a group with a number of traits in common, the Shanghai School has mainly been defined by a process of exclusion, the repository of whatever the New Culture elite looked down upon: commercial, traditional, apolitical and non-didactic. So while studies of the Shanghai School have been very valuable in bringing to light some lesser known popular authors, one should hesitate before validating it as a stand-alone literary category.[43]

Late romanticists or late modernists

Xu Xu and Wumingshi are frequently mentioned together. The comparisons between the two writers started soon after Wumingshi's publication of *North Pole Landscape Painting* in 1943, which became a bestseller.[44] By this time, Xu Xu was already a prominent author with a number of popular novels, essay collections and plays to his credit. Readers found that Wumingshi's style was fairly similar. According to later biographies, Wumingshi was rather averse to the comparison, claiming that his style was fundamentally different from Xu's.[45] Thus, the similarities were never accepted by the writers themselves.

When considered as a group in contemporary academic studies, the two authors are usually seen as the main proponents of 'late romanticism' or 'late modernism'. The tendency among scholars to group Xu Xu and Wumingshi together mainly derives from Yan Jiayan's influential classification of groups and categories of writers of early modern Chinese fiction.[46] According to Yan's system, Wumingshi and Xu Xu are the most representative authors in a category labelled 'second generation romanticists' ('*houqi langmanpai*' 後期浪漫派). Works that mention the two authors generally adopt this appellation.[47] Yan's grouping has also meant that most scholars have felt that they could not write about one of the two without at least acknowledging the relationship with the other. The category is also noted by Yingjin Zhang, who mentions the two authors together.[48]

Yan Jiayan argues that both Xu Xu and Wumingshi were romantic authors, but he distinguishes them from the earlier New Culture Movement romantic writers, such as Yu Dafu 郁達夫 (1896–1945) and Guo Moruo 郭沫若 (1892–1978).[49] Yan credits Xu Xu and Wumingshi with having several important characteristics in common. In addition to writing widely popular romantic works, they were both good at describing the characters' emotions and using their novels as platforms to convey their philosophical insights.[50] Equally important, their writings depart from realism and contain modernist elements in their narrative style. Concerning political content, Yan notes approvingly that Wumingshi's *Love of Russia* (*Luxiya zhi lian* 露西亞之戀) and Xu Xu's *The Rustling Wind* both display patriotic anti-Japanese sentiment and that some of their early works are sympathetic to the revolution.[51] Nevertheless, he criticises both writers for lacking a solid political message in most of their fiction, so, in his view, the principal value of their art lies in their literary technique.[52]

Using a similar term, Jiang Shuxian 蔣淑嫻 and Yin Jian 殷鉴 call Xu Xu and Wumingshi 'late romanticists' ('*houlangmanpai*' 後浪漫派).[53] They argue that Xu Xu and Wumingshi stand out among romantic authors by dealing with contemporary social issues and political events. For example, the protagonist of Wumingshi's *North Pole Landscape Painting* is a Korean freedom fighter and the seductive ghost in Xu's *Ghostly Love* previously worked as an undercover Communist agent.[54] Consequently, Xu Xu and Wumingshi share a progressive notion of liberty and exalt the attainment of individual freedom.

Other studies have focused more on Xu Xu and Wumingshi in terms of modernism. Wu Daoyi 吳道毅 similarly classifies Wumingshi and Xu Xu as late romanticists, but further argues that they straddle the divide between modernism and popular literature.[55] Wu classifies their works as 'legendary fiction' ('*chuanqi xiaoshuo*' 傳奇小說), reminiscent of the supernatural tales from the Tang dynasty (618–907), in his view a kind of writing that appeals to a large readership through melodramatic plots involving passionate love and superhuman characters who are almost excessively beautiful, accomplished, learned, etc.[56]

In a study of Chinese romantic fiction, Zhu Xi 朱曦 and Chen Xingwu 陳興蕪 describe Wumingshi and Xu Xu as authors who shift from romanticism to modernism.[57] They argue that both authors' early works were mostly romantic, whereas many of their later works dating after the mid-1940s, such as Wumingshi's *Beast, Beast, Beast* (*Yeshou, yeshou, yeshou* 野獸, 野獸, 野獸), were more strongly influenced by modernism.[58] According to Zhu and Chen, the shift towards modernism by both authors marks the end of romantic literature in China.[59]

Focusing more on the modernist aspects of their fiction, Kong Fanjin 孔范今 and Pan Xueqing 潘學清 argue that Xu Xu and Wumingshi belong in a category labelled 'second generation modernists' ('*houqi xiandai pai*' 後期現代派) together with Zhang Ailing.[60] They note that these authors have much in common with the New Sensationists, but they also differ in important ways, such as attaining greater philosophical depth and are seen as attempting to combine religion, philosophy and culture in search of a new spiritual path to guide people during troubled times. On the whole, compared with China's earlier modernist writers, Kong and Pan value the late modernists quite highly:

> Only few people know about the late modernists these days, but at the time they caused a much greater furore in society than the New Sensationists did and furthermore, their works are special and have better stood the test of time. Their transcendental thinking on life and existence, their broad and minute explorations of the psychological world, their complex variations of artistic expression as well as their holistic approach to every cultural aspect all serve to distinguish them strikingly from their predecessors.[61]

Yet Kong and Pan note somewhat disapprovingly that Xu Xu, Zhang Ailing and Wumingshi all essentially produced escapist literature that entertained readers with philosophical explorations and discourses concerning spiritual transcendence but neglected current social problems.[62]

Specifically regarding their philosophical outlook, Song Jianhua 宋劍華 calls Wumingshi and Xu Xu existentialists.[63] Their works contend that the ultimate purpose of life is the realisation and emancipation of the self – independent of all outside influences.[64] Song concludes his analysis of their thought with a critique of their transcendentalism, arguing that they fail to recognise the limits to escapism imposed by social circumstances.[65] Concerning their style of writing, Song notes that they are modernists and have much in common with the earlier New Sensationist authors.[66]

In a manner similar to the modernist authors of the 1930s, Xu Xu and Wumingshi focus on the inner worlds of the characters, using first-person narratives, and psychological issues play a predominant role in their development. It is also characteristic of these modernist authors to have first-person narrators. Typical of modernist fiction, their narrative style draws upon all sorts of sensory perceptions and metaphors in order to convey striking images and settings.

Several studies that have focused on the authors individually have similarly attempted to determine how their works balance between popular romanticism and modernism.

Individual studies of Xu Xu and Wumingshi

As mentioned earlier, Xu Xu and Wumingshi have remained largely neglected by scholarly studies until quite recently, particularly among Western scholars. In English, Frederik Green stands out as the sole person to put some effort into writing about Xu Xu's work, including looking at his essays and plays (neither of which are considered here).[67] Green sees Xu's work during the war as showing defiance against calls for Resistance Literature and moral collectivism.

> The transcendental power of individual fulfilment and love that the fictional pro-
> tagonists of Xu's novels rescued from the clutches of history thus must have brought
> much comfort to his readers whose personal salvation was rarely addressed in official
> wartime narratives that depicted the nation in peril and called for collective sacrifice.[68]

In the People's Republic until the 1990s, the neglect of Xu Xu was partly influenced by political sensibilities, since he was critical of Communist ideology.[69] The situation has been somewhat better in Taiwan and Hong Kong where Xu Xu's works have remained in circulation. His works are now available in mainland China, and the importance of his fiction from the 1940s is also gradually being recognised.

Chen Xuanbo's 陳旋波 monograph from 2004 is one of the main contributions to our understanding of Xu Xu today.[70] Chen sees Xu's works as reflecting various cultural trends that changed from one period to the next, and he traces Xu's writings from his first leftist works, noting how it was influenced by various philosophical trends and styles of literature. After an early leftist period, Xu Xu was heavily influenced by Freud, Bergson and Kant in the 1930s and 1940s. In this manner, his works are seen as reflecting practically every major intellectual trend that influenced China during these years. Pointing out these varying sources of inspiration is the major aim of Chen's study. In 2008, a biography of Xu Xu was written by Wu Yiqin 吳義勤 and Wang Suxia 王素霞.[71] Compared with Chen's study, this biography is more concerned with Xu Xu's personal life, including his three marriages. It sets out to portray a life full of drama and emotion. While analysis of his wartime writings is very brief, this biography is still a useful resource for understanding Xu Xu.

On Taiwan, where Xu Xu's anti-Communist stance is less of an obstacle, the author is better known. His complete works were published there in 1966 in a planned eighteen volumes.[72] Some of his writings have even been made into films, but there is still remarkably little research. Following his death in 1980, a collection of memorial articles was published, *A Few Things About Xu Xu* (*Xu Xu er san shi* 徐訏二三事), in which a number of friends and students pay tribute to him.[73] Some of the authors recollect the impact of reading Xu in their youth in the 1930s and 1940s, and recount a number of anecdotes about him after he left the mainland. While only rarely providing insights into his fiction in and of itself, the book does serve as a reminder of Xu's importance in the 1940s. A few of the contributors mention the popularity of his works as they were distributed in both free and occupied areas.[74] One of them notes Xu's frustration with the political infighting among writers and intellectuals during those years, and that he saw himself as politically independent.[75]

Wumingshi remains practically unstudied in the West and mentions of his work remain few and far between.[76] He is mostly known for his political writings about Chinese labour camps, not for his literary production.[77] Since his works were banned in mainland China for decades, there was no scholarship on his writings there. It was not until his elder brother Bu Shaofu 卜少夫 (1909–2000), an editor in Hong Kong, wrote a long essay about Wumingshi in 1976 that the author's life became known to the public again.[78] The volume was printed in Hong Kong and Taiwan and contained reprints of some of his works. It sparked an interest in the author that resulted in several articles and essays being written about him, many of which were gathered by Bu Shaofu and published in a separate book in 1981.[79]

Along with a more relaxed official attitude to Wumingshi's writings, Bu Shaofu's work has generated greater interest in his person. His mysterious *nom de plume*, his disappearance from the literary scene for several decades, his writings about the inhumane conditions in Chinese labour camps, and his marriage to a much younger wife in Taiwan in 1985 have all stirred considerable interest in his personal life. Between 1998 and 2001, three full biographies of Wumingshi were published on the mainland.[80] As a rule, these biographers relegate his writing to a secondary position. Wumingshi's private history, especially his dramatic and mostly unhappy love life, is the chief interest and is covered in great detail. In all of these works Wumingshi is presented as an enigmatic character, isolated and mysterious. The titles alone suffice to indicate their view of the subject: *The Legend of Wumingshi* (*Wumingshi chuanqi* 無名氏傳奇), *The Mysterious Wumingshi* (*Shenmi de Wumingshi* 神秘的無名氏) and, last, *Traces of a Solitary Walker: A Biography of Wumingshi* (*Duxing ren zong: Wumingshi zhuan* 獨行人蹤: 無名氏傳). One of the reasons for the portrayal of Wumingshi as such a mysterious entity is, of course, partly that 'Wumingshi' translates as 'Mr Anonymous'. Another frequent focus of attention is that in spite of his fame in the early 1940s, he vanished quite suddenly from the literary scene a few years later. He left no traces of his whereabouts and there was much speculation that he had left the country, moved to the interior or perhaps gone mad.[81]

Among the biographies, *The Legend of Wumingshi* by Wang Yingguo 汪應果 and Zhao Jiangbin 趙江濱 is the most academic.[82] It dedicates several chapters to analysing his magnum opus, *The Nameless Book* (*Wumingshu* 無名書) in six volumes, which is hailed as a masterful contribution to Chinese literature.[83] The two other biographies contain passages about his writings as well, but with a predominant focus on the people who later became the characters in his novels. Several of his protagonists, including those in *North Pole Landscape Painting* and *The Woman in the Tower*, are based on real people whom Wumingshi knew. All of the biographers value Wumingshi's works quite highly and agree that his writing should be accorded greater respect than is presently the case.

Looking at the academic studies, a few trends have emerged. A number of scholars commenting on Wumingshi's writings identify two main periods in his work: his early novels are considered romantic popular literature, whereas his later works – particularly the volumes that comprise *The Nameless Book* – are considered far deeper in thought, and as having greater artistic merit and philo-sophical and literary importance.[84] Zhu Xi 朱曦 and Chen Xingwu's 陳興蕪 study of romantic literature presents an example of this division of Wumingshi's work into two distinct periods. The authors explain that they will only deal with the two early 'romantic' novels, *North Pole Landscape Painting* and *The Woman in the Tower*, since his later modernist fiction falls outside the scope of their study.[85] Wang and Zhao see a similar shift and argue that Wumingshi is mostly known for his romantic works and that consequently his modernist experiments are less recognised.[86] Geng Chuanming 耿傳名 presents the shift to modernism in Wumingshi's authorship rather grandiosely:

> Wumingshi's traversal from popular love stories to the spiritual realm of *The Nameless Book*'s [final volume] *The Grand Bodhi of Genesis* (*Chuangshiji da puti* 創世紀大菩提) was the result of his continuously surpassing himself, persistently seeking out the edge of life's fulfilment. For this he paid a martyr's cost. Such people are very rare in literary history.[87]

This notion of a shift from romanticism to modernism has been supported by Wumingshi himself. The novels written prior to the publication of the first volume of *The Nameless Book* in December 1946, he has called his 'stage of com-position exercises' ('*xizuo jieduan*' 習作階段), while the later works belong to his 'stage of creative writing' ('*chuangzuo jieduan*' 創作階段).[88] The later works are thus seen by the author himself as more accomplished in both style and content.

Several scholars have focused exclusively on *The Nameless Book*. Chen Sihe 陳思和 sees it as a largely romantic, utopian work and likens it to Goethe's (1749–1832) *Faust*.[89] He argues that it should be read more as a treatise than as fiction. The volumes that treat various passages of the protagonist's life are more like essays that explain the author's religious and philosophical message about the purpose of life and enlightenment and ultimate truth. Song Jianhua sees *The Nameless Book* as an exposition of existentialist thought.[90] As with Xu Xu, Wumingshi has been compared with the New Sensationists. Wang and Zhao find Wumingshi far superior, arguing that his literary experiments in *The Nameless Book* are more thoughtful and radical than those of the 1930s modern-ists.[91] The merging of fiction, essay and philosophical treatise further distin-guishes *The Nameless Book* from earlier modernist writers in China. They also praise him for his language with its extended use of metaphors and extravagant descriptions.

As seen above, there is a tendency to see Wumingshi's works as progressing from romanticism to modernism. This classification invariably leads to seeing his authorship as undergoing a process of improvement and maturation as it moves from one sort of writing to another. A closer look at his writings reveals, however, that this notion of a simple shift from romanticism to modernism is faulty, since it is based on overly narrow interpretations of a few select works while ignoring others. His earliest short stories were very much inspired by modernist writing and the New Sensationist narrative style. Even his later supposedly 'romantic' novels are in fact hybrid works that cross back and forth between different modes of writing, switching between romantic melodrama and modernist explorations of subconscious fears and desires. Here he is deliberately mixing 'high' and 'low' forms of literature, which casts a very different light on these novels and their position in the literary field. In different ways, his works across a broad span of years combine elements from both the popular and the avant-garde.

Notes

1. Edward Gunn, *Unwelcome Muse: Chinese Literature in Shanghai and Peking 1937–1945* (New York: Columbia University Press, 1980), p. 5.

2. Wang Yingguo 汪應果 and Zhao Jiangbin 趙江濱, *Wumingshi chuanqi* 無名氏傳奇 (*The Legend of Wumingshi*) (Shanghai: Shanghai wenyi chubanshe, 1998), pp. 31–4.

3. Chen Xuanbo 陳旋波, *Shi yu guang: 20 shiji Zhongguo wenxueshi geju zhong de Xu Xu* 時與光: 20世紀中國文學史格局中的徐訏 (*Time and Light: Xu Xu in the Landscape of 20th-century Chinese Literary History*) (Nanchang: Baihuazhou wenyi chubanshe, 2004), pp. 328–9.

4. Tang Zhesheng 湯哲聲, 'Lun 40 niandai de liuxing xiaoshuo: yi Xu Xu, Wumingshi (Bu Naifu), Zhang Ailing, Su Qing de xiaoshuo weili', 論40 年代的流行小說: 以徐訏、無名氏 (卜乃夫) 、張愛玲、蘇青的小說為例 ('On the Popular Fiction of the 1940s: using the Fiction of Xu Xu, Wumingshi (Bu Naifu), Zhang Ailing, and Su Qing as Examples'), *Huadong chuanbo gongye xueyuan xuebao* 華東船舶工業學院學報 4(2) (June 2004): 1; Wu Yiqin 吳義勤 and Wang Suxia 王素霞, *Wo xin panghuang: Xu Xu zhuan* 我心彷徨:徐訏傳 (*My Wavering Heart: A Biography of Xu Xu*) (Shanghai: Shanghai sanlian shudian, 2012), p. 180.

5. There is unfortunately little agreement on how to render *xinganjuepai* 新感覺派 in English. Variations include 'New Sensibilities School' (Kirk A. Denton (ed.), *Modern Chinese Literary Thought: Writings on Literature 1893–1945* (Stanford, CA: Stanford University Press, 1996), p. 504); 'Neo-sensationalism' (Leo Ou-fan Lee, *Shanghai Modern: The Flowering of a New Urban Culture in China, 1930–1945* (Cambridge, MA: Harvard University Press, 1999), p. 405); 'New Sentiment Group' (Gregory B. Lee, *Troubadours, Trumpeters, Troubled Makers: Lyricism, Nationalism, and Hybridity in China and its Others* (London: Hurst, 1996), p. 71); 'New consciousness school' (Anonymous preface in Shi Zhecun, *One Rainy Evening*, trans. Wang Ying et al. (Beijing: Panda Books, 1994)); 'New Perceptionism' (Yingjin Zhang, *The City in Modern Chinese Literature and Film: Configuration of Space, Time, and Gender* (Stanford, CA: Stanford University Press, 1996), pp. 154–5); 'New Sensationalists' (Michel Hockx, *Questions of Style: Literary Societies and Literary Journals in Modern China, 1911–1937* (Leiden: Brill, 2003), p. 221); and 'New Sensationism' (Steven L. Riep, 'Chinese Modernism: The New Sensationists', in Joshua Mostow (ed.), *The Columbia Companion to Modern East Asian Literature* (New York: Columbia University Press, 2003), pp. 425–30).

6. Chang-tai Hung, *War and Popular Culture: Resistance in Modern China, 1937–1945* (Berkeley, CA: University of California Press, 1994), pp. 78–92.

7. See, for example, Charles J. Alber, *Enduring the Revolution: Ding Ling and the Politics of Literature in Guomindang China* (Westport, CT: Praeger, 2002); Yi-tsi Mei Feuerwerker, *Ding Ling's Fiction: Ideology and Narrative in Modern Chinese Literature* (Cambridge, MA: Harvard University Press, 1982).

8. Examples of the latter include David Holm, *Art and Ideology in Revolutionary China* (Oxford: Oxford University Press, 1991); Tsi-an Hsia, *The Gate of Darkness: Studies on the Leftist Literary Movement in China* (Seattle, WA: Washington University Press, 1971).

9. Poshek Fu, *Passivity, Resistance, and Collaboration: Intellectual Choices in Occupied Shanghai, 1937–1945* (Stanford, CA: Stanford University Press, 1993).

10. Carolyn FitzGerald, *Fragmenting Modernisms: Chinese Wartime Literature, Art, and Film, 1937–49* (Leiden: Brill, 2013).

11. FitzGerald, *Fragmenting Modernisms*, p. 26.

12. Gunn, *Unwelcome Muse*, pp. 249–62.

13. Perry Link, *Mandarin Ducks and Butterflies* (Berkeley, CA: University of California Press, 1981), pp. 23ff.

14. Nicole Huang, *Women, War, and Domesticity: Shanghai Literature and Popular Culture of the 1940s* (Leiden: Brill, 2005). Also see Amy D. Dooling, *Women's Literary Feminism in Twentieth-century China* (New York: Palgrave Macmillan, 2005), pp. 137ff.

15. Chang-tai Hung, *War and Popular Culture*.

16. See, for example, Kam Louie (ed.), *Eileen Chang: Romancing Languages, Cultures, and Genres* (Hong Kong: Hong Kong University Press, 2012); Theodore Huters, *Qian Zhongshu* (Boston, MA: Twayne, 1982).

17. Tommy McClellan, *Zhang Henshui and Popular Chinese Fiction, 1919–1949* (Lewiston, NY: Edwin Mellen, 2005).

18. Ng Mau-sang, 'Popular Fiction and the Culture of Everyday Life: A Cultural Analysis of Qin Shou'ou's *Qiuhaitang*', *Modern China*, 20(2) (1994): 131–56; David Der-wei Wang, 'Popular Literature and National Representation: The Gender and Genre Politics of *Begonia*', in Carlos Rojas and Eileen Cheng-yin Chow (eds), *Rethinking Chinese Popular Culture: Cannibalizations of the Canon* (London: Routledge, 2009).

19. Chang-tai Hung, *War and Popular Culture*, pp. 190–1.

20. Perhaps to escape such polarisation, the term 'middlebrow' is used in one anthology of popular Chinese literature. It has not found widespread usage. See Liu Ts'un-yan (ed.), *Chinese Middlebrow Fiction from the Ch'ing and Early Republican Eras* (Hong Kong: Chinese University Press, 1984).

21. Pierre Bourdieu, *The Field of Cultural Production: Essays on Art and Literature*, ed. Randal Johnson (Cambridge: Polity Press, 1993); Pierre Bourdieu, *The Rules of Art: Genesis and Structure of the Literary Field*, trans. Susan Emanuel (Cambridge: Polity Press, 1996).

22. See Michel Hockx (ed.), 'Introduction', in *The Literary Field of Twentieth-Century*

China (Richmond: Curzon Press, 1999); Michel Hockx, 'Theory as Practice: Modern Chinese Literature and Bourdieu', in Michel Hockx and Ivo Smits (eds), *Reading East Asian Writing: The Limits of Literary Theory* (London: RoutledgeCurzon, 2003).

23. Both Qian Zhongshu 錢鐘書 and Zhang Ailing 張愛玲 are usually seen as Shanghai School (*haipai* 海派) writers. See discussion below. They are classified as 'anti-romantic' authors by Gunn, *Unwelcome Muse*, pp. 200ff.

24. Dooling, *Women's Literary Feminism in Twentieth Century China*, pp. 137ff.

25. Theodore Huters, 'In Search of Qian Zhongshu', *Modern Chinese Literature and Culture*, 11(1) (1999): 193–9.

26. Zhou Zuoren 周作人, 'Humane Literature', in *Modern Chinese Literary Thought: Writings on Literature, 1893–1945*, ed. Kirk A. Denton and trans. Ernest Wolff (Stanford, CA: Stanford University Press, 1996), pp. 150–61.

27. Liping Feng, 'Democracy and Elitism: The May Fourth Ideal of Literature', *Modern China*, 22(2) (1996): 180.

28. This is still the case in some studies, for example, Carlos Rojas uses 'Butterfly fiction' as a term covering popular Chinese literature generally. See Carlos Rojas, 'Introduction: The Disease of Canonicity', in Carlos Rojas and Eileen Cheng-yin Chow (eds), *Rethinking Chinese Popular Culture: Cannibalizations of the Canon* (London: Routledge, 2009), p. 1.

29. Denise Gimpel, *Lost Voices of Modernity: A Chinese Popular Fiction Magazine in Context* (Honolulu, HI: University of Hawai'i Press, 2001).

30. Link, *Mandarin Ducks and Butterflies*, p. 198.

31. Ng Mau-sang, 'A Common People's Literature', *East Asian History*, 9 (1995): 20.

32. Yang Yi 楊義, 'Lun haipai xiaoshuo', 論海派小說 ('On Shanghai School Fiction'), *Zhongguo xiandai wenxue yanjiu congkan* 中國現代文學研究叢刊, 2 (1991): 167–81; Yan Jiayan 嚴家炎, 'Lun xin ganjue pai xiaoshuo', 論新感覺派小說 ('On New Sensationist Fiction'), in Yan Jiayan 嚴家炎 et al. (eds), *Zhongguo xiandai wenxue lunwen ji* 中國現代文學論文集 (*Essays on Modern Chinese Literature*) (Beijing: Beijing daxue chubanshe, 1986).

33. Yang Yi 楊義, *Jingpai haipai zonglun (tu zhi ben)* 京派海派总论 (图志本) (*An Overview of Beijing and Shanghai Schools*, illustrated edition) (Beijing: Zhongguo shehui kexue chubanshe, 2003), pp. 56–7.

34. Yang Yi 楊義, *Jingpai haipai zonglun (tu zhi ben)*, pp. 56–7.

35. Yang Yi 楊義, *Jingpai haipai zonglun (tu zhi ben)*, pp. 56ff. See also Yingjin Zhang, *The City in Modern Chinese Literature and Film*, pp. 21–7; Shu-mei Shih, *The Lure of the Modern: Writing Modernism in Semicolonial China, 1917–1937* (Berkeley, CA: University of California Press, 2001), pp. 175ff; Wu Fuhui 吳福輝, *Dushi xuanliu zhong de haipai xiaoshuo* 都市旋流中的海派小說 (*Shanghai School Fiction in the Urban Maelstrom*) (Changsha: Hunan jiaoyu chubanshe, 1995), pp. 282–303.

36. Wu Fuhui, *Dushi xuanliu zhong de haipai xiaoshuo*, pp. 3–4.

37. Wu Fuhui, *Dushi xuanliu zhong de haipai xiaoshuo*, pp. 3–4.

38. Wu Fuhui 吳福輝, 'Zuowei wenxue (shangpin) shengchan de haipai qikan', 作為文學(商品)生產的海派期刊 ('Shanghai School Journals as Literary (Commodity)

Productions'), *Zhongguo xiandai wenxue yanjiu congkan* 中國現代文學研究叢刊, 1 (1994): 3–5. The division is accepted by Yingjin Zhang, *The City in Modern Chinese Literature and Film*, p. 27.

39. Yan Jiayan, 'Lun xin ganjue pai xiaoshuo', p. 429; Yang Yi, *Jingpai haipai zonglun (tu zhi ben)*, pp. 173–6; Yang Yi, 'Lun haipai xiaoshuo', p. 2.

40. Wolfgang Kubin, *Die Chinesische Literatur im 20. Jahrhundert*, Geschichte der chinesischen Literatur, vol. 7, ed. Wolfgang Kubin (Munich: K. G. Saur, 2005), pp. 158–64.

41. Gimpel, *Lost Voices of Modernity*, pp. 222ff.

42. Ma Yixin 馬以鑫, *Zhongguo xiandai wenxue jieshou shi* 中國現代文學接受史 (*A History of the Reception of Modern Chinese Literature*) (Shanghai: Huadong shifan daxue chubanshe, 1998), p. 240.

43. In contrast to 'Shanghai School', a relatively neutral term that might simply be translated as 'popular literature' (*tongsu wenxue* 通俗文學) has found some traction in Chinese scholarship, and this seems to be more promising. See, for example, Fan Boqun 范伯群 (ed.), *Zhongguo jinxiandai tongsu wenxue shi* 中國近現代通俗文學史 (*A History of Late Qing and Republican Popular Literature*) (Nanjing: Jiangsu jiaoyu chubanshe, 2000).

44. Li Wei 李偉, *Shenmi de Wumingshi* 神秘的無名氏 (*The Mysterious Wumingshi*) (Shanghai: Shanghai shudian chubanshe, 1998), p. 59.

45. Li Wei, *Shenmi de Wumingshi*, p. 59.

46. Yan Jiayan 嚴家炎, *Zhongguo xiandai xiaoshuo liupai shi* 中國現代小說流派史 (*A History of Schools in Modern Chinese Fiction*) (Beijing: Renmin wenxue chubanshe, 1989), pp. 295–6. In an earlier classificatory scheme, Yan has Wumingshi and Xu Xu grouped as simply 'romanticists' (*langman zhuyi liupai* 浪漫注意流派). Yan Jiayan 嚴家炎, *Lun xiandai xiaoshuo yu wenyi sichao* 論現代小說與文藝思潮 (*On Modern Fiction and Trends in Literary Thought*) (Hunan: Hunan renmin chubanshe, 1987), p. 9.

47. For example, Li Yeping 李掖平 (ed.), *Xiandai Zhongguo wenxue zuopin daodu 1900–1949* 現代中國文學作品導讀 1900–1949 (*A Guide to Reading Modern Chinese Literary Works, 1900–1949*) (Jinan: Shandong huabao chubanshe, 2002); Wang Wenying 王文英, *Shanghai xiandai wenxueshi* 上海現代文學史 (*The History of Modern Shanghai Literature*) (Shanghai: Shanghai renmin chubanshe, 1999), p. 490.

48. Yingjin Zhang, *The City in Modern Chinese Literature and Film*, p. 223.

49. Yan Jiayan, *Lun xiandai xiaoshuo yu wenyi sichao*, p. 37

50. Yan Jiayan, *Lun xiandai xiaoshuo yu wenyi sichao*, p. 9.

51. Yan Jiayan, *Lun xiandai xiaoshuo yu wenyi sichao*, p. 37.

52. Yan Jiayan, *Lun xiandai xiaoshuo yu wenyi sichao*, p. 37.

53. Jiang Shuxian and Yin Jian, *Zhongguo xiandai wenxue shi*, p. 272.

54. Jiang Shuxian and Yin Jian, *Zhongguo xiandai wenxue shi*, p. 272.

55. Wu Daoyi 吳道毅, 'Xu Xu, Wumingshi xiaoshuo chuanqi tezheng lun', 徐訏、無名氏小說傳奇特徵論 ('On the *chuanqi* Characteristics of the Fiction by Xu Xu and Wumingshi'), *Wuhan daxue xuebao* 武漢大學學報, 53(6) (2000): 864–9.

56. Wu Daoyi, 'Xu Xu, Wumingshi xiaoshuo chuanqi tezheng lun', pp. 864–6. For a

brief overview of the *chuanqi* 傳奇 genre, see Wilt Idema and Lloyd Haft, *A Guide to Chinese Literature* (Ann Arbor, MI: Center for Chinese Studies, University of Michigan, 1997), pp. 134–9.

57. Zhu Xi 朱曦 and Chen Xingwu 陳興蕪, *Zhongguo xiandai langman zhuyi xiaoshuo moshi* 中國現代浪漫主義小說模式 (*Modes of Modern Chinese Romantic Fiction*) (Chongqing: Chongqing chubanshe, 2002), p. 255.

58. Zhu Xi and Chen Xingwu, *Zhongguo xiandai langman zhuyi xiaoshuo moshi*, pp. 271–8.

59. Zhu Xi and Chen Xingwu, *Zhongguo xiandai langman zhuyi xiaoshuo moshi*, pp. 255–6.

60. Kong Fanjin 孔范今 and Pan Xueqing 潘學清 (eds), *Zhongguo xiandai wenxue buyi shuxi* 中國現代文學補遺書系 (*Supplemental Series to Modern Chinese Literature*) (Jinan: Mingtian chubanshe, 1991), pp. 724–44.

61. Kong Fanjin and Pan Xueqing, *Zhongguo xiandai wenxue buyi shuxi*, p. 725.

62. Kong Fanjin and Pan Xueqing, *Zhongguo xiandai wenxue buyi shuxi*, p. 744.

63. Song Jianhua 宋劍華, 'Shengcun de tansuo yu yishu de xuanze: lun Wumingshi yu Xu Xu de xiaoshuo chuangzuo', 生存的探索與藝術的選擇: 論無名氏與徐訏的小說創作 ('Explorations of Existence and Artistic Choice: On the Fiction of Wumingshi and Xu Xu'), *Hebei xuekan* 河北學刊, 3 (1995): 58–63.

64. Song Jianhua, 'Shengcun de tansuo yu yishu de xuanze', pp. 60–1.

65. Song Jianhua, 'Shengcun de tansuo yu yishu de xuanze', pp. 60–1.

66. Song Jianhua, 'Shengcun de tansuo yu yishu de xuanze', p. 58.

67. Frederik Green, 'The Making of a Chinese Romantic: Cosmopolitan Nationalism and Lyrical Exoticism in Xu Xu's Early Travel Writings', *Modern Chinese Literature and Culture*, 23(2) (2011): 64–99; Frederik H. Green, 'Rescuing Love from the Nation: Love, Nation, and Self in Xu Xu's Alternative Wartime Fiction and Drama', *Frontiers of Literary Studies in China*, 8(1) (2014): 126–53. Other mentions are minor, e.g. Xu Xu has entries in Bonnie S. McDougall and Kam Louie, *The Literature of China in the Twentieth Century* (London: Hurst, 1997), as well as in Milena Doleželová-Velingerová (ed.), *A Selective Guide to Chinese Literature, 1900–1949, vol. 1: The Novel* (Leiden: Brill, 1988).

68. Green, 'Rescuing Love from the Nation', p. 150.

69. Song Jianhua, 'Shengcun de tansuo yu yishu de xuanze', pp. 60–1.

70. Chen Xuanbo, *Shi yu guang: 20 shiji Zhongguo wenxueshi geju zhong de Xu Xu.*

71. Wu Yiqin and Wang Suxia, *Wo xin panghuang: Xu Xu zhuan.*

72. Xu Xu 徐訏, *Xu Xu quanji* 徐訏全集 (*The Complete Works of Xu Xu*) (Taipei: Zhengzhong shuju, 1973). Only fifteen of the eighteen volumes were actually published. See Wu Yiqin and Wang Suxia, *Wo xin panghuang*, p. 317.

73. Chen Naixin 陳乃欣 et al. (eds), *Xu Xu er san shi* 徐訏二三事 (*A Few Things about Xu Xu*) (Taipei: Erya chubanshe, 1980).

74. For example, Sima Zhongyuan 司馬中原, 'Chuntian de huahuan', 春天的花環 ('Flower Wreaths of Spring'), in Chen Naixin et al. (eds), *Xu Xu er san shi*, p. 179.

75. Xin Dai 心岱, 'Taibei guoke', 臺北過客 ('Visiting Taipei'), in Chen Naixin et al. (eds), *Xu Xu er san shi*, p. 38.

76. Xiaoping Wang, 'An Alienated Mind Dreaming for Integration: Constrained Cosmopolitanism in Wumingshi's "Modern Literati Novel"', *Journal of Australasian Popular Culture*, 2(3) (2012): 425–38.

77. Yenna Wu, 'Expressing the "Inexpressible": Pain and Suffering in Wumingshi's Hongsha', in Philip F. Williams and Yenna Wu (eds), *Remolding and Resistance Among Writers of the Chinese Prison Camp: Disciplined and Published* (Abingdon: Routledge, 2006), pp. 122–56. See also Mr Anonymous (Wumingshi 無名氏), *The Scourge of the Sea: A True Account of My Experiences in the Hsia-sa Village Concentration Camp* (Taipei: Kuang Lu, 1985); Pu Ning, *Red in Tooth and Claw: Twenty-six Years in Communist Chinese Prisons*, trans. Tung Chung-hsuan (New York: Grove Press, 1994).

78. Bu Shaofu 卜少夫, 'Wumingshi sheng si xialuo', 無名氏生死下落 ('The Life and Whereabouts of Wumingshi'). Unfortunately I have been unable to locate this text.

79. Bu Shaofu 卜少夫 (ed.), *Wumingshi yanjiu* 無名氏研究 (*Wumingshi Research*) (Hong Kong: Xinwen tiandi she新聞天地社, 1981).

80. Wang Yingguo and Zhao Jiangbin, *Wumingshi chuanqi*; Geng Chuanming 耿傳名, *Duxing ren zong: Wumingshi zhuan* 獨行人蹤: 無名氏傳 (*Traces of a Solitary Walker: A Biography of Wumingshi*) (Nanjing: Jiangsu wenyi chubanshe, 2001).

81. Li Wei, 'Preface', *Shenmi de Wumingshi*, p. 2; Wang Yingguo and Zhao Jiangbin, *Wumingshi chuanqi*, p. 2.

82. Wang Yingguo and Zhao Jiangbin, *Wumingshi chuanqi*.

83. Wang Yingguo and Zhao Jiangbin, *Wumingshi chuanqi*, p. 5.

84. Zhao Jiangbin 趙江濱, 'Yixiang "xiandai" de zuji: Wumingshi wenxue chuangzuo jianlun', 移向 '現代' 的足跡: 無名氏文學創作簡論 ('Moving Towards the "Modern": Comments on Wumingshi's Creative Writing'), *Shijie huawen wenxue luntan* 世界華文文學論壇, 4 (1999): 30–5.

85. Zhu Xi and Chen Xingwu, *Zhongguo xiandai langman zhuyi xiaoshuo moshi*, p. 272.

86. Wang Yingguo and Zhao Jiangbin, *Wumingshi chuanqi*, p. 14.

87. Geng Chuanming, *Duxing ren zong: Wumingshi zhuan*, p. 246.

88. Zhao Zhi 趙智, 'Lun Wumingshi de zongjiao qinghuai', 論無名氏的宗教情懷 ('On Wumingshi's Religious Feelings'), *Peixun yu yanjiu: Hubei jiaoyu xueyuan xuebao* 培訓與研究: 湖北教育學院學報, 21(3) (2004): 8.

89. Chen Sihe 陳思和, 'Shilun Wumingshi de *Wumingshu*', 試論無名氏的《無名書》 ('On *The Nameless Book* by Wumingshi'), in Chen Sihe陳思和 (ed.), *Zhongguo dangdai wenxue guanjianci: Shi jiang* 中國當代文學關鍵詞: 十講 (*Keywords on Modern Chinese Literature: Ten Talks*) (Shanghai: Fudan daxue chubanshe, 2002).

90. Song Jianhua, 'Shengcun de tansuo yu yishu de xuanze'.

91. Wang Yingguo and Zhao Jiangbin, *Wumingshi chuanqi*, p. 14.

Chapter 2

Tradition and Hybridity in Shi Zhecun and Mu Shiying

Both Shi Zhecun 施蟄存 and Mu Shiying 穆時英 are fairly well known today for their modernist short stories from the 1930s.[1] Shi Zhecun worked as an author, translator and poet, as well as the editor-in-chief of *Les Contemporains* (*Xiandai* 現代, 1932–1935), a Shanghai journal that aimed to introduce a cosmopolitan educated readership to the latest trends in literature and art from China and abroad.[2] His fiction combined and juxtaposed various sources and genres of foreign and Chinese literature, drawing upon Freudian ideas of the subconscious, neurasthenia, dreams and irrationality. Mu Shiying was a protégé of Shi's and a frequent contributor to *Les Contemporains*. His modernist short stories set in Shanghai experiment with various styles and typographical elements to achieve jarring fragmented effects that break with normal narrative flows and notions of plot progression.

Alongside primarily Liu Na'ou 劉吶鷗 (1905–1940), Shi Zhecun and Mu Shiying are usually considered members of the 'New Sensationist' ('*xinganjuepai*' 新感覺派) group.[3] Like some of the terms discussed in the previous chapter, this label originated as an insult. It designated a group of Japanese writers (*shinkankaku ha*) who were inspired during the 1920s by Western avant-gardist art movements such as Futurism, Expressionism and Dadaism.[4] The leftist literary critic Lou Shiyi 樓適夷 (1905–2001) was the first to use the name to designate Chinese authors. In a dismissive critique of two of Shi Zhecun's short stories written in 1931, Lou argues that Shi was influenced by Japanese New Sensationism and that this aesthetic was inseparable from the '*Erotic*' and the '*Grotesque*'.[5] Shi's fiction was 'the literature of those who live by reaping the interests of money capitalism'.[6]

The Shanghai modernist writers of the 1930s entered a contentious literary field. The most prominent literary organisation of the day was the Chinese League of Left-wing Writers (*Zhongguo zuoyi zuojia lianmeng* 中國左翼作家聯盟) founded in Shanghai in March 1930 under the leadership of the august Lu Xun 魯迅.[7] The League called upon writers to produce literature supporting the socialist revolutionary cause, taking a hostile stance towards independent writers. A resolution adopted in 1931 demanded that themes reflecting 'trivial everyday matters' were to be rejected, and proletarian art was promoted to influence the masses.[8] Writers should adopt dialectical materialism in the fight against imperialist, feudal and capitalist ideas. Writers who sought symbolic capital turned to leftist causes and organisations.

The New Sensationists deliberately went against such dogma, writing about the experiences and fantasies of middle-class, bourgeois urban characters. Unlike the New Literature elite, the New Sensationist writers took a defiantly apolitical stance. There are no solutions, political critiques or noble ideals in their fiction. Instead of promoting ideological issues, they attacked the ideals and precepts of their contemporaries while attempting at the same time to renew the language and form of narrative representation. Their short stories frequently change direction midway, playing with familiar settings, clichés and narrative conventions, only to dismantle them and put them out of context. While there is no single document that outlines the New Sensationist aesthetic programme, it is quite clear that they saw themselves as cultural iconoclasts going against current trends of art in society.[9] Indeed, Leo Ou-fan Lee notes that they were interested in the avant-garde phenomenon and related to it in their own writings:

> According to Shi, the term *qianwei* (avant-garde) was first introduced to China around 1926–1928 from Japanese sources on Soviet literature. Shi and his friends were initially attracted to this radical revolutionary metaphor because they believed that all the best Soviet writers active in the 1920s – Mayakovsky, Babel and others – were avant-gardists, which they equated with the 'modern' trend in art and literature in Europe as well. In other words, they saw themselves as both revolutionary and aesthetic rebels on an international 'front line'.[10]

This stance of independence can also be observed in the now well-known literary debate on authors who chose to write independently of political ideology: the so-called 'third category' of writers ('*di san zhong ren*' 第三種人).[11] Another important debate took place between Shi Zhecun and Lu Xun on the merits of reading certain works of classical Chinese literature.[12] During the 1930s, Shi added punctuation to several classical works, such as Mao Zipu's 毛子普 *Poetry of Sixty Famous Song Poets* (*Song liushi mingjia ci* 宋六十名家詞) from the Ming dynasty and the late Qing work *Emerald Mansion* (*Cui lou ji* 翠樓集).[13] He also punctuated the erotic Ming novel *Jin Ping Mei* 金瓶梅 in 1936.[14] Shi's support of traditional literature of this sort was contentious at the time and pitted him against the standard bearers of New Literature.

As discussed in the previous chapter, literature that did not engage with progressive issues was rejected by New Literature proponents as shallow bourgeois entertainment. It was roundly denounced as harmful to national progress. By the 1930s, this boundary between the elite and the popular, or New and Old Literature, had hardened according to principles determined largely by the New Culture Movement intellectuals. One of the arguments of this chapter is that it was these principles that the New Sensationist writers set out to overturn. In their hybrid modernist works juxtaposing modernity and tradition, the rational, urban, modern outlook becomes inherently self-contradictory and liable to collapse. Their works demonstrate a deliberate rejection of realism and the politicisation of literature.

Fiction and the supernatural in Shi Zhecun

Spring Festival Lamp (*Shangyuan deng* 上元燈) is one of Shi Zhecun's earlier short-story collections. It was first published in 1929 by Froth Bookshop (*Shuimo shudian* 水沫書店), run by Shi together with Dai Wangshu 戴望舒 (1905–1950) and Liu Na'ou. The volume clearly foreshadows some of the themes found in Shi's later authorship, revealing his interest in literature, psychology and sexual desire that are also found in his later works. Most of the short stories in *Spring Festival Lamp* are gentle unassuming tales that revolve around memory and people's recollections of events in their youth. Frequently this act of memory is linked to material objects and how the supposed memento eventually displaces the actual person or event as the focus of the protagonist's attention. In both 'Spring Festival Lamp' ('*Shangyuan deng*' 上元燈) and 'Fan' ('*Shan*' 扇) the male protagonists develop links with objects that border on the fetishistic. 'Spring Festival Lamp' is written in a diary format and shows Shi's interest in narrative style.[15] Several of the short stories contain references to China's historical past as it appears in the present, with references to historical landmarks in the area.

As an example of Shi's interest in Chinese history, the foreword to the first edition of *Spring Festival Lamp* is written entirely in classical Chinese.[16] In contrast to the ornate language, the content itself is unremarkable. Shi claims not to know what to write for the preface since readers will determine for themselves what is good and bad about the works. He is pleased that his short stories will be published and that he can now join the ranks of authors. This lack of notable content in the preface is in contrast to the distinctive nature of its language. By 1928, classical Chinese had already been denounced by the majority of progressive Chinese authors and, therefore by using it, Shi Zhecun is indicating that these works should be considered in relation to the classical heritage and, thus, to literature. It highlights the collection's status as fiction situated between the modern and the traditional.

One of the short stories in *Spring Festival Lamp* that is strongly linked to traditional literary forms is 'How Master Hongzhi Became a Monk' ('*Hongzhi fashi de chujia*' 宏智法師的出家).[17] The narrator wonders about the origin of a local Daoist monk who hangs a lamp outside the temple every night for travellers. When a friend from Jiangxi 江西 comes to visit, he recognises the monk and tells the story of his life.

It turns out that Master Hongzhi, whose secular name is Lu 陸, was once a gifted young scholar (*caizi* 才子) who earned a first place in the *xiucai* 秀才 examinations. On marrying, young Lu was particularly unhappy with his new wife because she did not live up to his ideals of femininity, which were based entirely on the literature of the scholar-beauty (*caizijiaren* 才子佳人) genre.

Lu's ideal of a wife was a composite that stemmed from several classical works of Chinese literature. The narrator lists *The West Chamber Story* (*Xixiang ji* 西廂記), *Peony Pavilion* (*Mudan ting* 牡丹亭), 'Gaotang Shrine *fu*' ('*Gaotang fu*' 高唐賦), and 'Licentious *fu*' ('*Haose fu*' 好色賦).[18] In a common plot line from such romantic fiction and popular drama, an effete scholar hero passes the *xiucai* with flying colours and thereby wins the heart of the beautiful lady (*jiaren* 佳人), who composes elegant verse couplets, plays the lute, paints and displays impeccable calligraphy.

Considering himself just such a gifted story-book scholar, Lu was disappointed that his actual wife had none of these required skills, even being unable to read and write. One day Lu met the woman of his dreams who seemed every bit as beautiful and elegant as he had hoped his wife would be. But since he was already married, he was unable to court her. When some time later a number of disasters struck the area, Lu's wife disappeared under mysterious circumstances, and Lu eventually returned to the village remarried to the second woman, his ideal of feminine accomplishment. As might perhaps be expected, the second wife's gentility and sophistication turned out to be merely superficial, and unlike the first wife, she was not a kind person. Lu found himself missing his first wife, and suddenly she returned in dramatic fashion:

> On a certain night, an autumn night, there was a raging storm. He [Lu] and his second wife and the maid were all in the central room of the house.
> After a booming clap of thunder, the long window pasted over with paper creaked open. A woman with dishevelled hair, draped in a soaked gown, poked her head halfway into the room.
> 'Ah! Forgive me!' He suddenly leapt up and hiding his face with his hands and trembling all over, he knelt.
> This woman was his first wife!
> 'Demonic woman, have I not driven you away yet!' his second wife screamed after recognising who she was.
> 'Ah! ...' The first wife gave a piercing wail, full of anguish. The door creaked shut again. The sloshing sound of her footsteps gradually disappeared into the distance.
> At this instant, he scrambled up from the floor and pursued her outside. Through the heavy wind and rain he cried out remorsefully, 'My wife! ...'[19]

Lu and the second wife ran after her into the storm, but only Lu returned and neither of the two women was ever seen again. A long time after this incident, someone reportedly saw the first wife in the area where the narrator now resided. The visitor's tale thus explains why Lu became a Daoist monk who hangs a lamp outside the monastery every night in case his first wife should ever return.

This short story contains several interesting layers of intertextual references, shifting gradually from one genre to another. In the first passages, the reticent Master Hongzhi appears as a character out of the martial arts tradition: unknown by the villagers, a mysterious stranger with his own unusual nightly routine. In the traveller's tale, however, he then becomes an entirely different person who has based his life on romantic literature and stereotypes. These delusions are presented in a matter-of-fact way with brief explanatory asides on the lack of free love during that period. Finally, the short story explodes into absurd gothic horror, taking on an unreal aspect as the first wife appears from nowhere during a stormy night, only to disappear again immediately afterwards.

By changing genres midway, the short story repeatedly defies the logic of its own narrative framework. The scene in which the wife reappears seems such a mixture of gothic clichés that it is most likely a parody on the genre as a whole. Thus, the entire short story moves from one sort of intertextuality to the next, from borrowing popular stereotypes to direct reference and, finally, to parody. The incompatibility of these different modes of storytelling serves to undermine the narrator's voice. In the initial paragraph, he explains that there is less light in countryside villages than in big cities, which is why the monastery lamp is useful for travellers at night. Together with the comments on free love in the modern age, the narrator thus presents himself as a modern, urban and enlightened person. By the end of the story, however, this modern rationality is completely undermined by the absurdity of the tale.

The General's Head

The first of Shi's short stories to gain wider public notice were published in January 1932 in a collection called *The General's Head* (*Jiangjun de tou* 將軍的 頭).[20] In this collection, Shi produced several more directly intertextual pieces that are retellings of well-known classics and legends. Shi continued with such experiments in his later works as well, such as 'Li Shishi' ('*Li Shishi*' 李師師) in *An Evening of Spring Rain* (*Meiyu zhi xi* 梅雨之夕, 1933) and 'Master Huangxin' ('*Huangxin dashi*' 黃心大師, 1937).[21] But the four short stories in the collection *The General's Head* are probably the most well known of these works.

The first story, 'Kumarajiva', relates how a Buddhist monk is gradually corrupted by sexual desire.[22] The historical character Kumarajiva (344–413) was born in Kucha (*Qiuzi* 龜茲) in modern Xinjiang and was transported to Chang'an by Chinese forces when Kucha fell to them in 384. In Chang'an, Kumarajiva spread the knowledge of Buddhism and translated many impor-tant scriptures.[23] According to the *History of the Jin Dynasty* (*Jinshu* 晉書), the historical Kumarajiva was offered ten girls so that his many offspring might preserve his brilliance.[24]

Shi Zhecun's short story begins with Kumarajiva as he travels from Kucha to Chang'an. Outside Chang'an his beloved wife dies and he kisses her goodbye, using his tongue. This wife was given to him by a foreign ruler, but his love of her clearly indicates his fall from Buddhist purity. In Chang'an, Kumarajiva is haunted by visions of her when he looks at other women, particularly a beauti-ful courtesan. Eventually, he falls to temptation and surrounds himself with prostitutes and luxury, claiming that they mean nothing to him. Throughout the story, Kumarajiva is plagued by his guilty conscience – he is painfully aware that he has lost his Buddhist purity and is now merely posing before his audiences and lecturing on the sutras without real conviction. The short story ends with his death. After his cremation, his tongue lies among the ashes on the funeral pyre untouched by the flames.

'The General's Head' is loosely based on the semi-historical character Hua Jingding 花驚定, of whose real life little is known.[25] He was a half-Han and half-Tibetan general of the Tang dynasty. According to legend, Hua's Chinese army was defeated by invading forces and Hua was decapitated. Yet Hua kept on riding until he reached a creek where he stopped to wash his face. A woman who saw him cried out in fear, causing Hua to see his headless reflection in the water. Thereupon he realised that he had been killed, and dropped to the ground.[26] In Shi's recounting, Hua decapitates a Han soldier in Xinjiang for trying to rape a Han girl, but he cannot help falling in love with her himself. During battle he and an enemy general simultaneously decapitate each other. The headless Hua picks up his enemy's head and rides back to the girl to show her this trophy. The story concludes with the girl sneering at him and the head in his hands laughing, while his own head cries far away.

'Shi Xiu' 石秀 is a rewriting of an episode in the famous Ming dynasty novel *Water Margin* (*Shuihu zhuan* 水滸傳).[27] In the original, Shi Xiu and Yang Xiong 楊雄 expose Yang's deceitful wife Pan Qiaoyun 潘巧雲.[28] But in Shi Zhecun's recasting, Shi Xiu secretly desires Pan though he dares not pursue her since he wishes to be included in Yang Xiong's brotherhood of outlaws. His thwarted desires are replaced by sadistic fantasies that find an outlet when he catches Pan having an affair with a monk. Shi Xiu manipulates Yang into exercising a brutal revenge upon her.[29] In the final scene, Pan Qiaoyun is killed by Yang, and Shi Xiu relishes every cut of the knife, deriving great sexual pleasure from seeing the blood and entrails spilling from her stomach.

William Schaefer has dealt with three of the short stories in some detail, showing how they relate to their source material, so there is no need to repeat that here.[30] Still, I would like to take a brief look at how these works relate to literature and the contemporary literary scene. According to Shu-mei Shih, the historical settings serve to make the short stories less controversial:

> In Shi's fictional world, [Shi Xiu's] masculine assertion, with its obvious misogyny, can only occur in a remote past of no immediate consequence to the present (and a textually simulated past at that, since the story is derived from another text). The interiority in Shi's fiction, whether contemporary or historical, thus tends to be a nonideological and apolitical space of textual dissimulation and erotic-grotesque fantasies.[31]

Taking exactly the opposite view, William Schaefer argues that these stories are to be read as a challenge to contemporary elite conceptions of the past as separated from the present. Shi's fiction challenges the way modernity positions itself as sharply divided from the past. The short stories in *The General's*

Head 'interrupt and pollute the language of the past, and pile layer upon layer of complexity and contradiction until a comforting resolution is impossible and the narrative has nowhere to go but to explode into violence or the fantastic, or both'.[32]

I think both scholars seem to overlook the fact that these short stories are not principally concerned with history, but rather with legend and myth. Shi is rewriting fiction and legend rather than historical fact. He is not concerned with the realities of history, but instead with the idea of fictionality and the rules that govern narrative within such fictional domains. The Ming novel *The Water Margin* operates within a fictional universe of heroism and martial virtues which remains well known to Chinese readers and is perpetuated in countless popular novels of knight-errantry and martial arts (*wuxia xiaoshuo* 武俠小說). In 'Shi Xiu', Shi Zhecun breaks the integrity of this genre by making Shi Xiu the sole narrator – a stylistic device that violates the traditional role of the storyteller/narrator in classical fiction. Not only is Shi Xiu recast as a scheming villain, he is also possessed by typical Freudian anxieties and drives, such as repressed sexuality and voyeuristic sadistic desire. As Frank Dikötter demonstrates, such motives and desires were considered the result of modernity.[33] By imbuing the characters with these modern traits, *The Water Margin*'s fictional universe is violated and thus its status as unitary and self-contained narrative erodes.

The departure from realism and the grounding of the settings and characters in legend, not history, makes these short stories a challenge to the New Literature precepts that fiction should reflect real life and social issues. This is fiction based on fiction, and the only tie to the modern world is the modern psychological processes that are the cause of the characters' undoing.

Apart from mixing modern psychology into the narratives, Shi also shifts subtly between different registers of language, using both passages of lofty description that would traditionally belong to the martial arts genre as well as passages with extended streams-of-consciousness indicating the confusion and uncertainty of the protagonists. This is also the case with the last short story in the collection, 'Princess A Lan' ('*A Lan gongzhu*' 阿襤公主), which achieves an effect similar to the crossing of genres in 'How Master Hongzhi Became a Monk'. The logic of the narrative comes apart and highlights the composite fictionality of the work.

In these works, the very fictionality of the settings is decisive as the reader brings prior knowledge of events and cultural expectations to the table while reading them. It is the explorations of psychological weaknesses that place these works firmly outside the traditional martial arts genre. While the language in passages with flapping sleeves and glaring eyes clearly pays homage to such genres of bold heroics, the characters' failings serve to undermine any notion of heroism that might be expected. And the crossing between the familiarity of tradition and the intrusion of the modern makes these works all the more unsettling.

A similar effect can be found in the short story 'The Haunted House'

('*Xiongzhai*' 凶宅) from *An Evening of Spring Rain* from 1933.[34] The first-level narrator presents a number of source materials concerning a Dutch-style Shanghai mansion in which three young wives have supposedly hanged themselves. Through a newspaper excerpt, a diary, an interview and, finally, the confession of a serial killer, the mysteries of the haunted house are presented, researched and gradually unravelled. Featuring suicides, murder, grief, illicit love, royalty and frightening shadows of women with ropes around their necks, this short story contains every imaginable ingredient of a cheap potboiler horror story or whodunit. Taken as a whole, this piece appears as Shi Zhecun's exercise in how many trite clichés from popular literature can be crammed into a single piece of text.

But in 'The Haunted House', it is not the content, but the complex layered narrative format that suggests that it is to be read as more than grisly entertainment. By presenting various sources in a scholarly manner with expositions about their origin and date of publication, the first-level narrator comes across as an academic scholarly person concerned with the facts of an interesting criminal case. The newspaper excerpt that introduces the mansion and the three suicides of young wives within is presented as a translation into Chinese from an article in the English-language *Shanghai Paper* (*Yingwen Hu bao* 英文滬報). A diary excerpt from the Russian owner of the mansion is translated from its publication in a French newspaper. The newspaper had altered the names to protect the characters' identities, but their real names are revealed during a conversation between an Italian husband of a now-deceased Romanian princess and a lawyer in Harbin. Finally, the recorded confession of an American five-time serial wife-killer wraps up the last trailing loose ends.

This meticulous attention to names, places, sources and dates stands in sharp contrast to the purposely hackneyed content and composite fictional imagery. It is this free mixture of fictional sources and genres, from gothic horror to detective story and romantic melodrama, which offsets and ultimately dismantles the supposed realism of the narratorial instance in a manner similar to 'How Master Hongzhi Became a Monk'. The narrator's relation to reality is grounded in his representation of 'real facts' based on references to sources, yet this position is invariably undermined by the submerged references to well-known fictional tropes and stereotypes throughout the short story.

Examples of short stories where Shi Zhecun mixes gothic elements with other literature include 'Yaksha' ('*Yecha*' 夜叉), 'Sorcery' ('*Modao*' 魔道) and 'The Inn' ('*Lüshe*' 旅舍), which were all included in the 1933 short-story collection *An Evening of Spring Rain*.[35] 'Yaksha' is a modern retelling of a traditional *zhiguai* 志怪 tale, the ghost stories dating back to the Han dynasty often featuring men encountering female ghosts and spirits.[36] The short story features a modern Shanghai protagonist who goes to a remote village to arrange his grandmother's funeral. After reading about a local yaksha, a beautiful evil creature who used to lure local villagers to their deaths a long time ago, he rushes out in the night and pursues and eventually strangles a woman whom he believes to be this alluring monster. After realising his error, he rushes back to Shanghai, racked with guilt. With these short stories, Shi tests the boundaries of realism by drawing upon newly introduced psychological processes to explore worlds of fiction, legend and fantasy. These works are neither psychological realism nor ghost stories in a traditional sense. In the end, the short stories cannot be categorised as belonging to either category. They cross back and forth between the boundaries of the two genres, thereby creating hybrid works that undermine both types of literature.

Tradition in Shi Zhecun's fiction

Shi Zhecun's fiction spans a wide variety of genres and styles from pastiche and gothic horror to psychological studies of everyday events. Similarly, his characters span a range from sadistically deranged and violent madmen to nostalgic dreamers who wistfully long for more exciting lives. Yet one of the single threads that can be traced throughout Shi's diverse oeuvre is the persistent concern with how memory, tradition and China's cultural past mix with fantasy, illusion and sexual desire. Neurasthenia and psychology also play an important role in most of Shi's short stories. But the use of Freudian concepts is rarely an end unto itself. Rather, the psychological explorations mostly reflect the character's outlook and they form a point of departure from which to engage with fiction, cultural tradition and legend.

Practically all of Shi's short stories establish a binary in which rationalism, enlightenment and modernity are juxtaposed with traditions, legends and dreams. Psychology and literature play an important part in the crossing from one realm to the other. In a number of his short stories, such as 'How Master Hongzhi Became a Monk', 'Yaksha' and 'Fog' ('*Wu*' 霧), classical texts undermine the modern sensibilities of the protagonists and make them susceptible to their delusions. Interestingly, the short stories in *The General's Head* demonstrate a similar pattern in reverse as modern sensibilities are applied to well-known characters from classical texts. This juxtaposition undercuts the status of the original texts and destroys their narrative unity. In every case, once the realms of modernity and its other collide, modern enlightenment becomes a pathway into delusions and repressed desires. Modern rationality turns out to be the simple facade that covers groundless fear, desperate sexual pursuit and, in extreme cases, sadistic violence.

Madness and nervous conditions had been a mainstay in New Literature fiction from Lu Xun's famous madman to Yu Dafu's 郁達夫 nervous and emasculated protagonists. Yet notions of Freudianism had not been used to move into the realm of fictionality and legend in the same way that Shi Zhecun does. Tradition and fiction undermine the positions of the narrators and protagonists. As literary genres are mixed and turned around, realism turns to absurdity. Modernity, rationality and restraint inevitably give way to madness, fantasy and violent desire.

Urban decay and stereotypes in Mu Shiying

Mu Shiying was a friend of Shi Zhecun's and a frequent contributor to *Les Contemporains*. He wrote modernist short stories set in Shanghai that experimented with various styles and typographical elements to achieve jarring fragmented effects that break with normal narrative flows and notions of plot progression. The modernist short stories that were published in his later short-story collections, such as *Public Cemetery* (*Gongmu* 公墓, 1933) and *Statue of a Platinum Woman* (*Baijin de nüti suxiang* 白金的女體塑像, 1934), are those that are now considered most representative of his work – with their cosmopolitan *femmes fatales* and the poor feeble men who are duped and dumped by them.[37] They are quite different from his earlier short stories collected in *North Pole, South Pole* (*Nanbeiji* 南北極, 1932), which features bandits and pirates railing against capitalism and modern women whom they cannot understand.[38] In Mu's later work, the emphasis is on narrative technique rather than plot progression. The plot is secondary to the narrative style, which is highlighted by broken fragments of sentences and words juxtaposed typographically in novel ways. The modernist narrative draws upon diverse elements from poetry, popular culture, current politics and advertising. Unlike much contemporary fiction that was set in a timeless countryside, Mu's rendition of Shanghai foregrounds the passage of time and space.

The short story 'Five in a Nightclub' ('*Yezonghui li de wu ge ren*' 夜總會裏的五個人, 1932) is perhaps the one that is most representative of this style. It features five main characters, and the narrative shifts between them until they converge in a nightclub to drown their separate sorrows. They are not individualised characters, but representatives of different aspects of Shanghai. Mu uses all varieties of sensory impressions – colours, temperatures and smells – to describe the jumbled sensations of the metropolis. The *locus classicus* in this regard is the following passage:

> The world of a Saturday night is a cartoon globe spinning on the axis of jazz – just as quick, just as crazed; gravity loses its pull and buildings are launched skyward.
> On Saturday night reason is out of season.
> On Saturday night even judges are tempted to lead lives of crime.
> On Saturday night God goes to Hell.
> Men out on dates completely forget the civil code against seduction. Every woman out on a date tells her man that she is not yet eighteen, all the while laughing inside over how easy he is to dupe. The driver's eyes stray from the pedestrians on the road to admire his lover's scenic contours; hands move forward to probe.
> On Saturday night a self-respecting man steals; a simpleton's head fills with intrigue; a God-fearing Christian lies; old men drink rejuvenating tonics; experienced women apply kiss-proof lipstick.
> Streets:
> (Puyi Realty accrued annual interest totalling 33% of capital investment taels 100,000
> Has Manchuria fallen

No, our volunteers are right now fighting in the snow with Japs to the last man
COUNTRYMEN COME PLEDGE MONTHLY DONATIONS
The Mainland Daily circulation now totals 50,000
1933 Bartok
free meal-line)
'Evening Post!' The newsboy opened his blue mouth to reveal blue teeth and a blue
tongue. The blue neon high-heeled shoe across from him pointed straight at his blue
mouth.[39]

The city is envisioned as an abstract place of speed, fluidity and sexuality with all
its modern thrills and vices. The staccato narrative style underscores the city's
confusion and depredation. The fight against the Japanese is mentioned only as
a headline, not a concern of the characters present. It is an image of decay and
allure that is both seductive and repellent in its decadence. But overall, there is a
sharp indictment against the modern urbanite's life. Underneath the superficial
polish of newness and neon lights, the modernity of Shanghai is negative, superficial and senseless in its fetishism with new items and fashions. Egotism, deceit
and hypocrisy are emblematic of modernity in this configuration. Mu Shiying
presents a style of life that is exotic and alluring, but ultimately fatiguing and
inhuman. This representation of the city can be seen in the oft-quoted opening
of Mu Shiying's 'Shanghai Foxtrot' ('Shanghai de hubuwu' 上海的狐步舞, 1932):
'Shanghai. A Heaven built on Hell'.[40] The outward glamour of the city merely
disguises the lack of compassion of its citizens.

Likewise, casual sex devoid of romance or emotion is highlighted as syn-
onymous with the modern mores of Shanghai. The fleeting sexual encounter between anonymous partners is the quintessential modern experience. In
'Night' ('Ye' 夜), a foreign sailor meets a Chinese girl in a dance hall and later
they have sex at her place.[41] Their dancing and drinking together during the
evening is all dull, impersonal routine and going through the motions. They do
not reveal their names to each other until the very end, the next morning before
his departure, in which a glimmer of humanity surfaces between them. There
may be hope, but only during momentary exceptions when the characters let
down their guard.

Mu Shiying frequently uses the *femme fatale* stereotype as a symbol of the
new sexual mores in modern Shanghai. A typical seductress in Mu Shiying's
fiction can be found in the short story 'The Man Who Was Made a Plaything'
('*Bei dangzuo xiaoqianpin de nanzi*' 被當做消遣品的男子, 1931).[42] Here the narrator is a university student in Shanghai who cannot help falling in love with
a beautiful and glamorous woman despite his constant awareness that she is
treacherous and untruthful. He is fully aware of her allure and the danger she
poses to him from the very beginning:

The first time I saw her I felt: 'She's really a dangerous creature!' She had the body
of a snake and the head of a cat, a mixture of gentleness and danger. She was wearing

a long silk *qipao* and standing in a slight breeze that made its corners flap. As soon as I saw her feet, I knew that they were dancing feet, stepping on begonias in lovely red satin high-heeled shoes. They turned her waistline into the mouth of a flower vase above which opened a splendid peony ... a mouth that could tell lies and a pair of eyes which could deceive – a high-class piece of goods![43]

Despite the narrator being wary of her deceptions, he naturally cannot help but fall desperately in love with her. She claims to love him too, but she flirts and dances with other men which drives him to jealousy and despair. She insists that they are merely 'playthings' to her – she chews men like chocolate and spits them out again.[44] Choosing to believe her lies, the narrator thinks of himself as her one true love and eventually submits to her total control, reporting his every move to her while she goes on the town dancing and flirting. During the summer break, he pines for her and sends her letters, which are never answered. In the end, he realises that he was merely her plaything as well.

The femmes fatales of Mu Shiying's and Liu Na'ou's fiction were indebted to Hollywood's glamorous screen icons.[45] In 'The Man Who Was Made a Plaything', this is made explicit with repeated references to Clara Bow (1906–1965), Norma Shearer (1902–1983) and several other movie stars of the time. The narrative seems to indicate a certain level of textual self-awareness, an acknowledgement that the elusive seductress is a stereotype combining aspects of the *femme fatale* with the New Woman (*xin nüxing* 新女性): progressive, sensual and liberated. As confident New Women, flappers or vixens, they are well-known stock characters found in pulp fiction, romances, calendar posters and films. In using such stereotypes, Mu is repeating a common trope of popular fiction or Western cinema exemplified, among others, in Zhang Henshui's 張恨水 novel *Shanghai Express* (*Ping-Hu tongche* 平滬通車, 1935), where the male protagonist loses his money to a beautiful modern woman who seduces him on a train.[46] As stereotypes their role is to embody modern morals and sexual mores. They personify a modernity that is constantly out of reach and unattainable sexual gratification by embodying glamorous wealth, sophistication and urban leisure.[47]

In Mu Shiying's modernist short stories, there is little of the psychological depth that characterises Shi Zhecun's characters. Instead, Mu's characters are often deliberate stereotypes and their very superficiality is symptomatic of their meaningless petty bourgeois lives. In one way or another, they are all victims of modernity in the city that holds them in its grip and exerts a constant pressure on them to maintain their carefree outward facades.

But Mu Shiying's short stories also include instances of seductive modern women who are more complex. 'Black Peony' ('*Hei mudan*' 黑牡丹) is another short story from the collection *Public Cemetery*, published in 1933.[48] The female character in this tale is a seductive taxi dancer, but she is not a *femme fatale* to the narrator. The narrator, Gu 顧, is a young dandy who roams the nightclubs, but who has become tired of the speed and superficiality of big city life. One night he meets a breathtakingly beautiful Spanish-looking taxi dancer who is pursued by several other customers. She looks extremely tired. After a dance, they sit down at his table to talk:

> 'You look so tired!' [he said.]
> 'I've got a bit of a cold.'
> 'Why don't you take a rest for a day at home?'
> 'Once you're curled into the stream of life, you know, if you take a breath of air, you've already sunk to the bottom and you can't float back up again.'
> 'In our generation we're the slaves of our stomachs, slaves of our bodies … we're all oppressed by life!'
> 'Take me, for instance. I live a life of luxury, but take away the jazz, the foxtrot, the cocktails, autumn fashions, eight-cylinder cars, and Egyptian cigarettes … then I've got no soul. I am so deeply soaked in luxury, grabbing onto life, that in this luxury, in this life, I have become weary …'
> 'Yes, life is mechanical, sprinting forwards at full speed, but we are living beings after all! …'
> 'One day we'll collapse in the middle of the road.'
> 'One day we'll collapse in the middle of the road.'[49]

In this manner, the sophisticated narrator finds a soulmate who knows the pressures of trying to keep up with modern life. Their fatigue with life gives them a point in common and mutual understanding.

A month later, the narrator is contacted by a reclusive friend, Shengwu 聖五, who invites him to his mansion in the country for the weekend to see his black peonies. Shengwu tells Gu that he has met a flower spirit, Black Peony, just like those in the ghost stories from *Strange Tales from the Liaozhai Studio* (*Liaozhai zhiyi* 聊齋志異).[50] When Gu is introduced to Black Peony, he is shocked to recognise the taxi dancer he had met earlier. Later that evening, Shengwu tells Gu that not long ago a girl appeared, dreamlike, in the middle of the night while he was sleeping out in the open. She ran away, but his dog caught her. Mysterious and elusive, she refused to tell him her name, but she was seductive and showed Shengwu an enticing scar running from her stomach to her breast produced by the dog. Since then, she had remained in his house. He sees her as a flower spirit and she has made the plants in his house revive. Later the next day, the narrator meets Black Peony, who admits that she stumbled upon Shengwu's house while running away from a man who was after her. It was easier to pretend to be a supernatural spirit since he would probably have thrown her out if he knew the truth: that she was merely a taxi dancer. Shengwu's mansion is a refuge to her where she has found a place to relax and escape from the speed and pressure of Shanghai life. She has even managed to gain some weight. In the end, Gu leaves the countryside mansion feeling miserable. Inviting him to return every weekend, Black Peony cheerfully promises him 'a comfy bed, a full breakfast, a patio full of merriment, and a welcoming heart'.[51] Bereft, he feels that he has lost the one person who understood and shared the fatigue of modern life with him, and that he now has to shoulder this burden alone.

This brief short story establishes a simple contrast between the exhausting pressures of Shanghai and the pleasures of life outside the city. Shanghai is modern, sexual, oppressive and inhumane. The dance hall customers are all anonymous and unpleasant. In sharp contrast, Black Peony and Shengwu have found happiness in a countryside mansion that transcends the passing of time and the pressing events of real life. The total separation of this place from the life in Shanghai is reinforced by Black Peony's behaving like a flower spirit from traditional fiction. The deliberate tie with literature is established in several places during the narrative. Shengwu was already something of a traditional recluse, and Black Peony is likened to the figures of *chuanqi* 傳奇 ghost stories. In this manner, the mansion functions as a separate space isolated from the city, which becomes associated with the supernatural similar to the way in which Shi Zhecun made use of fiction and legend in his short stories. But unlike in Shi's fiction, this place does not undermine the rationality of the characters. Instead, it becomes a sanctuary from which to escape the pressures of life.

Apart from the use of the flower spirit trope to establish a distance from 'real life', this short story is also interesting in its use of changing narrative perspectives. We get several images of Black Peony presented in succession. First, we see her from the narrator's perspective as the poor taxi dancer, attractive but exhausted by working in the dance halls. Second, we get Shengwu's rendition of her as the marvellous and mystical apparition whom he cannot understand. Third, we are presented with her own story about herself and her escape from a man by running through the fields – battered and scratched from running – until she stumbles upon Shengwu's house. As the sum of these perspectives, she emerges as a good girl trying to find a way out of the pressures of modern life. From a narrative perspective, it is these different configurations that finally allow her to escape. Black Peony is able to recast her role and thereby achieve a measure of liberty that her profession could never have allowed.

Due to the narrative framework and various representations of her character, Black Peony cannot be considered a *femme fatale* in the usual sense, such as the woman in 'The Man Who Was Made a Plaything'. Black Peony is not primarily a seductress, but rather a woman who is worn out by the vicissitudes of modern life. In this respect, she is more like the stereotype of the poor prostitute who was also frequently seen as a victim of modernity.

Most of Mu Shiying's later short stories read as direct indictments against modernity. The characters are prisoners to the speed of life and the superficial glamour they pursue. Their surroundings all have a dehumanising effect. People become unfeeling machines who are racing to keep up with a constantly moving target. There is a prevailing sense of fatigue as the characters feel trapped or fail to come to terms with modern ways.

Mu Shiying's critique of modernity operates at another level as well. The vision of modernity tied to consumption, fashions and fads derives from the fragmentation of modernity created by popular literature and advertising that appropriated modern discourses on progress, rationality and enlightenment. In Mu Shiying's rendition, the spinning mosaic of neon lights, foreign advertising and media stereotypes lends his short stories an intertextual aspect. The incoherent jumble of cultural references builds upon well-known popular symbols of modernity, but uses them to undermine the modern in its original form. Progress, rationality and enlightenment are invariably the first to crumble in these short stories. The myriad modern images do not lead towards a meaningful plateau of development, but rather to its opposite: a jarring and random mixture of incoherent sensations. Amidst the collage of signifiers of modernity, the end result is chaos, exhaustion and alienation.

The New Sensationists and genre hybridity

Although the writings of Shi Zhecun and Mu Shiying are quite different in style and content, their use of a diverse mixture of intertextual references from foreign, native, classical and modern sources is similar. Their fiction borrowed themes, images and characters from both contemporary popular fiction as well as China's long cultural heritage, including ghost stories, martial arts novels and poetry. By calling attention to the inherent literariness of their fiction, these authors emphasised that their art was non-real and culturally fragmented. The intertextual links and the modernist narrative style highlight the short story's status as art, artifice and literary construction. In this manner it is self-referential in illuminating its own status as an instance of art that relates to other art. This is the diametric opposite of realism's aim for verisimilitude. The ideal of realism is rejected completely.

That is not to say that all of Shi Zhecun's and Mu Shiying's works should be considered nihilistic attacks on established cultural values. Their short stories have literary qualities in their own right and deserve to be read for their own literary value. Particularly Shi Zhecun was very much a part of the established cultural field with his editorship of *Les Contemporains*, so he cannot simply be seen as an iconoclastic outsider wishing to tear down petty bourgeois values in the field of literature. Similarly, a few of Mu Shiying's short stories read mostly like gentle love stories that contain little of the outrage or anger found in many of his other writings, and some of his short stories do contain a strong social message. Neither of the two authors ever reach the pure extremes of artistic rejection found in nonsense literature or the wilder outreaches of Dadaist unintelligibility. The New Sensationists produced writings with their own artistic value quite apart from challenging the principles of the literary field.

Yet rather than being largely culturally self-contained, these works frequently read as pastiche and parody. Such writing relates to both elite and popular fiction as cultural comment and critique. Thereby it situates itself outside the normal span of literary categories as meta-literature.

The use of history, legend and myth serves a purpose within the works as well. The references to the past are not rooted in historical reality, but rather manifest themselves indirectly by means of representation and construction. Through memory, delusion, legend and fiction, it is the depiction and refraction of the past and China's cultural heritage that are important, rather than the occurrence of actual events. The past and tradition are invariably seen through their representation in literature and myth, and, consequently, they become distorted. Mu Shiying and Shi Zhecun use this distortion to reflect back on current styles and genres of writing and the tenuous links between fiction and reality. The lingering presence of tradition subverts that which at first appears as real, modern and rational.

Rationality and progress come under attack as mental constructs that can be toppled by the dreams and displaced desires that are symptomatic of stressful modern life. Their fiction portrays the splitting forces of urban modernity – in subject matter as well as in style of writing. The expressionist staccato narrative style of Mu Shiying and the disjunctive narrative formats in Shi Zhecun's works convey the feelings of disorientation, loss and frustration of the protagonists. Apart from rejecting realism, the narrative style reflects the loss of rationalism in the face of modern progress.

Shanghai modernist literature of the 1930s was essentially hybrid. It adopted tropes and patterns from popular literature and tradition, combining them in novel ways that undercut each other. By adopting and subverting elements and stereotypes from popular literature and a negated cultural tradition, New Sensationist fiction of the 1930s was a sign of the times as well as a statement of opposition. These works not only depart from realism and reject the politicisation of art, they also undermine the image of modernity as progress. Modernity is instead associated with degeneration, neurasthenia, madness and absurdity. This constituted an avant-gardist attack on the notion that modernity and progress were meaningful goals with which the writer should engage in a constructive manner, as well as a rejection of the principles promoted by the League of Left-wing Writers.

Indeed, the League often wrote furious critiques of Mu Shiying's writings.[52] Mu came closest to articulating his defiance against their politicisation of literature in the preface to *Public Cemetery* from 1933:

> I am unwilling, as so many are today, to adorn my true face with some protective pigment, or to pass my days in hypocrisy shouting hypocritical slogans, or to manipulate the psychology of the masses, engaging in political maneuvering, self-propaganda, and the like to maintain a position once held in the past or to enhance my personal prestige. I consider this to be base and narrow-minded behavior, and I won't do it.[53]

Despite Mu's disavowal of politics, the New Sensationist style was contrary to the trends of the time, and by the 1940s the New Sensationist authors had disappeared or retreated from the literary field. Shi Zhecun moved to Kunming in 1937 and took up teaching at the History of Literature Department at Yunnan University.[54] Mu Shiying moved to Hong Kong in 1938, where he lived for a while with several other émigré writers and intellectuals, including Wumingshi's 無名氏 brother Bu Shaofu 卜少夫. Their residence, Tai Pak Lau 太白樓, became something of a cultural centre at the time.[55] Mu Shiying returned to Shanghai in 1939 and soon started working with the collaborationist government. This led to his assassination the following year.

Nevertheless, the New Sensationist works had a more profound impact on later writings than is generally recognised. During the 1940s, the writing style pioneered by the New Sensationists was adopted by other writers, but not as a stance of protest. The introduction of elements from the literary tradition was no longer seen as subversive, but rather considered as a kind of sophisticated intellectual game. Tradition and history stopped being contentious issues after the war broke out. Contrary to the attitude of the previous decade, China's cultural heritage became a source of pride and traditional literary forms were adopted as ways to reach and influence the masses.

Notes

1. Leo Ou-fan Lee, *Shanghai Modern*, pp. 190–231; Yingjin Zhang, *The City in Modern Chinese Literature and Film*, pp. 160–8; Li Junguo 李俊國, *Zhongguo xiandai dushi xiaoshuo yanjiu* 中國現代都市小說研究 (*A Study of Modern Chinese Urban Fiction*) (Beijing: Zhongguo shehui kexue chubanshe, 2004).

2. Leo Ou-fan Lee, *Shanghai Modern*, pp. 130–50.

3. *Zhongguo wenxue da cidian* 中國文學大辭典 (*Encyclopaedia of Chinese Literature*), s.v., 'Xinganjuepai 新感覺派', 8: 6070.

4. *Kodansha Encyclopedia of Japan*, s.v., 'Shinkankaku School', 7: 116.

5. Lou Shiyi 樓適夷, 'Shi Zhecun de xin ganjue zhuyi: Du "Zai Bali da xiyuan" yu "Modao" zhi hou', 施蟄存的新感覺主義: 讀《在巴黎大戲院》與《魔道》之後 ('The New Sensationism of Shi Zhecun: On Reading "In the Paris Cinema" and "Demon's Way"'), in Ying Guojing 應國靖 (ed.), *Zhongguo xiandai zuojia xuanji: Shi Zhecun* 中國現代作家選集: 施蟄存 (*Selections of Modern Chinese Authors: Shi Zhecun*) (Hong Kong: Sanlian shudian youxian gongsi, 1988), p. 306 (italic indicates wording in English in the original).

6. Lou Shiyi, 'Shi Zhecun de xin ganjue zhuyi', p. 305.

7. The history of the League is documented in Wang-chi Wong, *Politics and Literature in Shanghai: The Chinese League of Left-wing Writers, 1930–1936* (Manchester: Manchester University Press, 1991).

8. Other themes prohibited by the League were 'petty-bourgeois revolutionary zeal and subsequent disillusionment' and 'conflicts between romantic love and revolution'. Sylvia Chan, 'Realism or Socialist Realism? The "Proletarian" Episode in Modern Chinese Literature, 1927–1932', *Australian Journal of Chinese Affairs*, 9 (1983): 65.

9. Christopher Rosenmeier, 'The Subversion of Modernity and Socialism in Mu Shiying's Early Fiction', *Frontiers of Literary Studies in China*, 7(1) (2013): 2.

10. Leo Ou-fan Lee, *Shanghai Modern*, p. 134.

11. Wang-chi Wong, *League of Left-wing Writers*, p. 131.

12. Shi Zhecun's 施蟄存 debate with Lu Xun 魯迅 can be found in Lu Xun 魯迅, *Lu Xun quanji* 魯迅全集 (*The Complete Works of Lu Xun*) (Beijing: Renmin wenxue chubanshe, 1981), vol. 5, pp. 328–35.

13. Li Huibin 李惠彬, 'Lüe tan Shi Zhecun xiaoshuo chuangzuo de yishu jilei yu zhunbei', 略談施蟄存 小說創作的藝術積累與準備 ('A Brief Talk on the Artistic Accumulation and Preparation for Shi Zhecun's Creative Work'), *Zhongguo xiandai wenxue yanjiu congkan* 中國現代文學研究 叢刊, 1 (1994): 289.

14. Shi Zhecun 施蟄存, 'Zatan *Jin Ping Mei*', 雜談金瓶美 ('Rambling on *Jin Ping Mei*'), in Tang Wenyi 唐文一 and Liu Pin 劉屏 (eds), *Wangshi suixiang* 往事隨想 (*Random Thoughts on Past Events*) (Chengdu: Sichuan renmin chubanshe, 2000), p. 48.

15. Shi Zhecun 施蟄存, 'Shangyuan deng', 上元燈 ('Spring Festival Lamp'), in *Shi Zhecun wenji: Shi nian chuangzuo ji* 施蟄存文集: 十年創作集 (*The Works of Shi Zhecun: Ten Years of Creative Writing*) (Shanghai: Huadong shifan daxue chubanshe, 1996), pp. 14–20.

16. Shi Zhecun 施蟄存, '*Shangyuan deng* chuban zixu' 《上元燈》初版自序 ('Preface to the 1st edition of *Spring Festival Lamp*'), in *Shi Zhecun wenji*, p. 790.

17. Shi Zhecun 施蟄存, 'Hongzhi fashi de chujia', 宏智法師的出家 ('How Master Hongzhi Became a Monk'), in *Shi Zhecun wenji*, pp. 101–7.

18. Shi Zhecun, 'Hongzhi fashi de chujia', p. 103.

19. Shi Zhecun, 'Hongzhi fashi de chujia', p. 106.

20. Shi Zhecun 施蟄存, 'Jiangjun de tou', 將軍的頭 ('The General's Head'), in *Shi Zhecun wenji*, pp. 111–243.

21. For an analysis of the latter, see Lutz Bieg, 'Shi Zhecun und seine Erzählung Große Lehrerin Huangxin, oder die bewußte Rückwendung zur Tradition', in Helwig Schmidt-Glintzer (ed.), *Das Andere China: Festschrift für Wolfgang Bauer zum 65. Geburtstag* (Wiesbaden: Harrassowitz Verlag, 1995).

22. Shi Zhecun 施蟄存, 'Jiumoluoshi', 鳩摩羅什 ('Kumarajiva'), in *Shi Zhecun wenji*, pp. 111–38.

23. *Columbia Encyclopedia*, 6th edn, s.v., 'Kumarajiva'.

24. Shu-mei Shih, *The Lure of the Modern*, p. 363.

25. Shi Zhecun, 'Jiangjun de tou', pp. 139–71.

26. Shi Zhecun, 'Jiangjun de tou', p. 171.

27. Shi Zhecun 施蟄存, 'Shi Xiu', 石秀 ('Shi Xiu'), in *Shi Zhecun wenji*, pp. 172–211.

28. This is based on *Shuihu zhuan* 水滸傳 (*Water Margin*), chs 45–46. Leo Ou-fan Lee, *Shanghai Modern*, p. 161.

29. William Schaefer, 'Kumarajiva's Foreign Tongue: Shi Zhecun's Modernist Historical Fiction', *Modern Chinese Literature*, 10(1/2) (1998): 58–61. Schaefer demonstrates how Shi Zhecun carefully alters the original text through careful additions and deletions in order to change the narrative from traditional non-focalisation to strict focalisation on Shi Xiu and his inner monologues.

30. Schaefer, 'Kumarajiva's Foreign Tongue'. See also William Schaefer, 'Relics of Iconoclasm: Modernism, Shi Zhecun, and Shanghai's Margins', PhD dissertation, University of Chicago, 2000, pp. 210–95.

31. Shu-mei Shih, *The Lure of the Modern*, p. 366.

32. Schaefer, 'Kumarajiva's Foreign Tongue', p. 68.

33. Frank Dikötter, *Sex, Culture and Modernity in China: Medical Science and the Construction of Sexual Identities in the Early Republican Period* (London: Hurst, 1995), pp. 162–4.

34. Shi Zhecun 施蟄存, 'Xiongzhai', 凶宅 ('The Haunted House'), in *Shi Zhecun wenji*, pp. 356–79.

35. Leo Ou-fan Lee analyses 'Yecha' 夜叉 ('Yaksha') and 'Modao' 魔道 ('Sorcerer') in *Shanghai Modern*, pp. 176–8.

36. Shi Zhecun 施蟄存, 'Yecha', 夜叉 ('Yaksha'), in *Shi Zhecun wenji*, pp. 327–40.

37. See, for example, Shu-mei Shih, *The Lure of the Modern*, pp 302ff; Leo Ou-fan Lee, *Shanghai Modern*, pp. 211ff.

38. Rosenmeier, 'The Subversion of Modernity and Socialism in Mu Shiying's Early Fiction'.

39. Mu Shiying 穆時英, 'Five in a Nightclub', trans. Randolph Trumbull, *Renditions*, 37 (1992): 9.

40. Mu Shiying 穆時英, 'Shanghai de hubuwu', 上海的狐步舞 ('Shanghai Foxtrot'), in Yue Qi 樂齊 (ed.), *Zhongguo xin ganjue pai shengshou: Mu Shiying xiaoshuo quanji* 中國新感覺派聖手: 穆時英小說全集 (*The Chinese Master of New Sensationism: The Complete Fiction of Mu Shiying*) (Beijing: Zhongguo wenlian chuban gongsi, 1996), p. 249.

41. Mu Shiying 穆時英, 'Ye', 夜 ('Night'), in *Zhongguo xin ganjue pai shengshou: Mu Shiying xiaoshuo quanji*, pp. 241–8.

42. Mu Shiying 穆時英, 'Bei dangzuo xiaoqianpin de nanzi', 被當做消遣品的男子 ('The Man Who Was Made a Plaything'), in *Zhongguo xin ganjue pai shengshou: Mu Shiying xiaoshuo quanji*, pp. 151–76.

43. Mu Shiying, 'Bei dangzuo xiaoqianpin de nanzi', p. 151.

44. Mu Shiying, 'Bei dangzuo xiaoqianpin de nanzi', p. 153.

45. Li Oufan 李歐梵 (Leo Ou-fan Lee), *Xiandaixing de zhuiqiu: Li Oufan wenhua pinglun jingxuan ji* 現代性的追求: 李歐梵文化評論精選集 (*Pursuit of the Modern: Selected Cultural Critiques by Li Oufan*) (Taipei: Maitian chuban gufen youxian gongsi, 1996), p. 167.

46. Zhang Henshui 張恨水, *Shanghai Express*, trans. William A. Lyell (Honolulu, HI: University of Hawai'i Press, 1997).

47. Yingjin Zhang, *The City in Modern Chinese Literature and Film*, pp. 174–5.

48. Mu Shiying 穆時英, 'Hei mudan', 黑牡丹 ('Black Peony'), in *Zhongguo xin ganjue pai shengshou: Mu Shiying xiaoshuo quanji*, pp. 260–9.

49. Mu Shiying, 'Hei mudan', pp. 261–2.

50. Mu Shiying, 'Hei mudan', p. 264. Pu Songling's 蒲松齡 (1640–1715) *Liaozhai zhiyi* 聊齋志異 (*Strange Tales from the Liaozhai Studio*) is a collection of 491 *chuanqi* 傳奇 tales written in the early Qing dynasty.

51. Mu Shiying, 'Hei mudan', p. 269.

52. Shu-mei Shih, *The Lure of the Modern*, p. 302.

53. Quoted in Rosenmeier, 'The Subversion of Modernity and Socialism in Mu Shiying's Early Fiction', p. 18.

54. *Zhongguo xiandai zuojia da cidian* 中國現代作家大辭典 (*Encyclopaedia of Modern Chinese Authors*), s.v., 'Shi Zhecun 施蟄存', p. 425.

55. Bu Shaofu 卜少夫, 'Mu Shiying zhi si', 穆時英之死 ('Mu Shiying's Death'), in Mu Shiying 穆時英, *Mu Shiying quanji* 穆時英全集 (*The Complete Works of Mu Shiying*), ed. Yan Jiayan 嚴家炎 and Li Jin 李今 (Beijing: Shiyue wenyi, 2008), vol. 3, p. 484.

Chapter 3

Wartime Literature between Tradition and Modernity

Following the outbreak of the Second Sino-Japanese war in July 1937, the coastal cities fell quickly to the Japanese. Beijing and Tianjin were occupied within a month and the invading troops reached Shanghai in August. During the bloody battle of Shanghai, Chinese Nationalist forces mounted a fierce resistance for a few months, but eventually they also were forced to retreat and Nanjing, the national capital, had to be abandoned soon after in December. Despite the rapid initial Japanese advances, the invasion eventually slowed, and it had largely stalled by 1940.

The Nationalist government under Chiang Kai-shek 蔣介石 (1887–1975) remained in charge in most of China's interior (*guotong qu* 國統區) from Chongqing, the provisional capital from 1937 until 1946. In the region around Yan'an in north-central China, the Communists consolidated their control under Mao Zedong 毛澤東 (1893–1976). These were the 'liberated areas' ('*jiefang qu*' 解放區) in Communist parlance. The governments in these different regions advocated different policies regarding art and culture with varying degrees of interference and censorship.

For most writers, these were trying times. As a result of the chaotic national situation, identifying wider trends across wartime Chinese literature is complex. Shanghai lost its position as the pre-eminent centre of publishing as intellectuals relocated or fled inland, joining millions of other refugees. Publishing houses, universities and newspapers were relocated inland. Many writers moved to Hong Kong, still under British control. Some intellectuals chose to remain in Japanese-occupied areas, and many of those who did so, famously Zhou Zuoren 周作人 (1885–1967) who stayed in Beijing, were denounced as traitors or collaborators.

In Shanghai, the International and French concessions remained, respectively, under British and French control, while Japanese forces occupied the surrounding Chinese parts of the city. The International Settlement became known as the 'Solitary Island' ('*gudao*' 孤島), providing writers and intellectuals with a certain amount of freedom while the surrounding areas were engulfed by war. There was a lively scene for poetry and drama. Despite calls from the Municipal Council to tone down provocative rhetoric, resistance literature (*kangzhan wenxue* 抗戰文學) continued to be written and published there.[1]

44

This was naturally dangerous work, but despite assassinations and threats of violence against editors, the publishing world adapted and continued to function. Various types of fiction were still written. The major newspapers, such as *Shenbao* 申報 and *Da gongbao* 大公報, had literary and cultural supplements in which both political and entertainment pieces continued to appear, and there were several anti-Japanese publications in print.[2]

The Solitary Island period eventually came to an end when the Japanese attacked the American naval base on Pearl Harbor on 7 December 1941. With the outbreak of the Pacific War, Japanese troops took control of the International Settlement on 8 December.[3] Hong Kong surrendered to Japan on 25 December, following a brief resistance by British, Canadian and Indian troops. China was now divided into three main regions, variously under Japanese, Nationalist and Communist control.

Initially, the great Shanghai newspapers and publishing houses were closed, and the cultural milieu went quiet as cafés were shuttered and blackout curtains were hung.[4] More writers left Shanghai for the hinterland.[5] Yet despite the altered political situation, publishing and cultural production in Japanese-occupied areas recovered remarkably quickly. Journals and theatres in Shanghai reopened after a few months in 1942. A puppet government had been established in Nanjing in 1940 under Wang Jingwei 汪精衛 (1883–1944), which promoted collaboration in the cultural sphere under the banners of 'peace literature' ('*heping wenxue*' 和平文學) or 'Greater East Asian literature' ('*Da Dongya wenxue*' 大東亞文學). Not much literature was produced directly under such directives, but literary publishing resumed with more than a hundred cultural journals and magazines in print, including a great number devoted to movies and plays.[6] There was a surge in popular literature, but anti-Japanese literature became scarcer and more indirect in the occupied areas, and the Wang Jingwei government was harsh on dissent.[7]

The reconciliation between 'new' and 'old' literature

The Japanese invasion of China proper dramatically changed the nature of cultural production and the ways in which writers, publishers and audiences interacted with each other. In Bourdieu's terms, the system by which 'symbolic capital' was rewarded and maintained saw fundamental changes. In contrast to the situation before the war, it no longer makes sense to speak of a single or unified literary field. Still, there were several notable developments that can be observed across regions. One overall shift was that the previous distinctions between high and low culture were realigned, and this in turn opened up new positions in the field, particularly for popular literature.[8] The New Culture Movement ideals were challenged, and a number of prominent intellectuals set out to criticise its legacy. Some of these changes started sooner, in the mid-1930s after the Communists arrived in Yan'an, but arguably the war accelerated this process of reconfiguration and the re-evaluation of cultural priorities.[9]

On 1 October 1936, there was a concerted effort to bring writers and artists together across literary divides. Twenty-one artists joined together to produce 'A Manifesto of Fellows in Literature and Art, United against Foreign Aggression and in Defence of Free Speech' (*'Wenyijie tongren wei tuanjie yuwu yu yanlun ziyou xuanyan'* 文藝界同人為團結禦侮與言論自由宣言). Notable signatories among leftist writers included Zhou Yang 周揚 (1908–1989), Guo Moruo 郭沫若, Mao Dun 茅盾, Zheng Zhenduo 鄭振鐸, Bing Xin 冰心 (1900–1999) and Lu Xun 魯迅, who died only a few weeks later on 19 October. Writers associated with popular and politically independent literature included Lin Yutang 林語堂 (1895–1976), Bao Tianxiao 包天笑 and Zhou Shoujuan 週瘦鵑 (1895–1968).[10]

The Manifesto was a high-profile attempt to bridge the gap between 'new' and 'old' literature, respectively signifying politically engaged and popular literature. It also served to officially mark the end of the vicious 'Two Slogans Debate' (*liang ge kouhao zhi zheng* 兩個口號之爭) within the League of Left-wing Writers during which Lu Xun and some others tried to maintain the primacy of leftist views in the literature opposing Japanese aggression.[11] The following quote from the Manifesto demonstrates the attempt to reconcile opposing cultural camps:

> We are writers, and therefore we advocate that fellow writers across China should not distinguish between new and old [literary] groups, but rather unite to resist Japanese imperialism. Literature is a reflection of life, and life is complex, multifaceted, and multi-layered. Individual authors and literary groups in ordinary times have different opinions on literature, taste, and style. New and old literary groups are unlike, and leftist and rightist writers also have their differences, but regardless of whether we are new, old, leftist, or rightist, we are united as Chinese people, and we are united in refusing to be slaves in a conquered nation.[12]

The Manifesto not only demonstrates that some of the most influential writers and cultural intellectuals in China at the time wanted to look past cultural and political differences, it also shows a dramatically reconfigured intellectual field compared with just a few years earlier. And to some extent at least, the Manifesto was a real success. Attacks on popular literature receded, and the attempt to reconcile differences helped pave the way for a more formally established organisation to serve the national cause: the All-China Resistance Association of Writers and Artists (*Zhonghua quanguo wenyijie kangdi xiehui* 中華全國文藝界抗敵協會) founded eighteen months later.

In order to better organise artists and writers in their work against the Japanese enemy, the All-China Resistance Association of Writers and Artists was established on 27 March 1938 in Hankou (now Wuhan) and later moved to Chongqing.[13] The respected writer Lao She 老舍 (1899–1966) became its director, partly because he was politically neutral and therefore acceptable across ideological divides. Branches were eventually set up across major cities in China. Many writers, poets and playwrights devoted themselves to producing patriotic literature and a great number of plays were written to arouse audiences' passions against the enemy.

The All-China Resistance Association attempted to straddle political boundaries and had some success in this endeavour, gaining members from different sides of the political spectrum as well as from both 'old' and 'new' literature. As a result of these changes, old lines of opposition softened. Tradition became more acceptable, particularly when used in support of patriotism, and the division between elite and popular literature blurred as folk art forms and popular theatre found new respectability and political usage.

A few of the established New Culture Movement writers continued to produce novels in the hinterland, including Mao Dun and Ba Jin 巴金 (1904–2005), and new writers emerged. Still, literature overall suffered considerably during the war. According to C. T Hsia,

> the fiction in the Nationalist interior generally lacks excitement and distinction. Mao Tun's *Maple Leaves as Red as February Flowers*, Shen Ts'ung-wen's *The Long River*, and a few other titles compose a literature quantitatively much smaller than the best fiction of the pre-war decade. The stereotypes of guerrilla warfare and student romance and the ubiquitous note of patriotic propaganda mar most of the wartime novels.[14]

While intellectuals and writers tried to grapple with how best to deal with war and ideological differences, the period also saw notable advancements in popular literature.

In areas under Nationalist control, the three most important popular writers were arguably Xu Xu 徐訏, Wumingshi 無名氏 and Zhang Henshui 張恨水.[15] Zhang Henshui presents an interesting case that is also illustrative of wider developments. He was already a famous writer well before the Second Sino-Japanese War, and some of his early works were towering bestsellers in Shanghai, most notably his tragic romance *Fate in Tears and Laughter* (*Tixiao yinyuan* 啼笑因緣, 1929–1930), which in Perry Link's estimation was 'probably the most widely read Chinese novel in the first half of the twentieth century'.[16]

Following the outbreak of the war, Zhang Henshui relocated to Chongqing in January 1938 and took up a position on the board of the All-China Resistance Association of Writers and Artists. He soon expanded his literary repertoire considerably, turning out a great number of novels and short stories. According to Kong Qingdong 孔慶東, these wartime works can be divided into three main categories:

> The first type is war literature, e.g., *Nights of Street Fighting* (*Xiangzhan zhi ye* 巷戰之夜, 1938), *The Great River Flows East* (*Da jiang dong qu* 大江東去, 1938–1940), and *Long Live the [Huben] Warriors* (*Huben wan sui* 虎賁萬歲, 1946). The second type is satire, e.g., *Eighty-one dreams* (*Bashi yi meng* 八十一夢, 1939–1941), *Goblin Market* (*Wangliang shijie* 魍魎世界, 1941–1945), and *The Carpetbaggers* (*Wu zi dengke* 五子登科, 1947–). The third type is historical fiction and romances, e.g., *A New*

Tale of the Water Margin (*Shuihu xinzhuan* 水滸新傳, 1940–1943), *Singsong Girls of Nanking* (*Qinhuai shijia* 秦淮世家, 1939), and *Crimson Phoenix Street* (*Danfeng jie* 丹鳳街, 1940–1942).[17]

While we need not subscribe strictly to this somewhat facile tripartite division, it is clear that Zhang's work from this period spans broadly, from grim portrayals of pitched battles to entertaining romances, and it shows how the author successfully transitioned from a focus on popular literature to embracing a far more diverse range of writing. Tommy McClellan has studied some of these works in detail, so there is no need to revisit them here. Several of Zhang's works echoed traditional forms with stock storyteller phrases and traditional narrative styles. More daringly, a few of his wartime works, such as *Eighty-one Dreams*, demonstrate a turn from popular literature to satirical 'nightmare realism' with references to Chinese myths and legends.[18] There is a modernist and experimental streak here that seems reminiscent of works by authors like Shi Zhecun. In contrast, a novel such as *Crimson Phoenix Street* is considered 'a dreary romance of latter-day knight errantry'.[19] The diversity of Zhang's output in these years confirms the notion that writers were able to cross literary divides in new ways that would previously have been almost impossible.

A re-evaluation of tradition

A number of studies in recent years have clearly identified the resurgence of tradition as one of the main trends in Chinese literature and art produced during the Second Sino-Japanese War.[20] Traditional forms of literature, drama and art, as well as historical settings and narratives, found renewed favour in a stark reversal of the castigation of such forms since the New Culture Movement. The traditional narrative elements and motifs in Zhang Henshui's writings from the 1940s would seem to confirm this.

Already in the mid-1930s, a discussion had started among intellectuals about the extent to which traditional forms of art, such as folk opera and oral storytelling, could be used to inculcate correct political views and encourage greater resistance against the Japanese. Leftist cultural theorists in 1938, including Mao Dun, started promoting the slogan 'National Forms' ('*minzu xingshi*' 民族形式), which implied a rejection of the New Culture Movement's embrace of Western literary methods, such as realism and narrative experiments, as well as first-person narrators.[21] Mao Zedong came out in support of such views in his influential 'Talks at the Yan'an Forum on Literature and Art' in 1942. Eventually, working with tradition and popular forms of art was promoted in both Nationalist and Communist areas as a means to reach wider audiences.

From the early 1940s onwards, historical drama became a significant trend in many cities of the interior, including Chongqing.[22] For example, Guo Moruo 郭沫若 wrote three patriotic plays all set in the Warring States period.[23] Tradition was embraced in several other ways, for example, Chiang Kai-shek's ordering that various Confucian ethics and classical texts should form the core of a revised curriculum in schools.[24] This was a natural extension of the New Life Movement (*xin shenghuo yundong* 新生活運動) from 1934, which upheld traditional Confucian values, partly as an alternative to Marxist ideology.

In a parallel development, academic interest in traditional Chinese popular literature (*su wenxue* 俗文學) flourished. This was largely focused on folk literature and art from China's past, including various types of drama, songs, storytelling, etc. The leftist intellectual Zheng Zhenduo published *A History of Popular Chinese Literature* (*Zhongguo suwenxue shi* 中國俗文學史) in 1938, and his study became the basis for a good deal of further interest and research in the field.[25] Several journals were devoted to traditional folk art and culture during the 1940s.

This focus on the past and traditional art forms fits within a larger historical arc. Facing a direct threat to national unity, many intellectuals ceased to see China's historical traditions and popular literature as the main challenge holding the nation back. China's progress towards modernity was no longer impeded by neo-Confucian ideology or a moribund cultural past, but rather by the Japanese occupation and ideological differences. And as a result of this re-orientation, tradition and popular forms of literature were thus freed to be re-evaluated and reconstituted in novel ways, including as a means of delivering political education or rousing national pride.[26]

Yet while this embrace of historical topics and traditional art forms was indeed a factor for many intellectuals, particularly in the Communist areas, the issue becomes rather more complex when looking at popular literature. While some writers joined the trend, others were doing the opposite, adopting modern narrative forms and promoting a greater awareness of science, rationality and contemporary events.

Nationalism and tradition in popular literature

In popular literature written during the war, tradition and history became sources of entertainment and several writers increasingly turned towards historical topics and settings. Ping Jinya 平襟亞 (1892–1980), the editor of the popular Shanghai journal *Phenomena* (*Wanxiang* 萬象), wrote several short stories in which he retold classical tales, sometimes in modern settings.[27] In one of these, 'Confucius' Concern' ('*Kongfuzi de kumen*' 孔夫子的苦悶, 1941), Ping Jinya takes a few lines from *The Analects* (*Lunyu* 論語) and rewrites them into a humorous story in which Confucius is deeply worried about his disciples' ability to pay their tuition fees.[28] It comes across as an irreverent and playful piece of entertainment that still shows a hint of sophistication by quoting the original classical text at the end. Ping Jinya wrote more serious satirical pieces as well in which he ridiculed prominent figures, and for these he was eventually arrested and jailed for a month.[29]

Social satire was a fairly popular genre. This type of literature is somewhat borderline when considered as popular literature, and only a single example will be mentioned here. Jin Yi 靳以 (1909–1959) was an influential journal editor in Shanghai in the 1930s who went to Chongqing in 1938. In 1944, he published a collection of short stories, *The Gods* (*Zhongshen* 眾神, 1944). The title story, dated 1942, is similar to 'Confucius' Concern' in its humour and irreverence towards religious authority. The main character is one Liu Guodong 劉國棟 (his given name translates as Pillar-of-the-state), an obese, wealthy and deeply corrupt financial speculator. As the narrative begins, Liu dies and goes to Heaven where he meets Jesus, angels, etc.[30] A panel reviews his various immoral and nefarious deeds in life, but these acts become twisted as virtues in Liu's retelling. Moreover, the panel members are all greedy speculators like himself, so they cheerfully admit him to Heaven and a welcoming party is held. With even Heaven controlled by evil financiers and harmful deeds being grossly mis-represented, there is some humour in this short story, but it also reads as a thinly veiled satire, a critique of a China controlled by self-serving and hypocritical bankers and bureaucrats who have no interest in the well-being of common people.

The re-evaluation of tradition also benefited the popular genre of martial arts or *wuxia* novels. These works had been a mainstay of popular literature since the early 1920s. In the late 1930s, northern China saw the appearance of a new generation of *wuxia* writers, five of whom became popular enough to earn them the soubriquet 'the Five Masters of the North' ('*Beipai wu dajia*' 北派五大家).[31] Their works, usually serialised in journals through the early 1940s, expanded the scope of the genre by mixing the traditional stories of knight-errant heroes and bandits with elements from other genres, including romantic love stories, mystery novels and descriptions of social problems. The genre was revitalised with greater character depth and moral complexity, and this in turn led to a flourishing of the *wuxia* genre centred around Beijing and Tianjin.

The work of Wang Dulu 王度廬 (1909–1977) might be mentioned as an example. His major production was the highly popular five-volume Crane-Iron Series (*Hetie xilie* 鶴鐵系列) serialised in occupied Qingdao between 1938 and 1944.[32] In 2000, one of the volumes, *Crouching Tiger, Hidden Dragon* (*Wohu canglong* 臥虎藏龍), was filmed by Ang Lee (b. 1954), generating much greater interest in Wang Dulu's writings. One of the interesting aspects of the series is that it challenges several *wuxia* conventions while still staying firmly within the genre. Where most *wuxia* novels take place in a somewhat mythical land, the so-called *jianghu* 江湖 (the land of Rivers and Lakes), the Crane-Iron Series takes place specifically in late Qing China with countless references to real places scattered across the country. In a similar break from convention, there are no gods, spirits, monsters or magic, and while the main characters do have superhuman abilities, they are not completely untethered from human limitations. The series is thus an attempt to move the boundaries of this genre towards something more realistically grounded and less aligned with complete fantasy. This goes for the characters as well. Li Mubai 李慕白, a main protagonist, largely remains a typically virtuous *xia* 俠 (knight-errant) throughout, but various other characters are multifaceted and morally complex, for example, the young couple Yu Jiaolong 玉嬌龍 and Luo Xiaohu 羅小虎 who are still considered *xia* despite being some-what misguided in their actions and certainly less than entirely virtuous. The notion of what constitutes the noble *xia* thereby starts sliding. One virtuous female character is even pronounced to be *xia*, despite not having any fight-ing ability.[33] This demonstrates that by the late 1930s, the *wuxia* genre was so established that deviations from its standard conventions could be experimented with more freely. And while the text is not nationalistic in and of itself, the his-torically accurate Chinese setting and the powerful characters roaming across it would presumably appeal to readers thinking about the present state of the country.

Such popular works revisiting history and tradition were not primarily nation-alistic or political, yet perhaps the reminder of China's history and rich culture would for many readers call to mind its past greatness and the current sorry state of the nation, while at the same time providing some escapist entertainment. To that extent, the war thus provided a veneer of respectability to such works as they could now be represented as somewhat aligned with the efforts of intel-lectuals in promoting national awareness.

Nationalism found its way into popular literature in other ways as well. The most widely read work of literature during the war was arguably Qin Shou'ou's 秦瘦鷗 (1908–1994) *Begonia* (*Qiuhaitang* 秋海棠), serialised in the Shanghai newspaper *Shenbao* 申報 from February 1941 during the Solitary Island period.[34] It was published as a book in 1942, and by January 1944 it was in its seventh printing. Opera, drama and film versions soon appeared, and they found considerable success as well.[35] A play based on the novel was successfully staged from December 1942 to May 1943 at the Carlton Theatre (*Ka'erdeng* 卡爾登) with an impressive run of 153 performances.[36] When Qin refused to produce a sequel, Zhou Shoujuan 周瘦鵑, the former editor of the popular journal *Saturday* (*Libailiu* 禮拜六) and other journals in the 1910s and 1920s, and the current editor of the fiction supplement of *Shenbao* in which *Qiuhaitang* was published, wrote one. Zhou's *New Begonia* (*Xin Qiuhaitang* 新秋海棠) came out in the journal *Violet* (*Ziluolan* 紫羅蘭) in 1943, and this was also widely read.[37]

Set in the period from the 1910s to the 1930s, the plot of *Begonia* revolves around a tragic and melodramatic love triangle between a warlord, his concubine and a male Peking Opera singer who achieves fame playing female roles in his performances. The Tianjin warlord, Yuan Baofan 袁寶藩, pursues the singer, Wu Yuqin 吳玉琴, who has adopted the stage name Qiu Haitang (begonia). Wu manages to escape the general's clutches, but has an affair with Yuan's unwill-ing concubine, the beautiful Luo Xiangqi 羅湘綺, who gives birth to a little girl. General Yuan learns of the affair and has Wu's face mutilated in punishment. His career ruined, Wu raises the child in a small village, facing numerous hard-ships. Years later, just as a reunion with Xiangqi is finally in sight, Wu catches tuberculosis and takes his own life, jumping from the hospital window. Between these overarching events, there are numerous jealousies, abductions, fights, loyal brotherhoods, retribution, swapped babies, etc. Political events like the Northern Expedition and the Japanese invasion rumble on in the background.

At first glance, the novel is a meandering, convoluted melodrama that comes across as a 'tearjerker' aiming to maximise its emotional impact. Despite this, David Der-Wei Wang argues that even in this superficially trite work, 'a stale convention of Butterfly fiction is turned into an allegory of national self-renewal'.[38] Wu Yuqin's stage name, Qiu Haitang, is chosen to allude to the state of the nation. With a shape that resembles China, the begonia leaf is eaten by caterpillars, much as China is torn apart by foreign powers. Qiu Haitang's role on stage as a *dan* 旦 actor is similarly emasculated, echoing China's suffering in the 1940s, and through this there is an allegorical element to the novel as well.

Ng Mau-sang argues that works such as *Begonia* helped audiences during the war to deal with the social and political changes sweeping the nation, showing that there was still value in upholding and revering traditional values, such as friendship, righteousness and self-sacrifice. According to Ng, 'it is a world in which prescribed morals bring about social cohesion and, in turn, the social-ethical network reinforces the individual meaning of existence in the modern setting of Shanghai'.[39] By promoting traditional values in a modern world, popular literature was intricately linked with evaluations of modernity. The allusion to patriotic sentiment shows that love for the nation was an important part of the virtuous ideals being espoused.

Modern psychology and character depth

The depth of character portrayal generally increased in 1940s popular literature, and, as mentioned, Wang Dulu's work provides an example of this in transcending traditional *wuxia* stereotypes. In many other popular works, we similarly see more conflicted and multifaceted characters. Of course, this merely draws attention to the problematic issue of characterising such works as popular literature in the first place.

An example of this is Zhang Ailing's 張愛玲 'Jasmine Tea' ('*Moli xiangpian*' 茉莉香片) from 1943.[40] The short story starts with a light-hearted storyteller introduction in which the audience is encouraged to pour some tea for themselves, but the narrative quickly turns into a darker character study of the male protagonist's conflicting emotions, despair and self-hatred. Set in contemporary Hong Kong, the young male student Chuanqing 傳慶 is somewhat morose and withdrawn, with no friends at university as well as having a repressive father and cruel stepmother. Despite his withdrawn nature, he is approached by the vivacious and pretty Yan Danzhu 言丹朱, a fellow student whose father, professor Yan Ziye 言子夜, had many years before loved Chuanqing's now deceased mother. Unable to deal with his own emotions about this, Chuanqing fails his classes and his poor performance humiliates him in front of Danzhu and the other students.

Through the course of the short story, Chuanqing sinks ever deeper into depression and goes through various stages of self-pity, apathy, remorse and, eventually a senseless combination of self-loathing and fury directed at Danzhu. This culminates in his almost simultaneously declaring his undying love for her and beating her to the brink of death on a mountain path after a Christmas Eve party. The description of violence gives way to something more ephemeral or dreamlike, perhaps reflecting Chuanqing's weakening grasp on reality:

> After the first kicks, she moaned softly. Then she was silent. He kept kicking fiercely. He had to. He was afraid that she might still be alive. And yet he was also scared to go on. His legs were shaky and numb from kicking. Torn between these two fears, he finally left her there. He began to run down the hill. His body seemed to be moving in a nightmare, sailing on the clouds, riding on the mist like an immortal, his feet skimming above the ground, the moon shining on row upon row of stone steps that pranced boldly before his eyes, like agile lines of calligraphy.[41]

Such work clearly parallels Shi Zhecun's 施蛰存 interest in psychology, sexual desires and the fantastic. In a pattern similar to 'Yaksha' ('*Yecha*' 夜叉) and other gothic short stories, the disturbed urban male fails to comprehend his love interest and constantly projects various emotions onto her. This eventually descends into distress and madness culminating in misguided violence. Yet unlike Shi's work in which urban rationality is undermined by tradition, literature and myth, Zhang Ailing here presents a more mundane process of deterioration, mainly caused by family relationships and intellectual inferiority.

A very different type of example is provided in the writings by Cheng Xiaoqing 程小青 (1893–1976). He is mainly known as a writer, translator and critic of detective fiction. From the 1920s to the 1940s, he wrote more than a hundred such works. His detective fiction frequently features the heroic and aloof detective Huo Sang 霍桑 and his assistant Bao Lang 包郎, who serves as his biographer and the chronicler of his adventures. Huo ingeniously solves crimes across Shanghai, engaging with all levels of society, from educated elites to the criminal underworld. The characters themselves are even aware of their obvious parallel with Sherlock Holmes and Dr Watson, with Huo Sang referring to Bao Lang as 'Dr Watson of the East'.[42]

Cheng Xiaoqing saw his works as having an educational function, so Huo Sang solves cases through rational reasoning and modern science, thereby exposing superstition, denouncing medical quackery, and criticising various failings and corruption in Chinese society. Jeffrey C. Kinkley notes that promoting patriotism was part of the vision for much detective fiction in this period.[43] As a part of this effort, Cheng Xiaoqing saw his short stories as a vehicle by which to introduce readers to modern theories of psychology. According to King-fai Tam,

> the world of Huo Sang constantly alludes to the latest theories of criminology and abnormal psychology, and Huo enjoys quoting from both well-known and obscure

western scholars. The reader, it is assumed, will be inspired enough by Huo Sang's success to pay attention to the sciences.[44]

A brief example illustrates the point. Cheng's 'The Ghost in the Villa' ('*Bieshu zhi guai*' 別墅之怪) from 1947 sees Huo Sang and Bao Lang contacted by one Hua Bosun 華伯蓀, who reports that his new villa in the countryside is haunted by ghosts: fireballs, eerie whistling, a guard waking up under his bed.[45] Despite Hua's initial refusal to believe in such supernatural phenomena, he is unable to explain the various strange occurrences. Echoing Shi Zhecun's gothic ghost stories from the 1930s, Hua Bosun finds himself unravelling and desperate. Finally accepting the case, Huo Sang goes off to explore the matter and soon discovers that a Manchurian criminal gang is orchestrating the uncanny events in order to be able to take over the property cheaply. Huo Sang warns them off and the matter is thus resolved. The motives of the criminals are explained and thus science and rationality once again thoroughly debunk any supernatural explanations.

Yu Qie's 予且 (1902–1990) work provides another example of an expanding interest in psychological character development.[46] He was active on the Shanghai literary scene in the mid-1930s, writing short stories for several periodicals, including the popular *The Young Companion* (*Liangyou* 良友). He also wrote essays and a few works on drama theory and critique. After a stint as an editor with the Chunghwa Book Company (*Zhonghua shuju* 中華書局), he left Shanghai following the outbreak of the war. He returned in 1939 and became a prolific author of popular literature, producing several novels and many short stories over the next few years. His short story 'Cigars' ('*Xuejia*' 雪茄) from 1943 is an example of his work.[47] Most of the narrative consists of dialogue with little description, so the short story reads almost like a play. The male protagonist, Mr Zhao 趙, has decided to stop smoking on a whim, the main reason being that he finds carrying cigars around in his pockets to be a bother. Yet having made this solemn promise, he finds that everything soon conspires against him, tempting him to smoke again and break this vow; his wife and child both prefer that he continues to smoke, his friends smoke and his favourite brand is even on sale. Health issues are, of course, not raised as a concern of any sort, so Mr Zhao's continued reason for not smoking ends up being that he had declared that he would not to his family earlier. He gradually becomes more and more conflicted over this, taking a stroll into town and ending up buying matches without having anything to use them for. Over the course of a single day, he becomes completely obsessed with cigars, even licking some old cigars that his wife found in a jacket pocket. He eventually concedes defeat and smokes one, bringing about a reconciliation with his wife with whom he was testy earlier.

On the surface, this is just a story about a middle-class man's entirely self-imposed and imagined problems. He decides to quit smoking for no good reason, but his declaration of this means that he cannot go back on his word since this would cause him to lose face. His wife senses this predicament and teases him gently about it to his great annoyance. There is some humour in this and the dialogue between them, and that is, of course, the main theme of this short story. But 'Cigars' also contains gentler echoes of the fetishism and madness in Shi Zhecun's short stories from a decade before. Mr Zhao's constant worries and subconscious urges about cigars seem to be almost directly inspired by the delusions and displaced desire of the earlier Shanghai modernist writers. Yet the end result is, of course, very different since there is no nervous collapse, irrational violence or undermining of the modern outlook.

Another of Yu Qie's short stories, 'A Gentleman's Contract' ('*Junzi qiyue*' 君子契約) from 1943, shows a different aspect of his writing, featuring an elusive *femme fatale*.[48] Set in Shanghai in 1936, the first-person narrator is a young university student who decides to rent a house on his own rather than stay on campus. He lives near an elementary school where he notes that the young teacher, Miss Lu 陸, is very attractive. To his surprise, she knocks on his door one day and proposes to move in with him. She turns out to be a bold young woman, entering his home uninvited and even casually sitting on his bed.[49] In order to placate his worries about the seemliness of this arrangement, Lu suggests 'a gentlemen's contract' stipulating that there should be no romantic entanglements between them. He relents and she moves in upstairs. It turns out that she is very much a vivacious 'modern woman', lighting his cigarettes, entering his room uninvited, engaging in flirtatious banter, etc. Predictably, he is unable to resist her charms and falls in love with her. But it turns out that there was another undisclosed reason for her engagement with the narrator and her desire to move in with him: Miss Lu is also very friendly with the headmaster at the school where she works, Mr Wan 萬, but Wan's wife is very jealous of her. As a result of the wife's disapproval, Lu could no longer live in the school building and therefore moved in with the narrator in order to convince the wife that she was no longer a threat. Upon figuring out this relationship, the narrator feels used and deceived, and he is furious and jealous, despite both Miss Lu and Mr Wan trying to be friends with him. The short story ends with the girl leaving in order to prevent the two men fighting over her. The narrator makes peace with Mr Wan and takes up her vacant teaching position in the school.

The focus of this short story is the awkward love triangle relationship between the narrator, the seductive new neighbour and the headmaster. But there is little actual romance in this text. Instead, it is mostly about the narrator being dumbfounded by Miss Lu's confounding modern ways, trying to understand her actions and her relationship with the headmaster. The narrator is from Nanjing and, as an outsider to Shanghai, his perspective is mostly one of continuing incomprehension. Despite considering himself quite modern and liberal, he is still concerned with traditional notions of faithfulness and female virtue, whereas Miss Lu simply seeks fun, friendship and another drinking companion. Compared with Mu Shiying's seductresses and taxi dancers, Miss Lu is a more straightforward *femme fatale* stereotype. There is no intertextual self-awareness or deeper critique of Shanghai modernity here. But equally importantly, she is not a bad character either. It is rather the narrator who is naïve and fails to keep his part of the gentleman's contract.

Both of these short stories by Yu Qie were published in *Collected Short Stories of Yu Qie* (*Yu Qie duanpian xiaoshuo ji* 予且短片小說集, 1943). Other short stories in the volume similarly portray various episodes and bourgeois relationships set in Shanghai. Yu Qie garnered some praise for these writings, and he was given an award for this volume at the Japanese-sponsored second Greater East Asia Writers Congress (*Da Dongya wenxuezhe dahui* 大東亞文學者大會) in Nanjing in 1944.[50] As might be expected, this award has done little to improve his profile in the history of modern Chinese literature. The other writer to win an award at this event was Mei Niang 梅娘 (1920–2013), whose novel *Crabs* (*Xie* 蟹, 1941) describing the decline of a family in Manchuria was acclaimed as 'novel of the year'.[51] Her works often featured strong female characters and she has been seen as a feminist writer.

Arguably more influential as feminist writing was Su Qing's 苏青 autobiographical *Ten Years of Marriage* (*Jiehun shinian* 結婚十年, 1943), which set new heights in presenting complex female characters and relationships. It portrayed a woman torn between an unfaithful husband, oppressive in-laws expecting sons, a duty to her children, and a desire for her own career as a writer and teacher. The novel was initially serialised in *Wind and Rain Chats* (*Fengyutan* 風雨談) in Shanghai, and as a book it achieved such popularity that it had reached twelve reprints by 1945.[52] The novel is important as both a character portrait of a woman dealing with complex issues as well as an indictment of social injustices facing Chinese women in daily married life. In the end, the only viable option for her is to seek a divorce. As Edward Gunn demonstrates, the aim here was to portray a woman who is not shockingly modern or some sort of *femme fatale*:

> The heroine Su, however, is deliberately portrayed as a conventional young woman, so that her break with conformity cannot be laid simply to eccentricity. Further, Su is an ordinary woman with hardly more than a middle-school education, so that her ability to find employment and independence is an achievement addressed to other ordinary women who fear divorce, rather than to women of heroic ambitions.[53]

In addition to the more famous Zhang Ailing and Su Qing, several other female writers emerged in Shanghai during the period of Japanese occupation, such as Shi Jimei 施濟美 (1920–1968). According to Wang Wenying 王文英, these emerging writers often reached new levels in exploring the minds and emotions of female characters.[54]

Modernist narrative styles

Most New Culture Movement writers espoused realism as the most proper narrative style, yet by the late 1930s, the continued value of realism was being questioned as well, partly due to the turn towards 'national forms'.[55] In a different kind of departure from realism, FitzGerald demonstrates that examples of modernist literature can still be found throughout the wartime period.[56] In some genres this clearly resembles the New Sensationist style from the early 1930s. After the bombing of Shanghai in 1937, Luo Binji 駱賓基 (1917–1994) expressed the confusion and fear of the experience in a style that echoes the fragmented passages of Mu Shiying or Liu Na'ou 劉吶鷗. In 'Blood in the Ambulance' ('*Jiuhuche li de xue*' 救護車裏的血), Luo describes some of his experiences doing relief work:

> The ambulance was going full throttle, rushing into the resistance of the air current, dashing forward almost in flight; the Red Cross flag stuck in front of the cab fluttered violently, too, as if in excitement. Surprised gazes, searching gazes, in row after row flashed past. The ambulance, with the anxious, unceasing cry of its siren, cut through the waves of people like a steamship, and after it went past the people came together again in clumps.[57]

The narrative style attempts to mirror the confusion and chaos of the city and the characters as they rush about. In other stories, a similar narrative style is used to describe the panic of wounded people and the terror caused by mortar attacks, flares and bombs.[58] A similar modernist style is seen in Ah Long's 阿瓏 (1907–1967) *Nanjing* 南京, originally written in 1939. Yunzhong Shu notes how passages describing the destruction and carnage after an air raid are reminiscent of the New Sensationists' writings about Shanghai.[59]

The echoes of modernist styles were found in popular literature as well. According to Shu-mei Shih, the fiction of the 1940s demonstrates,

> an increasing disintegration of the borders between high and low culture in Shanghai, as new sensationism broadened into a new form of writing that integrated both the Westernized/Japanized form of new sensationism and the middle-brow fiction of the Mandarin Ducks and Butterflies style. Most of Zhang Ailing's highly crafted yet infinitely readable short stories were published in popular magazines such as *Phenomena* (*Wanxiang*), which fluctuated between advocating serious and popular literatures.[60]

As Shih notes, Zhang Ailing's work serves as an example here, and to some extent it represents a hybrid, for example, 'Jasmine Tea' discussed earlier. Zhang's writing was received as popular literature, widely read at the time, but it also contains modernist elements, including an interest in narrative experimentation and occasionally featuring disturbing psychological tales, more akin to Shi Zhecun's earlier works full of absurdity and violence. Zhang Ailing's works are also occasionally similarly reminiscent of the New Sensationist narrative style in her descriptions of the city.[61] The opening passage from the short story 'Sealed Off' ('*Fengsuo*' 封鎖, 1943) illustrates how such methods of introducing urban space found their way into popular literature.

The tramcar driver drove his tram. The tramcar tracks, in the blazing sun, shimmered like two shiny worms oozing out from water: stretch, then shrink, stretch, then shrink. Soft and slippery, long old worms, slinking on and on and on ... the driver stared at the wriggling rails, and did not go mad.

The tramcar would have gone on forever, if the city hadn't been shut down. It was. The streets were sealed off. 'Ding-ding-ding-ding' rang the bell. Each 'ding' was a small, cold dot: dot after dot, they formed a line that cut through space and time.

The tramcar stopped, but the people on the street started rushing around: those on the left rushed over to the right, those on the right rushed over to the left. The metal shop gates came rattling down.[62]

A subsequent passage notes how the city has fallen asleep and is drooling onto people's clothing. This narrative style is not distinctly modernist, but it takes a definite step away from realism. In the following paragraphs, the narrative gradually zooms in on the characters in the stopped tramcar and eventually focuses on two characters and the brief relationship that develops between them. The two strangers feel connected and even consider marriage, but as soon as the blockade is lifted, the tramcar starts up again and their connection instantly vanishes as though it had never happened. The story revolves around the two characters' relationship, but Zhang Ailing's careful attention to literary technique demonstrates narrative sophistication and, of course, helped to distinguish her short stories from other potboiler fiction. Her subtle portraits of characters and their strained family relationships are similar to Shi Zhecun's short stories about women's aspirations and failing relationships in *The Exemplary Conduct of Virtuous Women* (*Shan nüren xing pin* 善女人行).

Rather than trying to present a complete overview of popular Chinese literature during the 1940s, this chapter has been an attempt to highlight a few trends. Popular literature during the war was remarkably diverse, crossing cultural boundaries and expanding or even breaking normal genre conventions. The distinction between 'old' and 'new' literature became less sharp, and this is reflected in the works of the writers as they tried out new narrative styles and techniques in character portrayal. Popular writers continued to grapple with modernity and change during the war, and there was certainly no embrace of tradition as a whole. Yet the writers of the 1940s rarely displayed the sort of avant-gardist defiance or experimentalism found in New Sensationist short stories from the decade before with their attacks on narrative coherence and modern progress. The two Chinese writers who most deliberately adopted elements of modernism in their popular works were Xu Xu and Wumingshi.

Notes

1. Gunn, *Unwelcome Muse*, pp. 21–2.
2. Chen Qingsheng 陳青生, *Kangzhan shiqi de Shanghai wenxue* 抗戰時期的上海文學

(*Shanghai Literature during the Sino-Japanese War*) (Shanghai: Shanghai renmin chubanshe, 1995), pp. 73–4.

3. The French Concession lasted longer, remaining under the control of Vichy France until 1943, after which sovereignty was transferred to Wang Jingwei's pro-Japanese government.

4. Chen Qingsheng, *Kangzhan shiqi de Shanghai wenxue*, p. 194.

5. Gunn, *Unwelcome Muse*, p. 25.

6. Chen Qingsheng, *Kangzhan shiqi de Shanghai wenxue*, pp. 72ff.

7. Poshek Fu, *Passivity, Resistance, and Collaboration*, p. 79.

8. Shu-mei Shih, *The Lure of the Modern*, p. 380.

9 Qian Liqun, 'An Overview of Chinese Theories of Fiction from the 1940s', *Modern Chinese Literature* 1995, no. 9: 59–64.

10. Gloria Davies, *Lu Xun's Revolution: Writing in a Time of Violence* (Cambridge, MA: Harvard University Press, 2013), p. xxv.

11. For details on this debate, see Leo Ou-fan Lee, 'Literary Trends: The Road to Revolution 1927–1949', in John K. Fairbank and Albert Feuerwerker (eds), *The Cambridge History of China*, vol. 13 (Cambridge: Cambridge University Press, 1986), pp. 439–45.

12. Ba Jin 巴金 et al., 'Wenyijie tongren wei tuanjie yuwu yu yanlun ziyou xuanyan', 文藝界同人為團結禦侮與言論自由宣言 ('A Manifesto of Fellows in Literature and Art, United against Foreign Aggression and in Defence of Free Speech'), *Wenxue* 文學, 7(4) (1936): 744. Japan is denoted by an 'X' throughout the text, but the meaning is quite clear, so I have made the replacement here.

13. Charles A. Laughlin, 'The All-China Resistance Association of Writers and Artists', in Michel Hockx and Kirk A. Denton (eds), *Literary Societies of Republican China* (Lanham, MD: Lexington Books, 2008), p. 379.

14. C. T. Hsia, *A History of Modern Chinese Fiction* (New Haven, CT: Yale University Press, 1971), p. 317

15. Kong Qingdong 孔慶東, 'Guotongqu de tongsu xiaoshuo', 國統區的通俗小說 ('Popular Fiction in the Hinterland'), *Fuling shi zhuanxuebao* 涪陵師專學報, 16(1) (2000): 1.

16. Link, *Mandarin Ducks and Butterflies*, p. 12.

17. Kong Qingdong, 'Guotongqu de tongsu xiaoshuo', p. 3. See also Fan Boqun 范伯群 and Kong Qingdong 孔慶東, *Tongsu wenxue shiwu jiang* 通俗文學十五講 (*Fifteen Talks on Popular Literature*) (Beijing: Beijing daxue chubanshe, 2003), pp. 132–3. Dates of publication and English translations are from McClellan, *Zhang Henshui and Popular Chinese Fiction, 1919–1949*, pp. 329–44. The latter also provides a more complete list of Zhang's writings.

18. T. M. McClellan, 'Change and Continuity in the Fiction of Zhang Henshui (1895–1967): From Oneiric Romanticism to Nightmare Realism', *Modern Chinese Literature* 10 (1998): 113–14.

19. McClellan, *Zhang Henshui and Popular Chinese Fiction, 1919–1949*, p. 228

20. See, for example, McDougall and Louie, *The Literature of China in the Twentieth*

Century, ch. 6, 'Return to Tradition', pp. 189–207. See also Chang-tai Hung, *War and Popular Culture*, ch. 3, and Gunn, *Unwelcome Muse*, ch. 4.

21. Marston Anderson, *The Limits of Realism: Chinese Fiction in the Revolutionary Period* (Berkeley, CA: University of California Press, 1990), pp. 70–1. For Mao Dun's views, see Mao Dun 茅盾, 'Literature and Art for the Masses and the Use of Traditional Forms', trans. Yu-shih Chen, in Kirk A. Denton (ed.), *Modern Chinese Literary Thought: Writings on Literature, 1893–1945* (Stanford, CA: Stanford University Press, 1996).

22. Chang-tai Hung, *War and Popular Culture*, p. 64.

23. Hsia, *A History of Modern Chinese Fiction*, p. 320.

24. Yutaka Otsuka, 'Japan's Involvement with Higher Education in Manchuria: Some Historical Lessons from an Imposed Educational Cooperation', in Glen Peterson, Ruth Hayhoe and Yongling Lu (eds), *Education, Culture and Identity in Twentieth-century China* (Ann Arbor, MI: University of Michigan Press, 2001), p. 211.

25. Ellen Widmer, 'The Rhetoric of Retrospection: May Fourth Literary History and the Ming-Qing Woman Writer', in Milena Doleželová-Velingerová and Oldřich Král (eds), *The Appropriation of Cultural Capital: China's May Fourth Project* (Cambridge, MA: Harvard University Press, 2001), p. 201.

26. Chang-tai Hung, *War and Popular Culture*, pp. 275ff.

27. Fan Boqun 范伯群, Tang Zhesheng 湯哲聲 and Kong Qingdong 孔慶東, *20 shiji Zhongguo tongsu wenxue shi* 20世紀中國通俗文學史 (*A History of Chinese Popular Literature in the 20th Century*) (Beijing: Gaodeng jiaoyu chubanshe, 2006), p. 228.

28. Ping Jinya 平襟亞 (Qiu Weng 秋翁), 'Kongfuzi de kumen', 孔夫子的苦悶 ('Confucius' Concern'), *Wanxiang* 萬象, 1(1) (1941): 54–7.

29. Gunn, *Unwelcome Muse*, p. 46.

30. Jin Yi 靳以, 'Zhongshen', 眾神 ('The Gods'), in *Zhongshen* (Hong Kong: Xinyi chubanshe, 1958), pp. 139–67.

31. See Fan Boqun, Tang Zhesheng and Kong Qingdong, *20 shiji Zhongguo tongsu wenxue shi*, p. 209. The five writers were Huanzhu louzhu 還珠樓主 (Li Shoumin 李壽民) (1902–1961), Wang Dulu 王度廬 (1909–1977), Zhu Zhenmu 朱貞木 (*c.* 1905–?), Bai Yu 白羽 (1899–1966) and Zheng Zhengyin 鄭証因 (1900–1960).

32. Deborah Sang Tze-lan, 'The Transgender Body in Wang Dulu's Crouching Tiger, Hidden Dragon', in Larissa Heinrich and Fran Martin (eds), *Modernity Incarnate: Refiguring Chinese Body Politics* (Honolulu, HI: University of Hawaii Press, 2006), pp. 98–112.

33. Hubertus van Malssen, 'Redefining Xia: Reality and Fiction in Wang Dulu's Crane-Iron Series, 1938–1944', PhD dissertation, Manchester University, 2013), p. 133.

34. Der-wei Wang, 'Popular Literature and National Representation', p. 212.

35. Ng Mau-sang, 'A Common People's Literature', p. 1. See also Gunn, *Unwelcome Muse*, p. 29.

36. Michelle Yeh, 'Chinese Literature from 1937 to the Present', in Kang-I Sun Chang and Stephen Owen (eds), *The Cambridge History of Chinese Literature*, vol. 2 (Cambridge: Cambridge University Press, 2010), p. 585.

37. Ng Mau-sang, 'A Common People's Literature', p. 4.

38. Der-wei Wang, 'Popular Literature and National Representation', p. 214.

39. Ng Mau-sang, 'A Common People's Literature', p. 9.

40. Zhang Ailing 張愛玲, 'Jasmine Tea', in *Love in a Fallen City*, trans. Karen S. Kingsbury (New York: New York Review Books, 2007), pp. 77–108.

41. Zhang Ailing, 'Jasmine Tea', p. 107.

42. King-Fai Tam, 'The Detective Fiction of Ch'eng Hsiao-ch'ing', *Asia Major*, 5(1) (1992): 115.

43. Jeffrey C. Kinkley, *Chinese Justice, the Fiction: Law and Literature in Modern China* (Stanford, CA: Stanford University Press, 2000), p. 239.

44. King-Fai Tam, 'The Detective Fiction of Ch'eng Hsiao-ch'ing', p. 118.

45. Cheng Xiaoqing 程小青, 'The Ghost in the Villa', in *Stories for Saturday: Twentieth-Century Chinese Popular Fiction*, trans. Timothy C. Wong (Honolulu, HI: University of Hawai'i Press, 2003), pp. 175–89.

46. The author is also known as Pan Yuqie 潘予且, but Yu Qie seems to be the more common form.

47. Yu Qie 予且, 'Xuejia', 雪茄 ('Cigar'), in *Qianshui guniang* 淺水姑娘 (*Miss Stranded*), ed. Wu Fuhui 吳福輝 (Beijing: Huaxia chubanshe, 2011), pp. 123–30.

48. Yu Qie 予且, 'Junzi qiyue', 君子契約 ('A Gentleman's Contract'), in *Qianshui guniang* 淺水姑娘 (*Miss Stranded*), ed. Wu Fuhui 吳福輝 (Beijing: Huaxia chubanshe, 2011), pp. 131–48.

49. Yu Qie, 'Junzi qiyue', p. 133.

50. Gunn, *Unwelcome Muse*, p. 41.

51. Norman Smith, *Resisting Manchukuo: Chinese Women Writers and the Japanese Occupation* (Vancouver: UBC Press, 2007), p. xii.

52. Gunn, *Unwelcome Muse*, p. 72.

53. Gunn, *Unwelcome Muse*, p. 73.

54. Wang Wenying, *Shanghai xiandai wenxueshi*, pp. 481–2.

55. Anderson, *The Limits of Realism*, p. 180.

56. FitzGerald, *Fragmenting Modernisms*, pp. 25–6.

57. Translation in Charles A. Laughlin, *Chinese Reportage: The Aesthetics of Historical Experience* (Durham, NC: Duke University Press, 2002), p. 171.

58. Laughlin, *Chinese Reportage*, pp. 171–5.

59. Ah Long's *Nanjing* was not published until 1987 under the revised title *Nanjing Blood Sacrifice* (*Nanjing xueji* 南京血祭). Yunzhong Shu, *Buglers on the Home Front: The Wartime Practice of the Qiyue School* (Albany, NY: State University of New York Press, 2000), pp. 73–7.

60. Shu-mei Shih, *The Lure of the Modern*, p. 380.

61. Riep, 'Chinese Modernism: The New Sensationists', pp. 425–30.

62. Zhang Ailing 張愛玲, 'Sealed Off', in *Love in a Fallen City*, trans. by Karen S. Kingsbury (New York: New York Review Books, 2007), pp. 77–108.

Chapter 4

Boundaries of the Real in Xu Xu's Fiction

By the late 1930s, the New Sensationist authors had left creative writing behind. On the whole, the 1940s was a very different period for the production of Chinese literature and art. Wumingshi 無名氏 and Xu Xu 徐訏, who wrote during this period, worked under different conditions from those prevailing when Mu Shiying 穆時英 and Shi Zhecun 施蟄存 were active, and this is reflected in their writings. Both Wumingshi and Xu borrowed various elements from the New Sensationist style, but the different cultural milieu changed the way in which their works were written as well as how they were received.

Xu Xu was the pen name of Xu Boxu 徐伯訏. He was born in Cixi 慈溪 in Zhejiang province in 1908.[1] In 1931, he graduated from Peking University (*Beijing daxue* 北京大學) in philosophy.[2] He continued studying psychology for two years, but in 1933 he moved from Beijing to Shanghai. In April 1934, Xu was hired as an editor for Lin Yutang's 林語堂 new journal, *This Human World* (*Renjianshi* 人間世, 1934–1935).[3] The Lin Yutang journals, such as *The Analects* (*Lunyu* 論語, 1932–1937), gained a wide readership in Shanghai and many prominent authors wrote short stories and articles in their pages, including Yu Dafu 郁達夫, Hu Shi 胡適 (1891–1962), Liu Bannong 劉半農 (1891–1934), Shen Congwen 沈從文 and others.[4] *This Human World* carried articles on both foreign and Chinese literature as well as fiction, poetry, cultural news and essays. The articles were generally shorter than those found in Shi Zhecun's *Les Contemporains* (*Xiandai* 現代) and, in comparison, they were less concerned with cultural developments abroad. Xu Xu frequently contributed poems and essays to the journal.[5] His writings covered a wide range of topics, from a discussion of the New Life Movement (*xin shenghuo yundong* 新生活運動) in 1934 to current fashions.

Xu Xu also started writing fiction and plays in this period, and he published two short stories in *Les Contemporains* in 1933 and 1934, respectively. Details are scant about their connection, but we know that he met with Shi Zhecun and Mu Shiying, and considered Shi a friend.[6] Later he worked as an editor for *Cosmic Wind* (*Yuzhou feng* 宇宙風, 1935–1947) under Lin Yutang's younger brother, Lin Hanlu 林憾廬.[7] These journals were known for their elegant and light-hearted touch, as opposed to the more political and ideologically governed publications of the time. As might be expected, the journals were accused by leftist critics of being banal entertainment.[8] This was an approach to literature that influenced Xu Xu's work and fostered his disdain for literature carrying overt political agendas.

In March 1936, Xu Xu started his own bi-weekly journal, *People of Heaven and Earth* (*Tiandi ren* 天地人), which closed after five months.[9] In August, Xu went to France where he studied for a doctorate in philosophy. Frederik Green provides some further details about Xu Xu's stay in Paris, including his proposal to a Japanese classmate who turned him down.[10] According to an interview conducted much later, Xu began to have serious doubts about the merits of Communism during this period.[11] At the same time, he continued to write fiction and soon leapt to prominence with the novella *Ghostly Love* (*Gui lian* 鬼戀), published in 1937 in *Cosmic Wind*. It was among the top three bestsellers of that year, and over the following years it was reprinted nineteen times and was turned into a film in 1941.[12] Its success earned Xu the tag of *guicai* 鬼才, 'the unearthly genius'.[13] It also set a pattern in exploring a number of themes that reappear in much of his later fiction.

Xu Xu returned to China in January 1938 without having completed his doctorate.[14] He went on to write numerous plays, fiction, poetry and essays throughout the 1940s, with some of the plays being particularly well received.[15] In 1941, as the Japanese took over Shanghai, Xu Xu left the city. He eventually moved to Chongqing where he became a professor in the Chinese Department of Chongqing Central University 重慶中央大學 in 1942. Only two years later he left the university and began to write for the newspaper *Eradication* (*Saodang bao* 掃蕩報). This Republican paper was anti-Communist and is probably an indication of his political position. He was stationed in America for some time, but returned to China in 1946 after the Japanese surrender.[16]

Throughout this period, Xu kept on writing. He published several volumes of poetry written in the vernacular, but using the structures of classical poetry. His novels from Shanghai's 'lonely island' period were largely romantic love stories set in foreign countries, such as *The Gypsy's Seduction* (*Jibusai de youhuo* 吉布賽的誘惑, 1939), *The Absurd English Channel* (*Huangmiu de Ying-Fa haixia* 荒謬的英法海峽, 1940), and *The Lament of the Mental Patient* (*Jingshenbing huanzhe de beige* 精神病患者的悲歌, 1941). According to Chen Qingsheng 陳青生, these novels were less popular than some of his other work.[17] In addition, they were judged rather harshly by the literary critics of the time.[18] Critics of a nationalist and socialist realist bent criticised his work for having too much love and too little heroism.[19]

After *Ghostly Love*, Xu's next popular success was the love-story-cum-spy-thriller *The Rustling Wind* (*Feng xiaoxiao* 風蕭蕭), written in Chongqing and serialised in *Eradication* in 1943.[20] The book became a bestseller throughout China that year, resulting in some publishers naming 1943 the 'Year of Xu Xu' ('*Xu Xu nian*' 徐訏年).[21] In the late 1940s, Xu wrote less fiction than he had during the preceding years, but he republished several of his previous pieces of fiction through his own publishing house, Shanghai Night Window Studio (*Shanghai ye chuang shuwu* 上海夜窗書屋).

In 1950, soon after the People's Republic was declared, Xu Xu moved to Hong Kong, where he wrote a number of essays, some of which were strongly anti-communist, and worked as an editor for various journals.[22] He also resumed creative writing and published several popular novels, such as *Characters in Society* (*Jianghu xing* 江湖行, 1960).[23] Some of his works were filmed by Shaw Brothers, including *Ghostly Love* and *The Rustling Wind*.[24] From 1961 onwards, Xu Xu taught at various literature departments at universities in Singapore and Hong Kong. In his last years, he was dean of the School of Arts at Hong Kong Baptist College. A few of his novels were filmed and he also became popular in Taiwan.

Modernist beginnings

During his university studies in Beijing, Xu Xu was inspired by social realism and wrote some short stories and plays in that vein.[25] But already by the time he moved to Shanghai and joined Lin Yutang, this direction vanished from his writings. He mostly wrote poetry in this early period, but two of his short stories were published in *Les Contemporains*: 'Essence' ('*Benzhi*' 本質) in 1934 and 'Forbidden Fruit' ('*Jinguo*' 禁果) the following year. They both display a modernist narrative style that seems inspired by New Sensationist writings. The short story 'Essence' begins in the following manner:

> The lights went out and the curtains opened slowly like clouds. The audience easily associated the light on the stage with the sun. Thereupon Miss Shi's 史 smile floated onto this sun, floated beyond the clouds, floated into every person's pupils, into every person's optic nerves, into every person's central nervous system. Thereupon every person had a kind of movement with different organs, expressions and every sort of movement with the same organs, expressions. Some fluttered their eyelids, some stroked their lips with their hands, some pressed a smile onto their cheeks, some dribbled saliva, some had their hearts beating, and some used their hands to adjust the buttons in front of their pants ...[26]

The rest of the short story employs a similarly modernist narrative style. People are mostly faceless beings who react according to predefined patterns. The wealthy Miss Shi is the daughter of Professor Shi, an influential banker and academic. She is deeply in love with the poor poet and playwright Yin Yuan 殷 湲, and she has her father bring about a marriage with him, even though Yin is in love with somebody else. In Yin's play, the women have the looks and the men have the money, but in the story it is the other way around. The narration progresses through parallel repetition of story events and events on the stage.

The short story 'Forbidden Fruit' appeared in *Les Contemporains* in 1935 and follows a slightly different pattern.[27] The setting and characters are no longer worldly and urbane. Instead, they become abstract in a fairy-tale narrative style that focuses solely on the characters' relationship. Like 'Essence', it is one of the few pieces of fiction written by Xu Xu that does not have a first-person narrator. The story concerns a poet who is invited to live in an earthly paradise on the single condition that he does not fall in love with the supremely beautiful widow who lives there. Predictably, he cannot resist the temptation and falls in love with her. The unusual aspect of this short story is that it borrows the narrative style of Western children's fairy tales, which can be illustrated with the opening passage:

> Once upon a time, there was a poet who wrote a poem in which he condemned Adam and Eve for being unwilling to eat one type of fruit less in their world of happiness. This made the human race face endless suffering for all eternity.
>
> Surprisingly, there was an unimportant person who translated this unimportant poem into some language and printed it in some kingdom's unimportant newspaper.
>
> This newspaper's circulation was not very good, but in a certain coffee shop there was a wealthy widow who read it. She became happy and wrote to the newspaper's office to ask where the translation came from.[28]

The wealthy widow is a famous beauty with whom all men invariably fall in love. Her irresistible beauty is described at length, embellished with tales of men who became the victims of their own fascination with her. A painter never painted again and kings fell ill and died at the mere sight of her beauty. She contacts the author of the poem to make him an offer: he will be allowed to live in complete luxury in her beautiful park on the condition that he does not fall in love with her. If he does, he will be punished with death. He agrees, and an array of lawyers produce a contract about the arrangement, giving him the right to choose his own manner of dying if he should fail.

The poet moves into her paradisiacal garden where the widow reigns like a goddess. Predictably, he is unable to resist her and falls in love. This, of course, proves her point that humans cannot resist temptation, and he admits that he, like Adam, is merely human. As his manner of death he asks to be bitten to death by her. He is spared. In the end, she falls in love with him. When he is hit by a truck, she goes to the hospital to visit him and their roles are reversed for a brief while before he dies.

It is perhaps the presence of such works that has led some scholars to see Xu Xu's writings as containing deeper psychological analysis than those of most other authors of the time. As can be seen from his more popular novels and short stories, such works were the exception rather than the rule during the 1930s and 1940s.

Female ghosts and spies

Xu Xu's fiction from the late 1930s rarely displays a modernist influence on the narrative style to the same degree as his earlier short stories in *Les Contemporains*. They mostly follow a basic template: the male protagonist and narrator encounters a dazzlingly beautiful woman who is exotic and alluring. She is a modern

New Woman, cosmopolitan, sexy and often foreign. Frequently, she poses as a supernatural being or appears in some other way as a mystery to be solved. The male narrator is modern and cosmopolitan, but in other ways he is her diametric opposite. He is always Chinese, rational and intellectual. The relationship between the male narrator and the woman goes through various melodramatic developments involving secret lives and hidden agendas. In the end, they are resolved and the protagonist uncovers the truth behind the woman's facade.

Ghostly Love from 1937 is basically a *zhiguai* 志怪 tale transposed to a modern setting.[29] The male protagonist and first-person narrator encounters a beautiful woman while taking a stroll one night after meeting a friend on Shanghai's Nanjing Road, where he tried a new type of Egyptian cigarettes. The narrator is quickly characterised as a typical urban *flâneur* who is intellectual, cosmopolitan and someone who enjoys the sights and sounds of modern urban life. He is approached by a woman who has bought the same cigarettes and asks for directions to some street. She informs him very matter-of-factly from the start that she is a ghost. Being a modern person who considers himself above such superstitions, the narrator refuses to believe her. Nevertheless, she claims that she does not have a human name and insists on being called 'Ghost', and she addresses him consistently as 'Man'. Much as in traditional *zhiguai* tales, Ghost is neither scary nor repulsive. Instead, she is charming, intelligent and attractive. The dialogue between the two is mostly amusing and clever, demonstrating the sophistication of the interlocutors:

> 'A ghost,' I laughed. 'There are ghosts on Nanjing Road,' I thought to myself.
> 'Yes, I am a ghost!'
> 'A female ghost walking on Nanjing Road, buying rare Egyptian cigarettes from the tobacco store, and asking directions from a man who does not believe in ghosts?' I laughed, leaning against a wall with my hands in my coat pockets.
> 'Don't you believe in ghosts?'
> 'It is true that I have never believed in ghosts so far. And if I were to believe in them one day, it would not be on Shanghai's Nanjing Road from a beautiful woman who buys Era cigarettes and dares ask men for directions.'
> 'So are you afraid of ghosts?'
> 'I have never believed in ghosts, how could I be afraid of them?'
> 'So do you dare escort me to Xietu Road?'
> 'Would you like to invite me to escort you to Xietu Road?'
> 'Why do you say invite you?'
> 'Why didn't you say willing instead of dare?'
> 'Ok, I'll ask you if you are willing.'
> 'Why would you want to go to Xietu Road this late?'
> 'Because once we reach Xietu Road, then I know my way home.'[30]

Most of their conversations follow this pattern of flirtatiously teasing banter. The narrator agrees to escort her home despite continually refusing to believe her story. They decide to meet again later and eventually he falls deeply in love with her. Meeting regularly for a year, their relationship goes through various twists and turns. Throughout, the narrator remains deeply in love with Ghost. The love is not reciprocated, however, and she claims to be beyond human love. The narrator remains fully aware of the *zhiguai* aspect of his narrative. He even tells Ghost a traditional ghost story about a man who falls in love with a female ghost. After having visited her house one evening, the narrator returns during the day to check that it is not a burial tomb as is frequently the case in *zhiguai* stories about ghosts. When an old lady tells him that nobody lives in the house, he begins to believe that her story might be true. Soon after, the narrator is told that a young woman died a few years ago where Ghost now lives. But one day, the narrator surprises Ghost outside in broad daylight – something she had previously claimed was impossible. Pressed to tell the truth, she finally admits that she was merely pretending to be a ghost because she had become weary of life and no longer wished to be a part of human society after having worked as a secret agent. In her past life, she killed numerous people and narrowly escaped death several times. Some time after this, Ghost leaves him a farewell note and disappears. The narrator never sees her again.

There are several interesting parallels with some of Shi Zhecun's gothic short stories such as 'Yaksha' ('*Yecha*' 夜叉): the narrative in which a man from Shanghai strangles a young woman in a tomb, thinking that she is a ghost. The most obvious similarity between the two works is in their both using the *zhiguai* genre to tell the story of how a modern, urban male encounters and sees an attractive, mysterious woman. The protagonists are strikingly similar in the two stories and at some level both believe the women to be supernatural beings. In both works there is a return from the supernatural to the normal as the woman is revealed to be a normal human being. In this manner, the otherworldliness of the love interest is restricted to a certain delimited period. The differences are equally striking. In Xu's piece, the supernatural takes place in the middle of the city – it is no longer confined to a timeless rural space beyond urban modernity. And unlike the blind country girl in 'Yaksha', Ghost is very much a creature of modern urban life as she strolls through the city at night and engages unknown men in witty conversation. Ghost's supernatural status is self-imposed and presented to the narrator as fact. The rational urban male in Xu's story never quite gives up trying to prove that Ghost is a human being. He remains far more in charge of the situation than the males in Shi Zhecun's fiction. In 'Yaksha' and several other such short stories by Shi, the women's inscrutability is imposed on them by male gaze and fantasy. These male dreams about the female characters frame the women in a context of legend and myth, powered by sexual desire. But in *Ghostly Love*, the woman consciously represents herself as exotic and supernatural. It is an image she develops and projects in order to keep life – and men – at a distance. These differences between the women change the nature of the two narratives dramatically. In the end, *Ghostly Love* has few of the gothic and absurd qualities that characterise Shi Zhecun's short stories in this genre.

Another interesting parallel between the fiction by the New Sensationist writers and *Ghostly Love* is the manner in which Ghost has decided to retreat from war and modern life. She claims that she wants to avoid human society, much like Black Peony (*Hei mudan* 黑牡丹) in Mu Shiying's short story of the same name, or Su Wen 素雯 in Shi Zhecun's 'The Twilight Taxi Dancer' ('*Bomu de wunü*' 薄暮的舞女). Ghost's retreat is, however, no longer an escape from the dance halls and neon lights, but an escape from war and ideology. Her 'real' past career as a glamorous secret operative hardly makes her less exotic than if she were indeed a ghost. And unlike Black Peony or Su Wen, Ghost is no victim of modernity. Smoking cigarettes and remaining in charge of the situation throughout the story, she is more of an urban seductress than a victim of male control.

In and of itself, *Ghostly Love* is neither modernist nor avant-garde. With its clever dialogue and melodramatic plot, it is an entertaining and light-hearted love story that is a witty pastiche of a traditional genre. The setting is transposed to modern Shanghai and the characters are the popular stereotypes of modernity. The male *flâneur* is the quintessential modern urbanite, and the woman he meets is sexual, outgoing and assertive. As a *femme fatale*, she is also a mystery to him, and this is, of course, reinforced by her claiming to be a ghost. The similarity to New Sensationist fiction adds an extra intertextual layer to the novelette beyond the *zhiguai* references, which shows off the sophistication of the author as he playfully juggles between the contemporary and the traditional.

Following the pattern established in *Ghostly Love*, Xu's female characters often present themselves as supernatural beings or turn out to be secret agents. Their encounter with the uncomprehending urban male is a recurrent theme in much of his fiction. Another short story of this type is 'The Flower Spirit of the Gambling Den' ('*Duku li de hua hun*' 賭窟裏的花魂), dated 1939.[31] Much like the protagonist of *Ghostly Love*, the protagonist and narrator of 'The Flower Spirit of the Gambling Den' is an intellectual gentleman, an author in this case, who becomes enticed by a beautiful, otherworldly woman. He has started losing money in casinos, mostly on roulette, but wants to continue until he recoups some of his losses, after which he intends to quit gambling forever. One evening he meets a beautiful but tired-looking woman who tells him that he is like everybody else there: addicted to gambling. Yet she explains that there is still hope for him since he has only played for three months. She sees gamblers as flowers and he is still a bud that has not yet opened. She herself, on the other hand, is a withered flower who has been through it all before and become a 'flower spirit'. Flower Spirit is an expert gambler and on the following evenings she wins for him repeatedly. She wants to cure him of gambling by recouping his losses. In the casinos, she is more experienced than he is in every respect. She is outgoing, vivacious and takes charge of every situation, whereas the narrator, in comparison, is naïve and at a loss to understand how things work. Their relationship changes dramatically after they go to her house. It is revealed that she is mortal and spends most of the day smoking opium, so he reproaches her for letting herself go, and tells her to get her life in order. This introduces a role reversal between them. Where she was fully in charge of the situation before, hailing the taxis and making the decisions, he now has the upper hand, admonishing her for neglecting her appearance.

The remainder of the short story continues through a number of ups and downs, with the two of them taking turns trying to save or cure the other. She cures him of gambling and leaves him. He finds her again and has her cured of opium smoking. Throughout, their relationship is never consummated, but remains titillatingly out of reach as a vague promise of future happiness. This is finally broken when he leaves Shanghai to join his family in Hong Kong. When he returns a few months later, she is gone. They later meet by chance, and she has fallen back into her old ways and tells him she wanted his love, not his compassion, and leaves him. He starts gambling again to assuage his misery. By the time they finally meet in a casino much later, he has lost all his savings. She, on the other hand, has married a wealthy gentleman and tries, once more, to help him out. She reveals that she left him earlier because his daughter had written her a letter asking her to stay away so that his family could remain intact.

This lengthy short story starts much like *Ghostly Love*, but it develops quite differently. The relationship between the otherworldly woman and the modern urban male is far more dynamic. The beautiful flower spirit's exoticism and supernatural status do not last very long. The modern woman is brought down to male manageability and comprehension by her love for him and her opium addiction. Both of them have their weaknesses, which are in turn offset or magnified by the actions of the other. In this manner, they take turns being in charge. The changing power relationship between the couple is also repeated in some of Xu Xu's later works, such as *The Gypsy's Seduction* (*Jibusai de youhuo* 吉布賽的誘惑, 1939). The *femme fatale* is eventually unmasked and shown to be human and vulnerable. In general, the women in Xu's fiction have much in common with the typical *femme fatale* stereotype, always modern, inciting and mysterious. But there are also a few differences. First and foremost, the exotic women in Xu's fiction are not invariably unattainable. Frequently, they also fall in love with the narrator and thereby the fatal seductresses are rendered harmless.

Like Ghost in the previous short story, Flower Spirit is weary of life and has retreated into fictionality as a means of escaping the harsh realities of life. As in New Sensationist fiction, Ghost's and Flower Spirit's affiliation with otherworldliness and legend makes them more mysterious to the men they meet, but the mystery is of their own making, rather than imposed on them by male erotic fantasy. This also changes the short stories' relation with modernity. Their mysterious elusiveness is intriguing, but it does not undermine the rationality of the male observer. Although gambling is presented as an addiction and a vice, it does not become a clear-cut symbol of the depravity of modern life in general. Similarly, Flower Spirit's opium addiction is an individual failing, not a consequence of modernity. Thereby Xu's fiction does not constitute an indictment of modern life. Instead, the references to tradition are principally intriguing details in which the two women envelop themselves in order to place themselves beyond the pressures of ordinary life.

Dated May 1937, 'The Jewish Comet' ('*Youtai de huixing*' 猶太的彗星) features a beautiful woman who is a foreigner and not, this time, a supernatural being.[32] Otherwise, the story follows a pattern similar to that of *Ghostly Love*. An intellectual male narrator encounters an attractive but assertive woman, who turns out to be a secret agent in the end. Once again, most of the narrative concerns the protagonist's attempts to understand her. But unlike Ghost, the woman in this short story falls in love with the narrator.

The text begins *in medias res* with a mystery: the narrator, named Xu 徐, wakes up on a ship and wonders where a certain woman is, particularly considering their 'great plan'. Seeing her luggage, he concludes that she must have boarded the ship after he fell asleep at night and then left the cabin before he awoke the next morning. When they meet shortly afterwards, she introduces herself as Katharine 凱撒琳 and asks to be called by her first name since they are now husband and wife. In an extended flashback, the narrator explains the situation to the reader. While preparing for a trip to Europe, he had encountered a Norwegian Jew named Sherkels (She'erkesi 舍而可斯) who managed a shop in Shanghai. Sherkels asked him to accompany a young woman, the daughter of a deceased musician, to Italy, explaining that she was about to inherit a fortune, but needed to be married in order to obtain the money. Therefore the woman and Xu were to pretend to be married, both during the voyage to Italy and during their stay there. Out of curiosity and in good faith, the narrator agreed to the proposition, thus bringing the story back to the present: the narrator meeting the woman aboard the boat.

Pretending to be husband and wife, Katharine and Xu share the same cabin. But most of the time, she is out socialising with the other passengers and flirting with other men, particularly an Italian Fascist. Xu claims to be disinterested and spends his time reading books and playing chess with the other passengers, to the point where Katharine even reproaches him for not acting his part as husband better: he should be jealous when she is flirting with others. Gradually they get to know each other and they fall in love. Yet the narrator feels that he does not understand her or what she is doing all day. Finally, they arrive at Naples. For the next couple of days, Katharine goes about town alone, returning drunk to their hotel late at night. Xu is miserable with jealousy and incomprehension, but on the third day she tells him how much she cares for him and they make love. The following day, she is out gallivanting again and his misery is compounded after seeing her together with the Italian from the boat. The next evening she tells him the truth: she is a secret agent. She is carrying out sabotage against arms and munitions shipments to the Franco government in Spain. For her plan to succeed, somebody had to die. According to the original plan that she had devised with Sherkels, the narrator was picked to be sacrificed. But when they fell in love, she could not decide whether to sacrifice herself instead. In the end, she thought of the Italian Fascist and decided to use him. The narrator is much relieved and they declare their mutual love. The couple go to France and get married in Paris, but soon after she is killed while on a mission in Germany.

The major part of this short story thus reads like a love story with some mystery thriller and melodrama thrown in at the end. The male intellectual, yet again, fails to understand the modern, elusive, beautiful woman who is fully in charge of the situation. In the end, Katharine's revelation is obviously similar to that of the woman in *Ghostly Love*. Her inscrutability is also similar. Apart from being beautiful, clever and flirtatious, she also turns out to be an undercover agent and ardent patriot who is willing to die for her ideals.

There is one interesting aspect of this short story that does not quite fit into the simple love story scheme described above: Sherkels' long tirades against war. Soon after they meet, Sherkels and the narrator go out for dinner. Sherkels gives a speech about human fellowship and the horrors of war:

'During the Great War in Europe, we fought and fought, for what? What was gained? What was the cost? How many buildings were destroyed, how many people were killed? I think that I personally killed no less than a thousand. Why would I kill anyone? I had no enemies! ...'

I saw that he was very excited and interrupted to ask him: 'You took part in the Great War?'

'Who didn't? Back then even sixteen-year-old boys had to take part! During the four years of the war, I spent three of them in the trenches. And half a year in the hospital. Thousands of people got sick.'

'Well, then, you are a lucky man that you managed to stay alive.'

'Stay alive, why should it be considered lucky staying alive? Just so that I can see the next Great War? After you've lived through such a long career on the battlefield, everything alive is monotonous and hollow. Imagine that all your old friends are dead. I have seen them fall one by one with my own eyes, falling down never to see them rise again. My home was destroyed by the war, my mother, wife, son and daughter are all dead because of the war. What do you think is the point for me in living? The woman you saw in the coffee shop the other day in yellow, her father was a good friend of mine from childhood. But he died, he died for no good reason. If he hadn't died, he would certainly have been a great musician, he really had a gift for music and he was very hard-working as well. In the trenches he would never leave his violin. Well, what does it mean that this talented man was sacrificed for no reason? And we're not just talking [about] him alone. What were these sacrifices for? And why did those who killed him do it? Those who killed him were just the same as me. Among the thousand that I killed, naturally there were also quite a few scientific and artistic geniuses, of course there could also have been a musician. I really love musical people, so what if one among them had not been killed by me and had become a musician. He would have been my friend, that is our culture. Normally it is a crime to kill a person for love, why is it not a crime for me to kill about a thousand people for no reason whatsoever? I used to be a devout Christian, but when the clergy said that for glory and whatnot, that I had not committed a crime, I lost my faith in religion.'[33]

This extended monologue is quite unique for its time. In 1937, when it was written, the Chinese nation including its intellectuals were mostly caught up in war. Publishing such attack on war and the ideologies that lie behind it, even though it is a different war, would clearly be read as a comment on contemporary affairs. Xu Xu criticised war in other ways in a number of his essays. In some later pieces written in Hong Kong, such as 'Moral Demands and Moral Standards' ('*Daode yaoqiu yu daode biaozhun*' 道德要求與道德標準) from 1957, he also lashes out against Communist ideology and ideological movements.[34] Yet most of Xu Xu's fiction refrains from commenting on current political affairs. Sherkels' speech is a interesting exception.

Yet on the whole, this short story belongs to the category of love stories with alluring women who combine the modern and the mysterious – a favourite plotline that Xu Xu explored several times from various angles. Although these short stories may not be riveting in and of themselves, they do exemplify a change in what was considered acceptable subject matter. The inclusion of intertextual references to *zhiguai* and fairy tales was no longer a contentious issue by the late 1930s, and secret agents had entered the popular conscience as one more stereotype associated with drama and action. By integrating such elements into popular writing, Xu Xu was able to situate his works in the cultural field as non-ideological entertainment targeted at sophisticated readers.

Xu's longest novel of the 1940s, *The Rustling Wind* (*Feng xiaoxiao* 風蕭蕭), was serialised in the Chongqing newspaper *Eradication* in 1943. The complete novel was published the following year and became one of Xu Xu's most famous works. In two years, it underwent five printings and spread throughout most of the occupied areas.[35] At 513 pages in a modern edition, it is considerably longer than any of his previous fiction.[36] Unlike most of his earlier writing, *The Rustling Wind* is set in China. It is a thriller-cum-love story that takes place in Shanghai under the Japanese occupation. The novel combines many of the tropes and images from Xu Xu's previous work, replete with foreign spies, beautiful women, dance halls and gambling parlours. The protagonist and first-person narrator (again named Xu 徐) is a philosopher who frequents Shanghai's various dance halls. Eventually, Xu finds himself caught between three beautiful women and the events of the anti-Japanese war. Starting as a love story, the plot thickens and eventually the war comes to play an important role. Xu becomes an agent for the Americans following Pearl Harbor, and it turns out that two of the girls are secret agents as well. He suspects one of them of working for the Japanese, but it transpires that she is a double agent. In this manner, various events and stratagems propel the plot forward in an elaborate and melodramatic tale full of passion, sacrifice and love.

Frederik H. Green and Yingjin Zhang have both looked at this novel, showing how the narrator navigates the metropolis as *flâneur*, dandy and, finally, unwilling detective.[37] Zhang shows how Xu's voyeuristic strolls through the city, his wealth, elegance and cosmopolitan detachment make him a composite of such modern urban stereotypes. In Zhang's reading, this is another example of how

Shanghai is gendered and made an object of attraction, mystery and exploration in the same manner as exotic, inscrutable women.

Apart from the meaning of this novel as it relates to urban space, another element worth noting is how the war and the historical setting are used. The war simply furnishes a background against which a tale unfolds. It is not a vehicle for nationalism or agitating against the Japanese. Unlike many other works from this time, there is no social or patriotic outrage in this book. On the contrary, as in Xu Xu's previous novels, the roles as beautiful covert agents and spies demonstrate that they are passionate and superhuman characters who lead lives of danger and drama. Counter-espionage, stealth and international schemes shift the novel back and forth between love story and thriller – a clear sign that by the early 1940s agents and spies had entered mainstream entertainment as popular conventions.

Another element worth noting is the narrative style. The novel opens with a dinner invitation addressed to the narrator and his wife sent from a Mr C. L. Steven 史蒂芬 and his wife. The letter is printed on the page with a frame around it, ending with an RSVP. Echoing some of Shi Zhecun's short stories, a stream of consciousness follows:

> Steven and his wife? I started wondering. Did Steven really have a wife? Is this not very strange?
> So it must be a different Steven.
> But I only know one C. L. Steven.
> And how come C. L. Steven doesn't know that I am not married!
> There must be another C. L. Steven.
> And I do not know him.
> But he sent me this formal invitation.
> Perhaps it is that C. L. Steven playing games with me?[38]

Years later, Xu Xu mentioned that the novel's political independence might have been one of the reasons for its success:

> This novel [*The Rustling Wind*] is really not written very well, or at least not as well as the things I did later. At the time, Chongqing was full of propagandistic or leftist literature. There were no works that were as independent so that might be the reason it sold so well. Perhaps it was just by chance.[39]

Much like many of his other writings, the novel reads like a piece of escapist entertainment.

These works are all written according to a fairly rigid and standardised template in which the plots follow roughly the same pattern. The first-person narrator and protagonist falls in love with a beautiful and intriguing woman who is a mystery to him. Being a ghost or a spy, the woman is alluring, foreign, exotic, unknown. She is constructed along the lines of the New Woman stereotype by combining an air of modernity with an erotic appeal and suave self-confidence. These female characters have much in common with the *femme fatale*, but there is an important difference as they fall in love with the male narrator or the truth of their mysterious facades is unravelled.

Voyages and strange worlds

The appeal to exoticism in the spy and ghost stories is also found in the novels and short stories with foreign characters and settings. Many of Xu's works from the late 1930s and early 1940s take place in Europe or involve travel from one place to another. Apart from the Chinese narrator, the characters are foreign and – much like the ghosts and secret agents – their foreignness sets them apart from the everyday. The setting is otherworldly and becomes an abstract backdrop for love and drama in a place that is far away from present affairs and national concerns. While the place itself usually turns out to be relatively unimportant, its foreignness highlights the unfamiliar nature of the characters and events.

The novel, *The Absurd English Channel* (*Huangmiu de Ying-Fa haixia* 荒謬的英法海峽), dated 1939, is basically an extended love story that takes place on an island utopia situated in some secret, secluded corner of the English Channel.[40] As the story begins, the protagonist, a student in France named Xu 徐 (once more), is travelling from France to England to meet some professors and to take a few days off. En route, the ship is boarded by pirates. The pirate captain, named Smith 史密斯, convinces Xu to come see the land where they live. Xu agrees and sails with them to their secret hideout. Xu is invited to live with Smith, the island's leader, and with his mother and sister, and he is gradually introduced to their world. Throughout his stay, Xu is impressed by the islanders' various clever ways of doing things. People come from all over the world to stay there. Smith has no special prerogatives and therefore there are no other contestants for his position. He was chosen as leader by popular demand. Unlike China, there are no political parties and the society is egalitarian, so neither are there servants, much to Xu's surprise. After school, girls do the housework in people's homes and boys do the work outside like distributing papers and milk, collecting garbage and sweeping the streets. It is also an advanced society with factories, galleries and museums. In the streets, the people are happy, greet each other and have songs for every day of the week depending on their place of work.

Clearly the island is designed to be as different from China as possible. It is free of every ailment plaguing the nation. Yet the island utopia only provides the backdrop to the main plot of *The Absurd English Channel*: a love story in which Xu falls in love with Smith's sister, Peiyinsi 陪因斯, as well as becoming interested in another girl, the clever, flirtatious and beautiful Louise 魯慧斯, who is Peiyinsi's classmate.[41] Eventually, Smith reveals that his only motive in bringing Xu to the island was to help Smith win over a Chinese girl he loves, Li Yu'ning 李羽寧. Li loves Smith as well, but has decided to leave the island. Smith wants Xu's help in convincing her to marry him and then accompanying her on a trip back to China. Xu's presence on the trip would supposedly assure her return to Smith.

The criss-crossing love interests move the plot forward through various manoeuvres and jealousies. Xu worries that Peiyinsi may have fallen in love with him. Even though he is attracted to her, he decides to keep his distance since he is only temporarily on the island and fears that she would be deeply saddened by his departure. But he is jealous of a local boy, Peng Dian 彭點, who is also interested in her, and at the same time he is attracted to Louise. Throughout, he remains determined to return to China because he misses his family and wants to help rescue his suffering homeland.

The various subplots on the island end in Xu being deceived. Once a year, there is a special festival when the women can propose to the men, who cannot refuse. Xu agrees to a ruse with Li Yu'ning, who will propose to him so that they can leave the island together. But on the night of the festival, she proposes to Smith instead. Peiyinsi proposes to Peng Dian, which takes Xu by surprise since he was certain that she was in love with him. Finally, Louise proposes to him. It becomes clear that the deceit was intended to keep him on the island so that Louise could marry him. The novel ends with Xu finding himself alone on the docks in England where he was originally headed. We do not learn the results of the marriage or whether in fact a wedding ever took place. Back in the real world, it is as though the events on the pirate island never happened. The isolated nature of Xu's adventure on the island is underlined by the mirroring of the conversations among the other passengers, which are practically identical with those on the ship at the beginning of the novel.

Starting and ending among passengers crossing the English Channel, the events that take place on the island seem like a dream completely removed from real life. Falling into a rift between real destinations, the pirate island is a place of exploration, wonder and romance. In contrast, the beginning and ending passages are full of references to real places and contemporary political issues. The geography of real space is thus contrasted sharply to the exotic nature of the island and its people. This sense of unreality is reflected in the protagonist's own failure to understand the people around him. He completely misreads the women's intentions and erroneously attributes certain feelings to them. All the while, he has been endeavouring to control his own emotions since he is determined to return to China. Yet in the end, as the women propose to the men, it becomes evident that he had not understood anything after all – and quite clearly that he had never been anything but an outsider on the pirate island.

This is an escapist romance. The social system of the island utopia is diametrically different from that of China, free of strife, classes and bureaucracy, and people are at peace with one another and happy with their jobs and their duties. Yet the utopian setting of the story mainly serves as the background for the love story and the intrigues between the characters, so it would clearly be a mistake to try to read this primarily as a political comment along the lines of, for example, Lao She's 老舍 satirical novel *Cat City* (*Maocheng ji* 貓城記, 1932) set on Mars.[42]

The Gypsy's Seduction, first published in 1939, is also a love story in a foreign setting with various exotic characters.[43] The nameless protagonist and narrator is again a male Chinese intellectual who is in Europe. Before returning to China, he decides to spend a few days in Marseille because he has heard that it is an exciting city that offers many pleasures. After a few days, he meets a gypsy, Lola 羅拉, who tells people's fortunes and offers to introduce him to 'the most beautiful woman in the world'. The narrator agrees and goes to see a show full of dazzling beauties, nearly fainting when he sees the star attraction, a woman of divine beauty, Panrui 潘蕊, to whom he is helplessly drawn. Panrui and the narrator fall in love, and the rest of the story concerns the various troubles that develop during their relationship. At first, he worships her so he is deeply shocked to learn from Lola that Panrui also works as a prostitute in order to support her poor family, which has no other income. After much doubt and disbelief, the narrator pretends to be a customer one night in order to see whether the gypsy's story is true. Shocked to learn that Panrui was indeed prostituting herself, he leaves her. But due to his own lack of money, he in turn soon prostitutes himself with Lola's assistance, and this time his customer, a wealthy American woman, turns out to be Panrui in disguise. This parallel development is repeated throughout their relationship. They make up and in the second stage of the relationship, they marry and move to China despite Lola's objections. After moving, the narrator pursues his successful career while Panrui is lonely and miserable at home. Finally, they return to Marseille, where Panrui becomes a much sought-after model who is famous throughout the city. He is predictably miserable. On Lola's advice, he decides to join some gypsies headed for America, but he is followed soon after by Panrui, who is afraid that he might have fallen in love with a gypsy girl. Once again, their love is renewed.

The novel ends with the couple deciding to travel all over the world together like gypsies, thieving and telling people's fortunes. As with their other problems, it is Lola's advice on the nature of love that helps them get along. Only by living as gypsies like her can they be happy together, with each of them sacrificing their personal ambitions for their love of the other. The novel makes no attempt to be realistic. The double mirroring of emotions and events, joys and defeats, between the two main characters is purposefully artificial. The settings are not specified in any detail. Whether in China or in France, the narrative says nothing about the places in which they live. There are no details of place, weather or background situations. Similarly, little attention is paid to the few other characters in the story. Most of the narrative consists of dialogue between the narrator, Panrui and Lola. These three main characters fulfil narrowly determined roles. Panrui is the self-sacrificing beauty who prostitutes herself for her family. This is a well-known stereotype from Chinese literature and films.[44] Lola, the gypsy, is the wise adviser and mediator who knows all the secrets of love and is always one step ahead. She is also frequently underestimated by the narrator, such as when he refuses to believe that Panrui is a prostitute or refuses to heed her advice about not going to China. In every case, the narrator finds that Lola was right all along. This is, of course, reinforced with the ending as the couple turn to a life as vagrants and gypsies in a state of permanent travel.

The Gypsy's Seduction repeats the recurrent idea in Xu's fiction that love and travel are inextricably interconnected. Looking for adventure in Marseille, the narrator finds his true love. But after trying to settle down twice, they realise that only in a state of permanent travel can their love be maintained. This constant travel serves a function similar to that of the pirate island in *The Absurd English Channel*. It is a space outside real life in which adventure and passion can flourish. Not surprisingly, it is the gypsies who know the secret of a happy and carefree life. Exoticism, passionate feelings and geographical distance reinforce one another.

Another example of this pattern in Xu's fiction is seen in the short story 'The Spirit of the Arabian Sea' ('*Alabohai de nüshen*' 阿拉伯海的女神), dated 1936.[45] Set on a cruise ship, the tale concerns a male narrator who is out on deck one night, where he encounters a mystifying woman of indefinable age. Claiming to be a witch (*wunü* 巫女) of Arabian origin, she now travels all over the world telling people's fortunes. She has even spent nine years in China and speaks both Mandarin and the Shanghai dialect, and reveals to him that her knowledge of a great number of languages is her key to being able to tell people's fortunes. The narrator is equally international and cosmopolitan. He professes a great interest in philosophy and is on his way to Belgium, but then plans to live in France and England after that.

The witch tells him the tragic story of a woman who perished in the Arabian Sea. She was a beautiful Arab woman who sought to find truth in religion, but after having studied all the religions, she was still unable to find the true God, so in despair she threw herself into the sea to kill herself. Perversely, she was turned into a restless spirit who haunts passing ships, seeking now to learn from the passengers which God is the true God so she can learn which deity turned her into a wandering spirit. Soon after hearing this tale, the narrator meets a young woman of uncanny beauty on the deck of the ship and they talk about religion. She seems to be exquisitely beautiful, but she wears a veil so he cannot see her face clearly. Subsequently, they meet several times. Of course, he suspects that she may be the wandering spirit or perhaps the ageless witch in disguise. Despite his reservations, he falls in love with her and kisses her, removing her veil. She is flustered and runs away.[46]

The witch reappears and is furious with the narrator, who is still wondering if the spirit and the witch are perhaps the same woman. It turns out that the lovely young woman was merely the daughter of the witch, who as an enraged mother decides that in accordance with an old Muslim tradition, either her daughter or the narrator must be punished by death. After a teary farewell, the narrator leaps overboard, but he is followed by the daughter who kills herself with him. As they embrace in the water, the narrator awakens from what turns out to have been only a dream. He wakes up on a deck chair on a ship in the Mediterranean.

This short story again uses familiar elements from Xu Xu's fiction, and, once again, travelling plays a crucial role. The exotic and the supernatural come together in multiple layers which are framed by the ship and the voyage. The state of suspension between fixed destinations allows the narrator to live out the fantasies of the dream world that for him constitute voyaging on a ship in the Arabian Sea. Like Lola and Panrui, the women are exotic, beautiful, mystical and completely beyond comprehension. The story builds on successive revelations as the narrator acquires more knowledge or breaks various barriers. He learns how the witch tells people's fortunes, he strips away the spirit's veil and he learns the truth of their background. The mysteriously ageless witch becomes an angry mother, and the beautiful spirit becomes her mortal daughter. The repeated revelations finally culminate in the narrator's death and the ultimate revelation: that it was all just a dream. But waking up does not return the narrator to his home, but to yet another ship and yet another voyage. It is clearly the state of travel that makes the narrator susceptible to the mystical and the romantic in this short story – a theme that is repeated in Xu Xu's other works.

Another example of this pattern is found in the novel *The Lament of the Mental Patient* (*Jingshenbing huanzhe de beige* 精神病患者的悲歌).[47] It was first serialised in 1940 and later published as a novel with a few revisions in May 1941. Once again, the protagonist and narrator is an intellectual Chinese male who lives in France. This is a love story in which the protagonist finds himself between two beautiful women, a servant girl, Helene (*Hailan* 海蘭), and her mistress, Baidi 白蒂 who are, presumably, both French. The narrator, who remains nameless throughout the story, is hired by a psychiatrist, Dr E. Shelamei 奢拉美, to help cure Baidi of a mental disorder. In order to prepare for this job, Shelamei has the narrator undergo military training in which he learns to shoot and other combat skills. After another period of training working with mental patients in a hospital, he is finally deemed ready to meet Baidi. The patient, Baidi, is the daughter of a wealthy family who live in a luxurious manor house outside Paris. At first he cannot get close to her, but the equally attractive Helene, a servant at the manor, agrees to help him and writes reports for him regularly about Baidi's behaviour. It turns out that Baidi is consorting with criminals and gamblers, and has taken up drinking and staying out during the night. These are the symptoms of the mental affliction that the narrator is supposed to cure while working under the guise of ordering the books in the library. He attributes Baidi's behaviour to the misery brought on by the oppressive atmosphere in the manor and her cold parents. While working on the case, he falls in love with Helene and proposes that they leave. But Helene is so devoted to Baidi that she refuses to do so until Baidi is feeling better, thereby making it clear to the narrator that his own happiness depends on his patient's mental state. Baidi, who is both charismatic and domineering, is at the centre of the relationship. Like Helene, she is attracted to the narrator, but she is also attracted to Helene, telling her at one point that she wishes she were a man so that she might enjoy her tenderness. The three eventually become friends and spend much time going out together, and Baidi is eventually proclaimed well again.

Just as all looks fine, Baidi finds out that the narrator has been deceiving her: he had told her that he was working for her parents in their library as a cover story. In her fury she threatens to shoot him, but shoots herself instead. She is hospitalised with her wounds and when he visits, asks him to kiss her. The passage is typical of the constant outpouring of emotions in this novel.

> 'Tell me you love me!'
> 'Yes, I love you,' I said, obeying blindly.
> 'Kiss me!'
> Again I blindly obeyed and kissed her on the lips. As she used her right hand to hold my neck and stroked my hair with her left I changed completely against her bosom. In that instant I forgot everything in the world and I forgot myself. It was as though I had groundlessly leapt out of this world and stepped onto the clouds. I was unfettered by this world's contracts, mores, traditions, morals and even conscience. I just had the heart of a child.[48]

Soon after their kiss, Helene enters and the narrator is racked by guilt. Over the following days he is generally nervous and confused, and speaks with Dr Shelamei who tells him that all will be well. Helene declares her love for him and they have sex for the first time. Just as the narrator feels that everything is fine once again, tragedy strikes. Helene kills herself. In her farewell letters to Baidi and the narrator, she explains that the two of them love each other and should be together. She did not want to stand in their way. The novel ends with Baidi joining a convent to become a nun. The narrator has not seen her since.

Skipping between provocative women, shooting ranges, mental asylums and manor houses, the characters and settings seem taken out of a simple thriller or a B-film. The storyline is melodramatic and the personae are generally seen from only one angle. Baidi's ambivalent sexuality and domination of the other two are never spelled out sufficiently to make her seem different from the other alluring women in Xu's fiction. Yet *The Lament of the Mental Patient* does show an interesting direction in Chinese literature in some other respects. Most importantly, Freudian notions of madness, delusion and the subconscious are incorporated into romantic melodrama in this piece. The narrator repeatedly ponders the details of how Baidi is affected subconsciously, and he is also haunted by his own doubts and fears. As with the introduction of traditional Chinese superstitions in Xu Xu's earlier fiction, the subconscious has now moved into the mainstream.

The Freudian concepts are, however, deployed in a quite different manner from Shi Zhecun's earlier use. In Shi's novels, the subconscious provides the underlying motives for the characters who are tormented by their repressed fears and displaced desires. In Xu Xu's work, psychology plays a more direct and clear-cut part of the plot. The narrator is interested in psychology and takes the job with Dr Shelamei precisely because he is a renowned psychiatrist. He sees Baidi as a patient to be cured of a mental affliction. Much like the use of references to literary tradition, references to psychology and the subconscious are given a distinct role in the development of the plot. This further demonstrates how Xu Xu borrowed elements from the 1930s writers to spice up his works in various ways. The references to Freudian drives and notions lend the narrative a character of sophistication and learnedness.

Most of Xu Xu's fiction from the 1930s and 1940s is written in the first person and frequently features modern women who are somehow beyond male understanding. Particularly the supernatural and the exotic figure prominently in his work. The romantic tragedies, the mysteriously otherworldly women, and the suspenseful plots all place his works quite firmly outside the realist style. Yet given his hang for the melodramatic and the light-hearted touch in most of his creative writing, it is difficult to see Xu Xu as a modernist writer challenging narrative idiom with these works.

Voyages and the male traveller

As mentioned, Xu Xu's novels and short stories in foreign settings frequently follow a fairly distinctive pattern in their story and narrative structure. The narrator is an intellectual Chinese male who lives abroad. He is usually named Xu 徐 like the author, which seems to provide a link between the protagonists in these works as well as to the author's persona. There is no indicator that Xu Xu hoped that these works would be read in any autobiographical sense, but the male narrators are always alike and might as well be the same person. In these novels and short stories, Xu is modern, sophisticated, well educated and frequently interested in philosophy. Economically well off, he can afford to gamble and pay for entertainment wherever he wants. Culturally, he considers himself a knowledgeable insider. He speaks the local language, French or English, perfectly and is able to engage with people at all levels of society without hesitation or misunderstanding. By being Chinese, his foreignness is made distinct, but nationality is rarely an issue that is foregrounded. On the contrary, his national identity is downplayed in favour of international cosmopolitanism. His cultural fluency and knowledge reveal his sophistication. He is a world traveller whose self-confidence lets him feel at home in any setting.

As the polished *flâneur* and dandy on the lookout for new pleasures, he is the quintessential modern stereotype. Through his travels abroad, he is also an emblem of modernity. In addition, his belief in modern rationality and his interest in philosophy are complemented by his lack of restrictive native cultural grounding, which enables him to engage in affairs and adventures in foreign worlds. Frequently he has a wife and children at home. This is the case with the narrators in both *The Absurd English Channel* and 'The Spirit of the Arabian Sea'. But these families are never serious impediments to his freedom, and their chief function in the tales seems to be as silent background to point up both his liberal attitude as well as the irresistible allure of the women he encounters on his travels. They are so attractive that all moral conventions are cast aside. As a modern urbanite who feels free of cultural or geographical attachments at home, the narrator is not hampered by conventional hindrances, and he is able to embark on adventures and to woo and win the most desirable women in the world.

The Chinese nationality of the narrator encourages the reader to identify with him, but he is not a heroic figure. His being Chinese emphasises the cultural difference with the women he meets, adding another layer to their exotic other-worldliness and heightening the tension of the relationship. In Xu's fiction, the fact that the narrator is Chinese lets him act as the sophisticated guide for the implied reader, explaining cultural differences as he goes along.

Yet there always remains a barrier of understanding as the narrator, in spite of all his worldly accomplishments, struggles to grasp what is going on. This barrier is not directly related to nationality, but in every case the narrator's encounter with the exotic women is determined by his being an outsider. It is because he is a stranger that the narrator fails to understand the pirate island and the people there. Similarly, he fails to understand Lola and Panrui in *The Gypsy's Seduction* or the two women in 'The Spirit of the Arabian Sea'. On occasion he learns their secrets himself, but otherwise it is only through mediators, such as the gypsy Lola, that the narrator has a chance to comprehend what lies beneath the surface.

The foreign settings are intermediate places between fixed destinations. The pirate island appears on a trip between France and England, just as the spirit and witch appear on a voyage through the Arabian Sea. In *The Gypsy's Seduction*, the narrator has gone to Marseille to find adventure before returning to China. A different example is furnished in *Ghostly Love* in which the narrator encounters the beautiful Ghost while taking a midnight stroll on Nanjing Road in Shanghai.[49] Even if he is only taking a walk through the city, he is a detached tourist who can look upon the sights and sounds that are laid before him for his contemplation and enjoyment.

It is precisely the cosmopolitan act of travelling and looking that initiates the narrator's meeting with the uncanny. It is between destinations that modernity meets its opposite. Where the narrator is a symbol of modernity and enlightenment, the exotic women encountered during these travels are his opposite: otherworldly, timeless and elusive. Frequently, as in 'The Spirit of the Arabian Sea' or *Ghostly Love*, the beautiful woman represents both the supernatural and the traditional – the opposite of the rational and the new. As gypsies or spirits, the women are sensual and mystical and beyond rational comprehension. They belong to a realm of mystery and passion that is both intoxicating and strange. In this manner, voyages into foreign lands become the framework that enable encounters between the modern and the other.

Xu Xu's stories are about exploration and learning the secrets of the exotic. In most cases, the mysteries are eventually resolved. In this respect, his works are reminiscent of Cheng Xiaoqing's 程小青 detective stories. The ghosts are revealed to be mortal women, and in *The Gypsy's Seduction* the narrator learns the secret to a happy relationship with Panrui. There is a return to normality as the narrator wakes up from his dream or leaves the island utopia. The adventure and passion are invariably delimited in time and space. There turns out to be a rational explanation in the end and the narrators' cosmopolitan modernity is never truly undermined.

From New Sensationism to popular exoticism

One of the main characteristics of Xu Xu's fiction from his period in Shanghai is how freely he borrowed from various genres and styles of literature that he encountered. Xu Xu has stated that his early works from the late 1930s were inspired by Prosper Mérimée (1803–70) and aestheticism.[50] In a Chinese context, he comes closest to the New Sensationist writers who wrote in Shanghai in the 1930s. Other scholars have remarked upon this resemblance, as noted earlier. In a manner similar to the modernist authors of the 1930s, Xu focuses on the inner worlds of the characters using first-person narration. Psychological issues play an additional role in the characters' development. Xu Xu also freely incorporates references to earlier traditional genres of Chinese literature, such as *zhiguai* 志怪 and *chuanqi* 傳奇.

The plots have much in common as well. The urban intellectual's explorations of dreams, fantasy and exotic women are much like what occurs in the modernist writings of New Sensationist authors like Mu Shiying 穆時英 and Shi Zhecun 施蟄存. In Shi Zhecun's short-story collection *An Evening of Spring Rain* (*Meiyu zhi xi* 梅雨之夕) from 1933, there are several tales in which the modern protagonists are similarly confused by enigmatic, alluring women and their own irrational fears and desires.[51] They are also frequently intellectuals who have little sense of what is going on around them. In a similar manner, Xu Xu often makes use of psychology, philosophy and the supernatural to depart from realist modes of narrative. This was a main characteristic of Shi Zhecun's fiction in the early 1930s. Both Shi Zhecun's and Xu Xu's works are generally concerned with representing modernity and how it collides with an unknown other.

Yet there are important differences as well. Xu's stories are rarely as dark and unreal as Shi Zhecun's can be. The modernist opacity and dreamlike mystery are less heavily pervasive than they are in the New Sensationist narratives. Nor is the expressionist narrative style of Mu Shiying, for example, with its disconnected fragments, to be found in Xu Xu's works. Xu's fiction is far more concerned with the unfolding story. The modern protagonist is on a course to discover what is going on, and his gradual realisation goes through several stages or layers in the manner of a detective story. Where the New Sensationist writers often merely describe a setting, a mood or a state of mind, Xu's focus is more often on a train of events that eventually wend their way to an end in which the truth is revealed.

The mysterious women are also less dangerous in Xu Xu's fiction. They remain difficult to understand, but they are usually more attainable as wives and lovers. They often reciprocate the protagonist's love. It is also worth noting that as sources of mystery, their exoticism and otherworldliness are principally constructed by themselves. Frequently, as in 'The Spirit of the Arabian Sea', the women keep their true identities hidden from the narrator. In Shi Zhecun's stories, the women's exoticism is imposed on them by the male protagonist's imagination and fantasy. This gives the fiction of Xu Xu a dramatically different character. Eventually, their barriers are overcome and the truth is revealed, thus vindicating the male narrator's modern outlook. This is, once again, the opposite of what happens in most New Sensationist fiction where the narrator is usually reduced to confusion, neurasthenia and sexual frustration.

On the whole, Xu's works of fiction with foreign settings are romantic love stories with strikingly colourful characters and settings. The romances are part of an adventure spread out before the narrator as a challenge to be overcome. This is nothing like the New Sensationist works, which are far more experimentally daring in their modernist explorations of madness and desire.

Xu Xu's adoption of elements from earlier modernist fiction is an example of the process by which characteristic features of modernist New Sensationist literature are eventually picked up and disseminated into popular culture. Xu Xu adapted various New Sensationist styles and elements for his own purposes and spun them into tales of passion, adventure and high drama. He used these techniques to distance himself from the social realist style that was still predominant in much other Chinese literature of the time. Yet due to the changing cultural context, the usage of tradition and the departures from realism had ceased to be contentious. Similarly, when the exotic women turn out to be secret agents, as in *Ghostly Love* and 'The Jewish Comet', this is not to be seen as a political statement, but rather as a popular convention representing danger and drama.

Xu Xu's fiction is an important example of the escapist literature that was popular during the Second Sino-Japanese War. Considering the predominant trends among the intellectuals of the time, it is notable that there is little overt political or ideological message in Xu Xu's works from this period. He excelled in juxtaposing the exotic and the otherworldly with the faces of modernity. The exotic is frequently foreign, supernatural and female. In opposition to this stands that which is urban, cosmopolitan and rational. Similar juxtapositions are found in the works of the New Sensationist authors. But Xu did more than imitate the tropes of the previous avant-garde. His contribution to the Chinese literary scene was that he adopted and popularised this approach, thus disseminating previously avant-garde styles into other literature.

Smoke Rings

After the conclusion of the Sino-Japanese War in 1945, Xu Xu's style of writing changed in certain respects. Some of his short stories became less concerned with romantic melodrama and turned more towards exploring human nature. Two examples of this kind of writing can be found in the collection *Smoke Rings* (*Yanquan* 煙圈) in 1946: 'The Master of the Art of Smelling' ('*Qifen yishu de tiancai*' 氣氛藝術的天才) and the title story, 'Smoke Rings' ('*Yanquan*' 煙圈), first published in 1934.[52]

'The Master of the Art of Smelling' is a simple short story about an old man in a remote village who tells the narrator about his lifelong interest in smells.[53] Many years previously the old man had studied for several decades in France doing research into the basic categories of smells, and trying to develop shows for audiences based on various fragrances and the machines to produce the smells required. On the whole, his performances were not very successful. The old man argues that if people only had a better sense of smell, such shows would be the highest form of art, surpassing both music and painting. But since he is the only person who is gifted with an exceedingly strong sense of smell and the ability to appreciate this form of art, he feels isolated from the world. This short story is a melancholy piece as the old man tells the narrator about the failed projects of his life and his resulting loneliness. Yet it is hardly surprising that his contraptions failed to impress. The old man's machines and elaborate performances seem like exercises in futility that were bound to fail from the start. He has now settled as a hermit in remote countryside and abandoned his projects and machines. Instead, he simply enjoys the scents of the flowers and plants in the area.

'Smoke Rings' is one of Xu Xu's more experimental and modernist works in this collection.[54] A philosopher tries to work out the meaning of life by asking old school friends to put their understanding of this in writing before they die. The school-mates meet for a reunion after a few years and find that their lives have turned out very differently. They agree to meet regularly, and over the years the circle is expanded with friends. They also make a pact to write about the meaning of life shortly before their deaths. After they die, what they wrote is to be kept by one of them in a safe. The last person will then be able to read the others' letters and come closer to grasping the meaning of life. Over the years, the others die off in various manners from illness, suicide and accidents. Finally, only the philosopher remains with the letters written by all the others before they died. In the end, as he is dying he reads all the letters sent by the original students and their friends. He finds that they are vastly different, with only one thing in common: the final full stop which in Chinese forms a small round circle. In the end, the philosopher blows a ring of smoke before dying which naturally echoes the full stop of the others.

The narrative style is modernistic and most of the characters do not have names. During one of the meetings, one of them addresses the smoking philosopher:

'What is human life after all?' – the pink dimples and silver-coloured teeth flew over to the corner of the wall [where the philosopher was sitting] and broke through the spreading smoke. A dark grey long thin face appeared in the smoke with a smile hanging at the corner of his mouth. Everybody held their breath to listen carefully to the light sounds which came out of his mouth after the smoke.

'Human life?' after which a smoke ring came drifting out of his mouth. He and all the others at that time saw it slowly rolling larger, expanding, expanding, becoming thinner, thinner, dispersing, dispersing, until it vanished. 'That – is – life!' The smile once again hung from his lips.

The smoke which had dispersed in the room moved almost audibly.[55]

This is the most abstract of the short stories and the narrative style harks back to Xu's early works in *Les Contemporains*. The various characters are each representatives of different sorts of lives with a poet, soldier, musician, etc. Only the philosopher seems to stand above them all, regarding their lives from a distance. He is also given the final word on the impossibility of defining the true meaning of life. Their answers have nothing in common, only the full stop which ends each of their letters.

It is tempting to see these two short stories as indictments against the political machinations that were happening in China at the time. Writing a short story about the impossibility of finding a higher purpose in life flies directly against the ideological propaganda that informed much other literature being written. The modernist narrative style further sets it apart from the other literary forms being advocated. While the narrative style in 'The Master of the Art of Smelling' is relatively straightforward, it does point in the same direction. The old man's performances produced by modern contraptions fail to move the audience as intended. Instead, he reverts to the simple pleasures of life. The short story clearly portrays this as the more sensible option. Any attempt to change people's lives through modern art or contraptions of modernity is bound to fail.

These two tales are exceptions to the general tenor in *Smoke Rings*. This collection contains several of Xu's short stories from the mid-1930s until its time of publication in 1946. Given the mixture of styles and themes, it cannot be considered a homogeneous collection, like those Shi Zhecun aimed to produce. Yet looking at the dates of his short stories, there is a discernible shift in his style of writing. By the second half of the 1940s, after the Japanese surrender, Xu moves away from the romantic encounters between sophisticated Chinese gentlemen and foreign or supernatural beauties towards a wider number of concerns. This trend continues with his later writings from Hong Kong in which he often portrays the situation of emigrants and other groups.

While Xu's writings eventually moved on to deal with other topics, his widely popular novels and short stories from the 1940s still stand as a testament to the influence that the New Sensationists had on popular culture. Another author to use the techniques of the prior avant-garde is Wumingshi, but he did so in a very different manner which distinguishes his works quite clearly from those of Xu Xu.

Notes

1. Wang Wenying, *Shanghai xiandai wenxueshi*, p. 491. Xu's name has also been rendered as 'Xu Yu' (Kubin, *Die Chinesische Literatur im 20. Jahrhundert*, 246) or, in different transliteration, 'Hsu Yu' (e.g., Hsu Yu, *Bird Talk* 鳥語, trans. Lin Yutang (Hong Kong: Nantian shuye, 1971?).

2. Chen Xuanbo, *Shi yu guang: 20 shiji Zhongguo wenxueshi geju zhong de Xu Xu*, p. 328.

3. Chen Xuanbo, *Shi yu guang: 20 shiji Zhongguo wenxueshi geju zhong de Xu Xu*, pp. 85–7. For details on *Renjianshi* 人間世, see Tang Yuan 唐沅 et al. (eds), *Zhongguo xiandai wenque qikan mulu huibian* 中國現代文學期刊目錄彙編 (*Compilation of Tables of Contents of Journals in Modern Chinese Literature*) (Tianjin: Tianjin renmin chubanshe, 1988), p. 1595.

4. The journal was also published from 1946 to 1949, but under different editorship. Tang Yuan et al., *Zhongguo xiandai wenque qikan mulu huibian*, p. 1377. I share Qian Suoqiao's hesitation in accepting the notion of a so-called 'Analects School' (lunyu pai 論語派) since there was no shared programme or cultural agenda. See Qian Suoqiao, *Liberal Cosmopolitan: Lin Yutang and Middling Chinese Modernity* (Leiden: Brill, 2011), pp. 98–9.

5. Tang Yuan et al., *Zhongguo xiandai wenque qikan mulu huibian*, pp. 1595ff.

6. Chen Xuanbo, *Shi yu guang: 20 shiji Zhongguo wenxueshi geju zhong de Xu Xu*, pp. 55–6.

7. McDougall and Louie, *The Literature of China in the Twentieth Century*, p. 228.

8. Tang Yuan et al., *Zhongguo xiandai wenque qikan mulu huibian*, pp. 1595ff.

9. Qin Xianci 秦賢次, '*Jianghu xing* jin *Feng xiaoxiao*', 江湖行盡風蕭蕭 ('*Characters in Society* and *The Rustling Wind*'), in Chen Naixin 陳乃欣 et al. (eds), *Xu Xu er san shi*.

10. Green, 'Rescuing Love from the Nation', pp. 126–8.

11. Chen Naixin 陳乃欣, 'Xu Xu er san shi', 徐訏二三事 ('A Few Things about Xu Xu'), in Chen Naixin et al. (eds), *Xu Xu er san shi*, p. 26.

12. Green, 'Rescuing Love from the Nation', p. 127.

13. Huang Wei 黃煒, 'Guicai Xu Xu', 鬼才徐訏 ('The Literary Genius Xu Xu'), *Xin wenxue shiliao* 新文學史料, 4 (1996): 119.

14. Some of Xu Xu's plays, including *Brothers* from 1942, are discussed in Green, 'Rescuing Love from the Nation', pp. 144ff.

15. A chronological list of these works can be found in 'Xu Xu zuopin yilanbiao', 徐訏作品一覽表 ('A List of Xu Xu's Works'), in Chen Naixin et al. (eds), *Xu Xu er san shi*, pp. 269–73.

16. Wu Yiqin and Wang Suxia, *Wo xin panghuang: Xu Xu zhuan*, p. 315. According to one source he stayed in America until 1949. Wang Wenying, *Shanghai xiandai wenxueshi*, p. 491.

17. Chen Qingsheng, *Kangzhan shiqi de Shanghai wenxue*, p. 103.

18. Liu Hua 劉華, 'Luanshi qiju zhong de zhexue ganwu: Xu Xu xiaoshuo pian lun', 亂世棲居中的哲學感悟: 徐訏小說片論 ('Philosophic Understanding Gained from

Living in Troubled Times: on Xu Xu's Fiction'), *Jinzhou shifan xueyuan xuebao* 錦州示範學院學報, 21(3) (1999): 67.

19. Lü Qingfu 呂清夫, 'Xu Xu de huihua yinyuan', 徐訏的繪畫姻緣 ('Xu Xu's Affair with Painting'), in Chen Naixin et al. (eds), *Xu Xu er san shi*, p. 259.

20. Wu Yiqin and Wang Suxia, *Wo xin panghuang: Xu Xu zhuan*, pp. 179–80.

21. Tang Zhesheng, 'Lun 40 niandai de liuxing xiaoshuo: yi Xu Xu, Wumingshi (Bu Naifu), Zhang Ailing, Su Qing de xiaoshuo weili', p. 1.

22. Xu Xu 徐訏, 'Daode yaoqiu yu daode biaozhun', 道德要求與道德標準 ('Moral Demands and Moral Standards'), in Chen Naixin et al. (eds), *Xu Xu er san shi*.

23. McDougall and Louie, *The Literature of China in the Twentieth Century*, p. 229.

24. *Feng xiaoxiao* 風蕭蕭 was filmed in 1953 by Shaw Brothers in Hong Kong. *Ghostly Love* was filmed in 1953, with a remake in 1996 titled *Evening Liaison* (*Renyue huanghun* 人约黄昏). *Jianghu xing* 江湖行 was filmed in 1973, with *River of Fury* as the English title and Xu Xu transcribed as 'Hsu Yu' in the credits. On Taiwan, some of his works were turned into TV series. For further details, see Frederik H. Green, 'A Chinese Romantic's Journey through Time and Space: Cosmopolitanism, Nationalism and Nostalgia in the Work of Xu Xu (1908–1980)', PhD diss., Yale University, 2009, pp. 307–8.

25. Wang Qinghua 王慶華, 'Zuowei gushijia de Xu Xu: cong *Gui lian* dao *Feng xiao-xiao*', 作為故事家的徐訏-從《鬼戀》到《風蕭蕭》 ('The Storyteller Xu Xu: From *Ghostly Love* to *The Rustling Wind*'), *Nanjing shida xuebao* 南京師大學報, 4 (1994): 99; Chen Xuanbo, *Shi yu guang: 20 shiji Zhongguo wenxueshi geju zhong de Xu Xu*, pp. 29–31.

26. Xu Xu 徐訏, 'Benzhi', 本質 ('Essence'), *Xiandai* 現代, 4(2) (1934): 403.

27. Xu Xu 徐訏, 'Jinguo', 禁果 ('Forbidden Fruit'), *Xiandai* 現代, 5(3) (1935): 514–24.

28. Xu Xu, 'Jinguo', p. 514.

29. Xu Xu 徐訏, *Gui lian* 鬼戀 (*Ghostly Love*), in Kong Fanjin 孔范今 and Pan Xueqing 潘學清 (eds), *Zhongguo xiandai wenxue buyi shuxi* 中國現代文學補遺書系 (*Supplemental Series to Modern Chinese Literature*) (Jinan: Mingtian chubanshe, 1991), pp. 332–88.

30. Xu Xu, *Gui lian*, pp. 334–5.

31. Xu Xu 徐訏, 'Dukuli de huahun', 賭窟裏的花魂 ('The Flower Spirit of the Gambling Den'), in *Yanquan* 煙圈 (*Smoke Rings*) (Shanghai: Yechuang shuwu, 1946), pp. 41–88.

32. Xu Xu 徐訏, 'Youtai de huixing', 猶太的彗星 ('The Jewish Comet'), in *Yanquan*, pp. 2–40.

33. Xu Xu, 'Youtai de huixing', pp. 9–10. How Sherkels might have ended up Jewish after losing his Christian faith is never explained.

34. Xu Xu, 'Daode yaoqiu yu daode biaozhun', p. 85.

35. Yingjin Zhang, *The City in Modern Chinese Literature and Film*, p. 223.

36. Xu Xu 徐訏, '*Feng xiaoxiao*', 風蕭蕭 ('The Rustling Wind'), in Kong Fanjin 孔范今 and Pan Xueqing 潘學清 (eds), *Zhongguo xiandai wenxue buyi shuxi* 中國現代文學補遺書系 (*Supplemental Series to Modern Chinese Literature*), vol. 6, Jinan: Mingtian chubanshe, 1990.

37. Green, 'Rescuing Love from the Nation', pp. 135–8; Yingjin Zhang, *The City in Modern Chinese Literature and Film*, pp. 226–8.

38. Xu Xu, *Feng xiaoxiao*, p. 3.

39. Quoted in Xin Dai, 'Taibei guoke', p. 38.

40. Xu Xu 徐訏, *Huang-miu de Ying-Fa haixia* 荒謬的英法海峽 (*The Absurd English Channel*) (Shanghai: Yechuang shuwu, 1946).

41. Xu Xu might have had an Anglo-Saxon name in mind for Peiyinsi, but in cases where I have not felt able to assign one, such as here, I have retained the Chinese transcription.

42. Lao She 老舍, *Maocheng ji* 貓城記 (*Cat City*) (Hong Kong: Huitong shudian, 1976).

43. Xu Xu 徐訏, *Jibusai de youhuo* 吉布賽的誘惑 (*The Gypsy's Seduction*) (Shanghai: Yechuang shuwu, 1940).

44. The most famous example of this prostitute stereotype is perhaps to be found in the popular film *Shennü* 神女 (*The Goddess*), directed by Wu Yonggang 吳永剛, in which Ruan Lingyu 阮玲玉 plays a poor prostitute who struggles to put her son through school.

45. Xu Xu 徐訏, 'Alabohai de nüshen', 阿拉伯海的女神 ('The Spirit of the Arabian Sea'), in Kong Fanjin and Pan Xueqing (eds), *Zhongguo xiandai wenxue buyi shuxi*, pp. 305–31.

46. Xu Xu, 'Alabohai de nüshen', p. 323.

47. Xu Xu 徐訏, *Jingshenbing huanzhe de beige* 精神病患者的悲歌 (*The Lament of the Mental Patient*), in Kong Fanjin and Pan Xueqing (eds), *Zhongguo xiandai wenxue buyi shuxi*.

48. Xu Xu, *Jingshenbing huanzhe de beige*, p. 473.

49. Xu Xu, *Gui lian*.

50. Gui Wenya 桂文亞, 'Xu Xu lai Tai xiaozhu', 徐訏來臺小住 ('Xu Xu Visits Taiwan'), in Chen Naixin et al. (eds), *Xu Xu er san shi*.

51. Christopher Rosenmeier, 'Women Stereotypes in Shi Zhecun's Short Stories', *Modern China*, 37(1) (2011): 64–6.

52. Xu Xu 徐訏, *Yanquan* 煙圈 (*Smoke Rings*) (Shanghai: Yechuang shuwu, 1946).

53. Xu Xu 徐訏, 'Qifen yishu de tiancai', 氣氛藝術的天才 ('The Master of the Art of Smelling'), in *Yanquan* 煙圈 (*Smoke Rings*), pp. 89–115.

54. Xu Xu 徐訏, 'Yanquan', 煙圈 ('Smoke Rings'), in *Yanquan* 煙圈 (*Smoke Rings*), pp. 116–31.

55. Xu Xu, 'Yanquan', p. 120.

Chapter 5

Wumingshi and the Wartime Romances

Wumingshi 無名氏 is an unusual author on the Chinese literary scene of the 1940s. Spanning a range of styles, he combined modernist explorations of death and dreams with popular romantic melodrama, and at the same time he vividly portrayed the horrors of war and the errors of ideological conviction. Hoping to create a new platform for peace and human unity, he wrote soaring religious treatises advocating a new perspective on life, love, sex and ideology. Throughout these diverse writings, he frequently employed an ebullient, gushing narrative style laden with metaphor – a characteristic that became the hallmark of his creative writings.

Wumingshi was always somewhat isolated from the public literary sphere. Going against the currents of the time in his writings, he remained mostly separate from the groupings and associations that characterised contemporary literary life. His major work was written in hiding and this is symptomatic of his creative career: as a thinker and writer, he remained an outsider.

His isolation was partly of his own choosing. His *nom de plume*, 'Wumingshi', would translate as 'Nameless' or 'Anonymous'. It is hardly a name in any traditional sense and reads more like a commercial brand. He used it to that effect when he opened his own publishing outlet, The Nameless Studio (*Wuming shuwu* 無名書屋), which distributed his works.[1] It was also used in the title of his multi-volume work *The Nameless Book* (*Wumingshu* 無名書). But while promoting this public brand, he nevertheless kept his private persona one step removed. He did not encourage publicity about himself and remained mostly a recluse from the literary scene.

His original name was Bu Baonan 卜寶南. Later he used several other names, most frequently Bu Ning 卜寧 and Bu Naifu 卜乃夫, but Wumingshi was the name under which he became best known.[2] It was first adopted when he wrote the novel *North Pole Landscape Painting* (*Beiji fengqing hua* 北極風情畫), serialised in 1943.[3] It was hardly a distinguishing trait at the time. The 'wumingshi' label was frequently used to indicate that the author was unknown or wished to remain anonymous. It was a common label or concept used already in the 1920s to describe the aspiring young writers who had not yet made their names in the literary field. In fact, there were organisations and publications established solely for their benefit.[4] But the designation was rarely used for longer novels.

This might be taken as an indication that Wumingshi was still not ready to commit to his work or was afraid of its being poorly received.

Presenting the opposite view, Wumingshi's elder brother, Bu Shaofu 卜少夫, has since stated that the name was deliberately chosen to mock more famous authors of the time who were busy promoting themselves.[5] Wumingshi, on the contrary, wanted his literature to receive attention in its own right, not himself personally. Of course, the name also served to create a sense of mystery around the author. According to Bu's later explanation, the name was intended as a critical comment on the state of the literary field at the time.

Wumingshi was born in Nanjing in 1917.[6] His father was a doctor from a landowning family. After high school, he decided to drop the university entrance examinations (*liankao* 聯考), so he never received a diploma and consequently was unable to enrol at a university. Nevertheless, at the age of seventeen he moved to Beijing, where he audited many lectures in the Chinese department of Peking University and spent a great deal of time in the library there.[7] He eventually managed to enrol in the university's Russian department, which accepted students without diplomas, and completed a two-year degree in Russian, while also studying English at the same time.

When the war with Japan erupted in 1937, Wumingshi went inland where he worked in various positions, including a stint as government censor. Later he was employed by his brother as a journalist for the newspaper *Li Bao* 立報 in Chongqing and Wuhan.[8] In Chongqing he also edited and wrote articles for several other publications, including a number of patriotic essays and other pieces. In addition, he started writing fiction.

From 1940 onwards, he became interested in Korea, which had fallen under Japanese colonial rule in 1910. He interviewed prominent Korean politicians in exile, including the premier of the Provisional Government of Korea, Kim Koo 金九 (1846–1949), and he wrote articles about them in *Li Bao*. In 1941, he was invited to start working for the volunteer Korean Liberation Army (the Kwangbok kun 光復軍) in China as a representative and spokesperson.[9] He relocated to Xi'an with Lee Beom-seok 李范奭 (1900–1972), the leader of the Korean army, in order to get closer to the Japanese front. While the troops stationed there saw little actual fighting, the two men became close friends, and Wumingshi's experiences with the Korean military became a strong influence on his fiction from this period.[10]

Wumingshi's authorship took several interesting turns. He started writing short stories in the late 1930s, publishing a collection, *Love of Russia* (*Luxiya zhi lian* 露西亞之 戀), in 1940. His next major piece of fiction was the novel *North Pole Landscape Painting* from 1943, a love story about a Korean soldier stationed in Siberia. It became highly popular, and after first being serialised in 1943 it was published as a separate book in 1944. The printed novel also sold beyond all expectations, beating previous publication records in Xi'an.[11] This work gave Wumingshi some recognition as his reputation increased, and many readers started comparing him with Xu Xu 徐訏.[12]

His next novel, *A Million Years Ago* (*Yi bai wan nian yiqian* 百萬年以前) from 1944, was an anti-Japanese piece that received comparatively little attention. It was more political propaganda than fiction.[13] Wumingshi's next commercially successful novel was *The Woman in the Tower* (*Tali de nüren* 塔裡的女人), also from 1944, which became a bestseller throughout China.[14] *The Woman in the Tower* and *North Pole Landscape Painting* were filmed in Taiwan in the 1960s.

After the Japanese surrender in 1945, Wumingshi settled in Shanghai where he worked as an assistant editor for the popular *Free Talk* (*Ziyou tan* 自由談), a supplement to the newspaper *Shenbao* 申報.[15] In late 1946, Wumingshi moved to Hangzhou, supposedly to take care of his mother. He also started work on *The Nameless Book*, which was intended to be his *tour de force* in six volumes. His ambition was to produce nothing less than a grand synthesis of Eastern and Western religions. In 1946, he published the first volume, *Beast, Beast, Beast* (*Yeshou, yeshou, yeshou* 野獸,野獸,野獸). The next two volumes, *Golden Snake Nights* (*Jinse de sheye* 金色的蛇夜), and the first part of the third volume, *Ocean Splendour* (*Haiyan* 海艷), followed fairly soon after.

Wumingshi's work on the project was broken off by the establishment of the People's Republic in October 1949. His works were banned in mainland China and he disappeared from the literary scene. From 1956 onwards, he secretly continued writing the subsequent volumes of *The Nameless Book* and it was finally completed in 1960.[16] During these years, he also produced several collections of poetry. Wumingshi was arrested and put into police custody multiple times. During the Cultural Revolution, like countless other intellectuals, he was sent to do forced labour. Wumingshi's later writings about the abuses of the labour camps during the Anti-Rightist Movement and the Cultural Revolution were later published and translated into other languages, including English.[17] Throughout this period, *The Woman in the Tower* and *North Pole Landscape Painting* remained in wide underground circulation through handwritten copies that were passed around.[18] After China opened to the outside world again in 1978, Wumingshi managed to send the nearly 2-million-character manuscript of *The Nameless Book* to his brother in Hong Kong where it was finally published. On the mainland, he was rehabilitated in 1978.[19] He left the mainland in 1982 and moved to Taiwan soon afterwards where he continued writing.[20] He also married again, causing a great scandal by taking a bride who was forty-one years his junior. In the 1990s, *The Nameless Book* was published in mainland China as well. He died on 9 October 2002.

Early modernist short stories

Wumingshi started writing fiction in 1939 under the name Bu Ning. His early short stories were eventually collected and published in two collections: *Love of Russia* (*Luxiya zhi lian* 露西亞之戀, 1942) and *Dragon Cave* (*Long ku* 龍窟, 1943). The literary supplement in the *Citizen's Gazette* (*Guomin gongbao*

國民公報), *Literary Groups* (*Wenqun* 文群), published some of them as well as a few essays.[21] *Literary Groups* was edited by the prominent writer and intellectual Jin Yi 靳以, who quickly took a liking to Wumingshi's work and praised it on several occasions.[22] The two of them eventually parted ways due to political differences.

One of the notable aspects of these early short stories is their use of extensive passages that set the scene in a manner reminiscent of the New Sensationist style. In 'Love of Russia' (*Luxiya zhi lian* 露西亞之戀, 1940) the opening paragraphs describe Berlin at night:

> An April night, a Berlin night, a night of 卍 banners, a nightless night.
>
> Neon of every colour slithered like snakes, whirling up in rose-coloured, grape-coloured, and kumquat-coloured waves, dark red, ocean blue, ochre and duck green waves. Gorgeous serenades, sonatas, and concerts poured from orange coffee houses. The revolving glass doors of the department stores as bright as day kept on swallowing one group of customers and then spitting out another group of customers. In the torrential stream of people, swastika armbands rocked with the waves, black dovetails, brown Nazi insignia ...
>
> The broadest chests of all of Europe were thrust forward on the asphalt roads, creating a stomping of all sorts of boots and shoes. Those who had suffered losses in the Great War wore black armbands, lonely, walking with German shepherds on leashes. White poplars along the side of the street shook in the wind. The mourning *bass* voices of street singers drifted along through the violet night, their voices carrying countless sharp angles.[23]

The narrative style here seems to come directly out of Mu Shiying's descriptions of 1930s Shanghai. The use of disconnected images and metaphors to convey the bustle and speed of modern Berlin is almost identical. Similarly, there are several references to unsettling aspects that show the negative side of dazzling modernity in the metropolis. It is an enticing image, but also one that is somewhat menacing, even without an awareness of Nazi atrocities.

In other places, Wumingshi goes further than the New Sensationists in his use of modernist narrative techniques. It is certainly not limited only to representations of urban cityscapes. Later in the same short story, there is a description of riveting music produced by a band of Russian musicians in exile:

> When the black baton waved in the air, a flow of music instantly poured over the coffee house like a geyser. After a few seconds, the flow turned into a flood of music which inundated everything. The flood of music flooded, overflowed, this was the spilling over of the Nile beneath the pyramids, the overflowing of the waters of Venice. This music was boundless like the sea, endless. The sea of music was full of gleaming, gloomy, joyous, brooding waves which crested, rose, rose, swelled, swelled into one gigantic wave which surpassed everything and then collapsed, shattered into tens of

thousands of little wavelets which one by one washed far away, and washed back again one by one, washing away, overflowing, opening up ...[24]

The ecstatic description of the music continues at length, swollen with metaphors, in this manner for several more paragraphs, likening the music to fire, waves, cannons, etc. It gives the impression that the music is relentless and overwhelming as the narrative style attempts to carry on in the same way. It is a sensory overload of metaphor that is intended to convey the impression that the music was received by its audience in much the same manner as the reader is swamped by description.

In contrast to the ebullient narrative language, the plots of these short stories are relatively simple. The protagonist of 'Love of Russia' is a Korean soldier, Kim 金, who has just arrived in Berlin after an extended stay in Tomsk. A Korean friend takes him to a coffee house run by Russians in exile. There are some musicians with a small orchestra there, and Kim tells them stories about their homeland, which they have not seen for years. They are deeply moved by his stories and the atmosphere becomes highly emotional. To show their gratitude, the musicians play some Russian songs and there is much drinking of vodka. The modernist narrative style is not ideally suited to describing plot developments. Instead, it is the moods and environments that are highlighted in the text. The short story thus shifts between more straightforward expository passages that carry the plot forward and these extended sections portraying the setting or background.

Proving once again that the narrative style of juxtaposed fragments and metaphors can be utilized for more than describing urban spaces, the short story 'Red Demons' ('Hong mo' 紅魔), written in 1943, starts in the following manner:

Despair and madness!
    Fire was whirling about, running wild, gushing forth, leaping like a wild beast, flames grabbing each other, intertwining, fighting. Clusters of flame swirled in the air, soaring, inflaming rage and heat, striking one darkness after another, rushing from one space to the next. Flowing columns of smoke billowed out, spreading fury in a raging dance, snake-like breaking through the burning fires, turning madly like twisting dragons, whirling faster and faster, rushing along, reaching into the sky. The fire and smoke spread chaotically all around, becoming ever more ferocious, ripping through the dark of night, burning space, making the boundless sea of space a savage red, ghostly black, ghostly green. Myriads of sparks were glittering, myriads of pink maggots were jumping about ...[25]

This unrelenting torrent of narrative continues unabated for several more paragraphs, but the excerpt above gives a good impression of the remainder. The scene is a battlefield full of carnage and people dying. Towards the end of this introduction, the sixth paragraph reads:

Guns and bombs went mad with hunger, plundering blood and flesh like crazy, like drunk, as though they had opened a gaping blood-thirsty mouth like an endless chasm which could not be filled in a million years. Countless rockets flashed like lightning, madly sprinting, rushing. Sparks flew about, a beautiful fire. It magnified countless furious faces, phantasmal faces, faces exhausted like corpses. Black torsos rushed about madly in the yellow fog and mud and rain, like old Mongolian oaks with legs. Black people, red people, yellow people, and it was not heads that were swinging on their shoulders, but odd cartoonish balls of meat. The balls of meat rolled. All the piles of black flesh in human form rolled about and magically transformed into moistened gum arabic, turning from solid form into a sticky fluid, rolling horribly, with a gleaming malicious laugh holding a bayonet.[26]

The battle related is that of the Korean resistance fighting against Japanese invaders. The rest of the short story concerns two Korean soldiers who manage to survive the fight and try to find a place to hide. After some initial frustration, a family finally takes them in, with the family members struggling among themselves about whether to do their patriotic duty, concealing the soldiers, or whether to turn them out, thereby protecting themselves. Together with the short story 'Dragon's Cave' ('*Long ku*' 龍窟), 'Red Demons' was originally intended as a novel. As a short story, the most striking and memorable aspect is the narrative style of the first pages.

Most of these short stories are set against a backdrop of contemporary political events and situations. This is quite unlike the works of the other authors in this study who deliberately avoided ideology and politics. In Wumingshi's short stories, the Japanese are invariably the villains, cruel and murderous, and the heroes are the Korean soldiers, brave and stoic. Yet these are not rousing war stories like much other contemporary fiction. In essence they are mostly abstract stories of human nature.

Another example of this abstraction of the political can be found in 'A Story from the Seaside' ('*Haibian de gushi*' 海邊的故事), dated February 1940.[27] Here, an elderly man lying on a beach at night tells the narrator of the first time he cried. He was incarcerated in a Japanese prison for many years. The madness and darkness and cruelty of the prison were all without purpose, and no real explanation is provided for his imprisonment. After a long time in his cell, he was allowed outside the prison one day to do forced labour. The overwhelming sight of the beautiful scenery and nature made him cry. The tale of the dark prison also contrasts sharply with the beautiful view of the moonlit sea where the first-level narrator and the old man are talking. As with Wumingshi's other descriptive passages, the description of the sea is ripe with figures of speech: the sea is laughing, kissing the clouds, like a white flower, nude under the moonlight, etc. In the end, this short story comes across as an exercise in portraying an abstract contrast between freedom, light and vast expanses, on the one side, and incarceration, darkness and confined space, on the other. The specifics of the political situation fade into insignificance.

Wumingshi's early short stories do contain references to current political events. Like those mentioned above, the Japanese figure in most of them as a source of cruelty, injustice and inhuman violence. Several of the stories were inspired by Wumingshi's contacts with soldiers from Korea and hearing about the Japanese occupation there, and the Korean freedom-fighter was also a theme that Wumingshi pursued later in his novel, *North Pole Landscape Painting*. Of course, a Chinese readership would easily relate to seeing the Japanese playing the part of villains. Yet his fiction is quite different from contemporary Chinese war propaganda stories intended to arouse hatred against the Japanese invaders. The importance of the nation disappears in these war narratives. Instead, these short stories are to be seen as more abstract tales of the eternal human conflict between good and evil. Contemporary affairs fade away as Wumingshi's distinctive narrative style almost precludes any primary consideration of current social and political affairs.

There is no call to arms here and China is rarely mentioned. Instead, there is a sense of resignation in most of these short stories: there is not much hope of saving Korea or Russia anymore, and the Japanese prisons are presented as an unalterable reality of life. There is little to be done other than enjoying the simple pleasures that remain: a cigarette, some nice music, a beautiful view. In this manner, the politics of real events become somewhat abstract. The Japanese represent cruelty and violence, but in a symbolic, detached, and apolitical way. It becomes a background against which to describe violence and torment in a purely ahistorical form set apart from the battles and deaths plaguing China at the time of writing.

Extended passages of theatrically tempestuous narration are also present in several of Wumingshi's other short-story collections. Yet the narrative style is different from that of Liu Na'ou 劉吶鷗 and Mu Shiying 穆時英. It is not as staccato and fragmented. Wumingshi never uses creative typesetting to break the sentences as the New Sensationists did. Liu and Mu place disconnected bits of text on the page in various ways to break the textual flow and convey an image of chaos and incomprehensibility uniquely tied to the modern urban experience. The aim is to produce a narrative experience that is jarring in the same way. Describing the streets of Berlin or the Japanese invasion of Korea, Wumingshi is clearly aiming to achieve a similar effect of chaos. But generally his descriptions are more rhythmical, often flowing and persistent with long arcs. In the descriptions of music and the waves of the sea, the narrative style is not used to reflect disconnected confusion but, on the contrary, to render impressions of lyrical beauty. The technique tries to reflect the overpowering emotional effect of the music on the listeners. Like the modern cityscape, the music and sea produce a sensory overload that the author tries to reproduce in the text. This is where the metaphors of Venice, flowers and poetry enter the description. Wumingshi is striving to summon forth a rich array of scenes and emotional responses.

Seen as a whole, it becomes clear that Wumingshi's early short stories cannot simply be classified as 'romantic' as some studies have claimed.[28] They are a far cry from the love stories that made Xu Xu popular during the same period. Rather, they demonstrate that already from the start of his creative writing, he had a far more experimental and modernist strain than scholars have hitherto acknowledged. He adapted the expressionist narrative style of the New Sensationists for his own purposes in these works, but he took it further and experimented with it in an attempt to achieve a broader palette of stylistic effects. These short stories also demonstrate that the facile division of Wumingshi's oeuvre into two periods – romanticist and modernist – is not as simple as it seems. On the contrary, there are clear links in narrative style between these short stories and his later writings to be found in *The Nameless Book*.[29]

Despite the display of modernist narrative techniques, these short stories are not literary challenges in a wider sense against the literary establishment. On the contrary, they portray the Japanese as faceless, brutal villains and show the staunch resistance of a few heroic Koreans against overwhelming odds. With their abstract narrative style and foreign settings, these works cannot be considered as stirring or nationalistic war literature, but neither do they go against the trends of the time. Nationalism remains a virtue of the highest order, and thus neither modernity nor ideology come under attack.

North Pole Landscape Painting and *The Woman in the Tower*

The two novels *North Pole Landscape Painting* and *The Woman in the Tower* were published within a year of each other in 1943 and 1944, respectively, and are very similar in plot and structure. Both novels became top bestsellers in the occupied areas and remained in underground circulation in China for a long time. They were both filmed on Taiwan in the 1960s and are still highly regarded by many Chinese readers. One of Wumingshi's biographers, Li Wei 李偉, lavishes the following praise on *North Pole Landscape Painting*:

> *North Pole Landscape Painting* is fiction, but it can also be read as an essay or poetry. Wumingshi ingeniously uses the methods of classical Chinese poetry (*fubixing shoufa* 賦比興手法) in both narrative descriptions and in character dialogue. His writing is witty and the phrasing is often highly original. He has his own stylistic technique, texture, manner, and flair. His writing has a unique distinction, literary elegance, and lasting charm. He bravely experiments with forging an exceptional rhetoric based on his own processing of the essences of Eastern and Western languages.[30]

It is these two novels that are seen as most representative of Wumingshi's romantic period. In their study of romantic literature in China, Zhu Xi 朱曦 and Chen Xingwu 陳興蕪 pay particular attention to them.[31] They find that Wumingshi expanded the boundaries of romantic fiction in China in these works, writing about different sorts of love and the beauty of nature in elegiac tones that were new and unusual at the time.

Presenting a more radical picture, Wumingshi's brother Bu Shaofu 卜少夫 declared that the two novels were intended as statements of protest against the stifling political requirements of the current literary establishment. Wumingshi objected to the demands that literature should promote nationalist sentiment. According to Bu Shaofu, the novels 'used a new popular method to capture a large readership and present a challenge to some of the self-proclaimed popular artists' of this time.[32] Wumingshi himself has similarly claimed that the two books were written in opposition to the political demands put on literature. After moving to Taipei, he enlarged upon the historical role of the two novels in 1987:

> From the 1930s, a political force dominated the ideological trends of new literature and art in mainland China. The volcanic nature of many youths was directed towards social revolutionary movements which engulfed the expression of their young emotions with religiously socialist ideals. The anarchist Ba Jin 巴金 employed revolution-plus-love style fiction to attract many young people. The characteristic of his writings was merely the projection of volcanic expression, it was not the real thing. But based on his widely imitated splashing around of fire, he did indeed ignite the hearts of some young people at the time. Of course he benefited to a certain degree from the strong political dominating force mentioned earlier. The heavy influence of this domination lasted for a full fifteen years (1929–1943). In those years, there was a desolate lack of literature that truly reflected the volcanic nature of youth.
>
> It was not until 1944 with the publication of *North Pole Landscape Painting* and *The Woman in the Tower* that this desolate lack began to be rectified. This also broke the dominance of the literary ideology mentioned above and therefore intellectuals with a political inclination attacked it vigorously, criticizing the books for "diluting the wave of fighting for democracy". The two books were popular on the mainland for a while and if we were to objectively evaluate their importance (and not their art), I think they would not fall much behind the influence of *The Sorrows of the Young Werther* at the time. Almost all young people who liked reading fiction and were able to get a copy of these two books read them.[33]

It is clear that Wumingshi, at least in retrospect, saw these two novels as defiant works that challenged the literary establishment and broke new ground for Chinese literature. In his view, they even ended the domination of politics over of art and literature, not least by virtue of their commercial success. The historical record does not, however, accord these two works such an important position. The political discussions on the nature of art certainly did not change noticeably as a result of their influence. An attempt to evaluate their position in the literary field requires a closer reading of the novels.

Written in 1943, *North Pole Landscape Painting* was first serialised in *North China News* (*Huabei xinwen* 華北新聞) in Xi'an. Given its popularity, it was soon published as a novel on its own and proceeded to become a major bestseller. The initial print run of 2,000 copies was sold out almost immediately after publication. This was an unprecedented success. Normally, a sale of half that number within two years was considered profitable.[34]

The melodramatic plot of the novel is fairly straightforward. The narrative framework consists of a story in a story. The first-level narrator meets a mysterious man, a Korean named Lin 林, on Huashan Mountain 華山, who tells him his tragic love story. Ten years earlier, Lin was garrisoned in Tomsk in Siberia together with a large contingent of Korean troops who had been fighting against the Japanese occupation. Here Lin fell passionately in love with a Polish girl he met, and the two had an intense affair. After Lin and his troops were ordered to leave the city, the girl committed suicide out of grief. In her farewell note, she asked him to sing a certain song at the top of a mountain exactly ten years later. The narrator happens to encounter Lin as he is fulfilling this request.

While Lin's love story is of no extraordinary interest from a literary viewpoint, the novel as a whole nevertheless has a few features that are worth noting. The first-level framing narrative is used effectively, principally in establishing a pervasive setting of darkness and mystery. The first-level narrator has come to Huashan Mountain in the autumn of 1942 to recover from 'severe mental strain' (*julie de naopizheng* 劇烈的腦疲癥). This already signals that he is a modern urbanite of an intellectual bent. In the first paragraph, we learn that he had originally relocated to Xi'an from the battlefront, but that Xi'an was still too noisy to provide a restful atmosphere, so he has therefore come to Huashan to recuperate. There follows a long encomium praising the eternal beauty and curative powers of the mountain. Thus, we are quickly transferred from the brutal events of contemporary China to a remote place beyond ordinary time and place.

In the early 1940s, Wumingshi had himself spent some time on Huashan Mountain, one of China's holy mountains according to Buddhist beliefs.[35] Thereafter, Huashan was to become a recurring theme in most of his later works, where it often figures prominently, usually representing something primordial, elemental and wild, which is set far apart from ordinary human society. On the mountain, the narrator stays at a Buddhist monastery run by a monk who has stayed behind to watch the place through the winter. On New Year's Eve 1943, a fierce storm rages on the mountain. The following day, New Year's Day, everything is covered by heavy snow and the narrator goes out to admire the view. Here he encounters a mysterious and taciturn man in a ragged Russian coat, the only other person outside. Later, during the night, the narrator hears the mysterious stranger rummaging about and decides to sneak after him. The stranger eventually reaches the mountain peak where he starts howling into the night with uncontrolled grief. Finally, the narrator rushes forward to prevent the man from committing suicide as he heads towards a cliff. The two of them sit down and talk, and the narrator learns that the mysterious man is Korean and mourning a dead girl whom he claims to be able to see and hear. He states that he has no name, but suggests that he be called Lin.[36]

In this manner, suspense is built up prior to Lin's tale, which forms the second-level narrative. Throughout this first part, the setting and the characters all hint towards mystery, madness, death and the supernatural in a manner very similar to Shi Zhecun's 施蟄存 short stories. The stranger is rudely taciturn during the day and appears like a ghost as he walks through the night, making the narrator wonder whether he is perhaps not human.[37] He looks suicidal and communes with the dead. In addition, the setting with the barren snow-clad mountain, the raging storms and the solitary monastery forms an otherworldly scene that contributes to the mounting suspense and odd crossing between real and unreal events and locations. Much as in Shi Zhecun's gothic short stories, a remote place forms a delimited space set apart from normal life in which the unreal takes hold.

The first-level narrative contains multiple references to real names and dates and places. The place and setting – New Year's Eve 1943 on Huashan Mountain – is as specific as can be. This supposed realism is in direct contrast to the otherworldliness of the setting and characters. Again, this is somewhat similar to the New Sensationist mode of writing in which real times and places are rendered strangely unfamiliar through the narrative style. In Wumingshi's novel this appeal to reality is particularly striking in the end, as the first-level narrator makes a direct appeal to the supposed audience. Readers are asked to contact the author if they should have any knowledge of Lin's current whereabouts. To this extent, Wumingshi goes further than the New Sensationists, specifying not only dates and places, but also addressing his readers and referring to the publication of the work itself. Finally, the first-level narrative is remarkable in its contrast to the second-level narrative, which is far more conventional as a tragic love story. Lin's tale of passionate feelings and endless despair contains none of the modernist mystery that pervades the first-level narrative. Lin's story takes up the main part of the novel. For the remainder of the book until the last few pages, only the stranger's second-level narrative is given. Supposedly, the first-level narrator has recorded it verbatim.

In 1932, ten years prior to the narration, Lin was garrisoned in Tomsk as aide-de-camp with the Korean army. Here he meets a Polish girl, Aurelia (Aoleiliya 奧蕾利亞), and the two eventually fall deeply in love. Both characters are larger-than-life stereotypes. Aurelia is exquisitely beautiful, an accomplished guitarist, and enjoys listening to Lin's learned lectures on countless topics. He, too, is the epitome of the virtues of his sex: passionate, poetic, musical, scholarly, handsome, patriotic and brave. He is deeply emotional, has a tendency to brood and harbours a darker pessimistic streak, yet this only demonstrates his manly ability to overcome problems as well as a certain weariness with life that comes with experience – details intended to convey that Lin has seen it all before; there is little that is new to him or causes him surprise. He is worldly and sophisticated, but not an urban dandy like Xu Xu's protagonists, and he does not represent modernity in the same manner.

The many conversations between Lin and Aurelia follow a set pattern: Lin starts the dialogue with a paradox or other statement that goes against normal opinion. When Aurelia fails to understand him or questions his reasoning, Lin seizes the opportunity to lecture her on some subject, displaying his learning, wit and originality. In this manner, Lin covers a vast amount of ground throughout the book with his opinionated discourses on history, human nature, poetry, plays, music, etc. Here is part of their conversation after having seen *La Dame aux Camélias*.

'Strictly speaking, an opera (*geju* 歌劇) cannot be a success. If you look at the "songs" (*ge* 歌), then the "play" (*ju* 劇) will be a failure. If you look at the "play" part, then the "songs" will be a failure.'

'That is quite correct,' she nodded.

'To be even more precise,' I continued, 'tragedies (*beiju* 悲剧) cannot be a success! If you have the "tragic" (*bei* 悲), then you cannot have drama (*ju* 剧). And if you have drama, then you can't have tragedy!'

'Now this is not quite clear to me.'

'What I am saying is quite clear: For a real tragedy you have to read the script, it cannot be performed on stage!'

'Why is that?'

'If it is to be performed, a murder would have to be committed!'

'You are joking again.'

'No, I am not joking. Let's take *La Dame aux Camélias*. If I were a woman and had to play the main part, then I would only be willing to play the role under a single set of circumstances.'

'What set of circumstances is that?'

'When I wanted to commit suicide.'

'Commit suicide?' Her eyes widened as she looked at me.

'Yes. Only when I had made up my mind to commit suicide would I be willing to act in *La Dame aux Camélias*. If I were an actress and had decided to kill myself due to some unhappiness, I wouldn't need to throw myself into the river or take sleeping pills. I would only have to perform *La Dame aux Camélias*!'

'What you are saying is very strange,' she said, laughing.

'It is not strange at all. A genuinely good actress would have to die as she acts out *La Dame aux Camélias*' last moments. If she does not die, it proves that her acting is not real ...'[38]

Such expositions on various subjects range from Heine (1797–1856) and Goethe (1749–1832) to different sorts of coffee, and Aurelia is naturally overwhelmed by Lin's displays of humour, learning and breadth of mind. These qualities are also emphasised by Lin's own narrative style, which is heavy on description and metaphor. Here Lin notices for the first time how exquisitely beautiful Aurelia is:

Her long golden hair was shining like billowing wheat fields under the spring sun. Her eyes were two blue gems, more blue than a blue Indian sky, with a glimmer of dreaminess. Her face was white with black eyebrows and a high-bridged nose. No face was better suited for sculpting with its evenness and harmony. It was almost like a relief sculpture of a face made in veneration of an ancient goddess. Her figure was tall and slender, almost like a well-trained dancer's, every pose expressed a kind of gentleness, a kind of sweetness, a kind of harmony that was full of musical melody and rhythm.[39]

Yet even the most everyday actions become reasons for metaphor, exposition and displays of learning. In the following, Lin describes the sensation of drinking some beer:

When the rosy liquor slipped past my lips, the fragrance of barley arose in the air, even my pores seemed to exude an aroma. After the liquor had passed through the digestion in my stomach, it was absorbed into my veins and my whole body became incredibly warm and comfortable. The warmth from sorghum wine or whiskey is like a fast bomb explosion which suddenly goes off in your body. All of a sudden the body becomes very hot. The heat you get from beer is slow, very slow, degree by degree, gradually raising the person's temperature ...[40]

These opinionated disquisitions on countless topics give the novel a fairly distinct narrative style. It is equally characteristic of the narrative in *The Woman in the Tower*. But unlike the New Sensationist fiction or some of Wumingshi's earlier short stories, there is no sense of jarring or displacement. Rather, the technique seems intended to show off the narrator's (and perhaps the author's) wide learning.

Eventually, love for their respective nations binds Lin and Aurelia even closer together. Aurelia keeps her Polish identity hidden in the beginning, but when Lin learns about it, he launches into an extended eulogy of Marie Curie (1867–1934), the Polish-born scientist, which spans five pages of the book and sees Lin reeling off long letters written by Curie which he had learned by heart.[41] Thus, they are bound together by the joint fate of coming from countries that have been brutalised under foreign occupation. Polish sovereignty was restored in 1918 after the First World War, while Korea was still under Japanese occupation. As Lin explains with typical poetic pathos:

Poland today has already raised the flag of freedom. Poland's mothers no longer need to shed their tears in the dead of the night to raise the children of Poland from their beds.

But Poland's brother, Korea, is still trembling under the Japanese bayonets. Everywhere the tragedy of Polish mothers exists. On the Eastern shore of the Yalu River, in my beautiful motherland, there is no sun, there is no freedom, no warmth, no laughter, no spring. Like wounded beasts, people hide alone in their caves. Outside, the muzzles of the hunters' rifles are everywhere.[42]

Their passionate nationalism provides a new element in the story as contemporary events – hitherto not a major part of the novel – suddenly become an important factor in their relationship. It turns out that both Aurelia and Lin are ardent patriots. The introduction of this nationalistic aspect seems somewhat out of place compared with the rest of the novel. It is interesting that China is not mentioned at all in this context, even though the Japanese retain the well-known role of villains and brutal aggressors. This would, of course, resonate with the intended Chinese readership. Yet perhaps omitting China allows the reader to enjoy the novel more as entertainment rather than yet another attempt to rouse readers into action or reminding them of China's sorry state at the time. In another way, this highlights a development parallel to Xu Xu's use of secret spies and agents or Qin Shou'ou's 秦瘦鷗 nationalist sentiment in *Begonia* (*Qiuhaitang* 秋海棠). While not central to the plot, notions of patriotism were incorporated into popular literature, and *North Pole Landscape Painting* shows how the idealised stereotype of the strong fighter for the nation had entered into the mainstream imagination as a fictional type. Lin's successful military career and his nationalist sentiment reveal him to be a man of principles and vision – yet more of his numerous virtues.

The remainder of the novel details his affair with Aurelia through various twists and turns. Lin worries about a former boyfriend of hers, and she worries about one of her girlfriends who is pursuing him. As these various hurdles are overcome, she declares her undying love and that he has awoken unknown depths of passion in her. Finally, Lin learns that the troops have been ordered back to the areas of fighting and their last days of grief are in sharp contrast to their previous days of endless happiness. After Lin has left, he receives a letter from Aurelia's mother stating that she killed herself soon after his departure. Her note includes Aurelia's farewell letter with a few strands of her hair. The letter only has the word 'darkness' (*hei'an* 黑暗) written all over it. In a note in the corner, she writes how she cannot live without him and that as she writes, she is holding a dagger pointed to her heart. Her final request is that exactly ten years after the day they met, Lin should go to a tall mountain, face north and sing a certain Korean song that he had sung to her earlier. Thus, Lin's romantic tragedy thus comes full circle with the melodramatic ending.

The Woman in the Tower followed soon after *North Pole Landscape Painting*. It was published the following year in 1944. Rather than serialising it in a journal or newspaper supplement, Wumingshi decided to publish *The Woman in the Tower* himself through his newly established publishing outlet, The Nameless Studio.[43] The printing was financed through pre-orders based on the popularity of *North Pole Landscape Painting*. The initial print run of 3,000 copies was sold out in just twenty days. Within two months of its publication, Wumingshi had recouped the printing cost of 140,000 yuan and earned an additional 70,000.[44]

The plots of the two novels are similar and the narrative framework is practically identical. As in *North Pole Landscape Painting*, *The Woman in the Tower* features a first-level narrative setting that introduces the main part of the story, the second-level narrative. The framing device similarly builds upon dreams and fantasy and expository leaps that take place in an unreal and timeless setting.

Again, the main part of the novel is a highly romantic and tragic love story, much like its predecessor. As the novel begins, the narrator has just completed writing *North Pole Landscape Painting*. Life in Xi'an is too dull, so he decides to return to Huashan for recreation.[45] Once more, the appeal to realism is striking as the author refers to previously published work. Nevertheless, this realism is immediately offset by the otherworldliness of the events. During the night, he hears some strange and unearthly music playing so he goes to investigate by following the sound. In the middle of the forest, he finds a solitary man, Juekong 覺空 (a name that translates as 'Sensing emptiness'), playing a violin, and producing the most beautifully intoxicating music.

The mysterious Juekong at first avoids the narrator. But after much persistent pestering, Juekong agrees to give him a present. Some time later, the author is presented with a book in which Juekong tells the story of his life and why he has chosen to become a monk on Huashan Mountain. The content of the book is the second-level narrative. Juekong's lay name was Luo Shengti 羅聖提, and his story starts sixteen years prior to the first-level narrator's encounter with him. Luo is an eminent doctor and highly accomplished violinist. He is sophisticated, handsome, cultivated and wealthy. He is also pursued by a number of women.

At a wedding party, Luo meets a young university student, Li Wei 黎薇, who is stunningly, breathtakingly, predictably attractive. Luo plays his violin for the party and the audience roars with approval.[46] Other men find Li Wei arrogant and haughty. Although Luo believes that he perceives her true values underneath, he decides not to pursue her. This is a deliberate ruse to entice her. Over the following years they meet a few times and barely speak. Finally, she comes to his home seeking violin lessons. He agrees and starts to give her lessons. Throughout, he remains cool and polite. At last she is unable to resist him and confesses that she had fallen deeply and passionately in love with him. She gives him her diaries from which he learns that she has been in love with him for years. So they start a relationship, going sailing together, playing the violin, etc. Utter bliss and happiness. They complete each other's thoughts. After several years, he finally admits his dark secret: he is already married and has two children in the countryside. The existence of his estranged wife means that they cannot marry. Luo decides that if a better man than he appears on the scene, he should surrender Li Wei for her own good. A colleague at the hospital introduces Luo to a promising young man, Fang 方, who is wealthy, well educated, polite and everything he ought to be. So Luo sets up a meeting between Li and Fang, and insists that they spend some time together. Finally, Li relents and marries Fang in order to make Luo happy.

Years pass without the two being in touch. Luo travels all over China, and war rages in the background. Every now and again Luo hears from friends how Li is doing. It turns out that Fang was an imposter and a cheat. After Li became pregnant, Fang left her and the baby died. Finally, Luo decides to go and seek her out again. One winter day he finds her at a small missionary school out in the countryside. She has lost her mind and become more or less catatonic. She does not recognise him. So he leaves and retreats, eventually, to Huashan to live as Juekong.

In the epilogue, we return to the first-level narrative. The narrator, named Wumingshi, intends to publish Juekong's manuscript.[47] He recounts why it is named *The Woman in the Tower*, relating it to a tale with that title written by a friend without giving further explanation. En route to the publisher with the manuscript, he meets Juekong on the street, who flies into a rage and beats him up for breaking his promise not to tell the story to others. Later, the author wakes up in bed and discovers that it was all just a bad dream. He resolves to write down the story and have it published.

Like Lin's tale of his love in Tomsk, Juekong's story is a sentimental, melodramatic tragedy. The love affair between two witty, beautiful and accomplished people and the inevitable agonising tragedy that follows is predictable and trite. The plot with its relative simplicity often seems merely the excuse for the narrator to present and embroider upon various arguments and opinions on a wide number of subjects. One gets the sense that Wumingshi is trying to educate the reader as well as displaying his wide learning throughout the novel.

In both of these novels, the narrative structure and technique are arguably the most interesting aspects. Like Lin, Luo Shengti is fond of using elaborate figures of speech to describe various events and situations. Metaphors and similes abound in the narrative to describe sights, sounds and feelings. Quite far from the expressionist style of his earlier short stories, it is still unusual enough to give his fiction a fairly distinctive character. Nonetheless, compared with Wumingshi's earlier short stories, such as the dramatic opening in 'Red Demons', the narrative style in these novels is quite subdued.

As in *North Pole Landscape Painting*, the first-level narrative in *The Woman in the Tower* is also characterised by an otherworldly air of mystery, dreams and illusions. The first-level narrative framework with strange music in the night and being beaten by Juekong is written in a completely different vein than the second-level narrative. When the narrator claims to be the author of *North Pole Landscape Painting*, we again see fantasy being mixed with specific events and places in a self-referential manner.

Both of these novels thus use a contrasting set of narrative styles in the first- and second-level narratives. Clearly, Wumingshi is playing with different literary registers or genres that cast the framed love stories in a somewhat different light. The first-level narrators' tales are both grounded in supernatural settings and otherworldly encounters, thereby undermining their own supposed realism. By contrast, the love stories contain none of this mysticism and are completely straightforward. This clash between different genres within the same novel throws both love stories into sharp relief by calling attention to their fictionality. This crossing between genres is somewhat reminiscent of some of Shi Zhecun's short stories, such as 'How Master Hongzhi Became A Monk' ('*Hongzhi fashi de chujia*' 宏智法師的出家) and 'The Haunted House' ('*Xiongzhai*' 凶宅), which also moved between different narrative modes belonging to incompatible narrative voices.

Kirk A. Denton remarks that the use of a first-person narrator is somewhat unusual compared with the progressive literature of the time:

> the first-person story had become stale and hackneyed and was associated with the values of an anachronistic May Fourth romantic solipsism and self-consciousness, values that were viewed negatively as counter to urgent national and revolutionary interests. Only a sentimental novel such as *The Woman in the Tower* or the rather gothic romanticism of Xu Xu's 'Ghost Love' continued to use first-person narration in the 1940s.[48]

Yet the use of a first-person narrative voice hardly qualifies as challenging narrative idiom. When Wumingshi argued that these two novels challenged the political domination of the field of literature and art, as shown earlier, he was probably overstating their importance. Despite their popularity, their influence on the literary field was not as notable as he would like. But the two novels did indeed push the boundaries of established literary conventions. They both shift fluidly between simple romantic melodrama and more modernist narratives. As such, they take a middle position, crossing between high and low literature in what might be considered a self-consciously playful fashion. This in itself calls attention to the divide that had been established between popular romance and supposedly more serious modern literature.

It also demonstrates that these novels cannot merely be seen as examples of pure romanticism. It is, of course, the romance that take centre stage in both of these novels, but the presence of the distinctly contrasting modernist framework shows that Wumingshi was conscious of challenging contemporary trends in the literary field. Where the New Sensationists frequently juxtaposed traditional Chinese literature with the modern, Wumingshi is here juxtaposing highbrow literature with the popular. To that extent, these novels are indeed comments on the state of the literary field at the time.

The grand design: *The Nameless Book*

Despite the fame Wumingshi received on the Chinese literary scene of the early 1940s with the success of *North Pole Landscape Painting* and *The Woman in the Tower*, at the same time, he felt that they were not sufficiently deep and that he had more important things to convey with his writings. He had higher ambitions: to create a magnificent work that would change people's lives and thoughts.[49]

After moving to Hangzhou, Wumingshi started planning and writing this work, *The Nameless Book*, consisting of six volumes, titled: *Beast, Beast, Beast* (*Yeshou, yeshou, yeshou* 野獸, 野獸, 野獸), *Ocean Splendour* (*Haiyan* 海艷), *Golden Snake Nights* (*Jinse de she ye* 金色的蛇夜), *Dead Rock Formations* (*Si de yanceng* 死的岩層), *Blossoming Beyond the Stars* (*Kaihua zai xingyun yiwai* 開花在星雲以外) and, finally, *The Great Bodhi of Genesis* (*Chuangshiji da puti* 創世紀大菩提). In each of the six volumes, the protagonist, Yindi 印蒂, is in constant search of fulfilment in his life, but without knowing just what he is searching for. In each volume he explores a different aspect of life, finally reaching a synthesis of philosophical thought and religion that reveals the meaning of life and man's role in the universe. He ends as a messianic godlike figure above worldly constraints and concerns.

Wang Yingguo and Zhao Jiangbin argue that *The Nameless Book* made a great contribution to Chinese literature, being unique in three important ways.[50] First, Wumingshi is exceptionally pensive and philosophical in these writings. The protagonist of *The Nameless Book* explores different ideologies and religions before finally attempting to produce a synthesis of Western and Eastern learning. Second, the protagonist's explorations and personal development set him apart from other characters in Chinese fiction. The authors liken him to Goethe's Faust. Third, Wumingshi broke new ground in modernist Chinese literature by experimenting with novel narrative forms and content.

The first volume, *Beast, Beast, Beast*, was published in Shanghai in 1946, the second volume in 1948, and the first part of the third volume in the following year. The remaining volumes were written in secret after Wumingshi's works were banned on the mainland. *The Nameless Book* was completed in 1960, but it was not published until he managed to send the manuscript to his brother in Hong Kong. It has now been printed in the People's Republic as well.

In *Beast, Beast, Beast*, the narrative starts off grandly with the creation of the world and an overview of world history that randomly skims across numerous historical events. The stylistic crescendo and ornate language are once again brimming over in the modernist style that is characteristic of Wumingshi's earlier writings:

> Ah! A marvellous expanse! An unreal expanse! An eerie expanse! A gorgeous expanse! This endless miracle! These twists and turns blazing in a myriad of colours! This resplendence billowing and shifting! What is all this? What is all this? What is all this? Such ghostly visages! Such chaotic profusion! Such racing about! What is all this? What is all this? What is all this? Ah! A tune! A tune! A tune! One tune after another! One group of tunes after another! Ah! Music! Music! Endlessly beautiful music! Endlessly intoxicating music! But also endlessly devastating music! A boundless sonata! Sound without end! Calls without limit! Inexhaustible sound! Sound! Sound! Sound! Sound! Sound! Sound! Sound! ...[51]

The narrative carries on in this elegiac manner for several more pages as the cosmos is created and human civilisation develops. It far surpasses both *North Pole Landscape Painting* and *The Woman in the Tower* in narrative drive and shows instead a return to the style of his early modernist short stories. Throughout the novel, the narration shifts back and forth between such passages and more conventional exposition.

Later we meet the protagonist, Yindi, who drops out of school in 1920, and eventually joins the Northern Expedition in 1926. Aroused by a surging sense of nationalism and political determination, he joins the leftist cause but is caught and imprisoned by the Nationalists during the violent purge of Communists in Shanghai in 1927. Through his father's connections he is eventually freed, but after his release he is ignored by his Communist comrades and former friends. Giving him a chance to prove his loyalty, the Communists ask him to write a self-criticism. Yindi refuses since his political convictions never wavered during incarceration. This injustice finally makes Yindi conclude that ideology and political causes are empty and unfulfilling.

Through the course of the 1940s, we also see that Wumingshi's view on nationalist ideology gradually changes. In *A Million Years Ago*, the brutality of the Japanese in Nanjing is portrayed as an act of timeless, abstract savagery. In *North Pole Landscape Painting*, events taking place in China take a back seat to the love story, but nationalist fervour is still considered a virtue that binds Lin and Aurelia together. By the time *Beast, Beast, Beast* is published, however, Wumingshi has turned against nationalism and political ideology, rejecting them completely. The new message is that self-realisation is only possible through individualism.

In the second volume, *Ocean Splendour*, Yindi finds love instead and has a passionate affair with a beautiful and accomplished woman who also loves him deeply.[52] Nevertheless he also finds that this is not sufficiently fulfilling and is not the true purpose of his life. The third volume, *Golden Snake Nights*, is itself subdivided into two sub-volumes about Yindi trying to realise himself through indulging freely in luxury, wine and carnal desires. He engages in wild orgies and debauchery, but once again finds that his life must have a higher purpose. Similar to the previous writings, the narrative style is built upon a relentless barrage of metaphor. In one memorable orgy, Yindi teasingly feeds the assembled women each a piece of chocolate that matches their dresses. Like an aphrodisiac, this frees the women of all inhibitions and the party turns orgiastic:

It was as though numerous glasses of wine were dancing and fermenting in their bloodstream. A strange desire flooded over them. Suddenly, two or three women jumped out and spun their buttocks around repeatedly, dancing crazily in circles, on their chests two big red and white waves were pouring out all over, the round buttocks were turning over and over like gyroscopes, great big flames curled rising from the core of the deep valleys between their legs, rising, making all the women leap up in excitement. With a roar, all the men quickly embraced every brilliant red torso turning madly. Each and every torso was a stalk of barley waving slowly in the wind. Every chest was like a great bellows puffing and heaving. The cascade of lust was like countless hunting dogs ferociously pursuing their quarry. Buttocks like wheels! Lips red like the sun! Snake eyes! Flaming desire of wolves! Ripe breasts rippling in all directions like thick fruit juice! Destroy! Go mad! This is a night of crazy devastation![53]

The Nameless Book is without a doubt Wumingshi's most rebellious and subversive work, clearly going directly against the cultural diktats of the age. Yindi's denunciation of both nationalism and Communist ideology was a direct attack upon current trends and was certainly incendiary enough. With the orgies found in later volumes, it was hardly surprising that Wumingshi was harshly criticised and eventually found his works banned after the founding of the People's Republic.[54]

The remaining volumes of *The Nameless Book* were written secretly in the 1950s and were thus not a part of China's literary field. In the subsequent volumes, Yindi tries to find truth in religion, pursuing both Christianity and Buddhism. In the end, he forges his own belief system intended to bring about a new era of peace and progress.[55]

In some ways, it can be argued that *The Nameless Book* is actually a return to certain New Literature principles: representing modernity for China (and humanity more generally) and trying to serve a didactic function, aiming to improve people's lives. This is literature with a social function, much like the contemporary political propaganda and the New Culture fiction that preceded it. Regardless of whether or not one subscribes to Wumingshi's lofty visions of enlightenment, his views of the future were a radical departure from the nationalistic and ideological views that were current at the time. By speaking out against politics in these works, Wumingshi directly opposed the main trends in the literary field. In addition, he continued and expanded upon the characteristic narrative style that he had developed in his earlier works.

Moving against the current

Wumingshi is a remarkable author who stands out in Chinese literature during the Republican era. Throughout this period, his works depart from the mainstream as well as what was being demanded in terms of politics and ideology. On the whole, his fiction is more complex than has commonly been assumed. The notion that he simply shifted from romanticism to modernism during the course of his writings overlooks several important factors. In his earliest short stories he wrote modernist narratives that borrowed from the New Sensationist narrative style. But he moved beyond the descriptions of metropolitan cityscapes and also used expressionist narrative techniques to describe the horrors of war and cultural displacement. Later, in his novels, he situates popular romantic melodrama within a more modernist framework that breaks conventional barriers between high and low genres in fiction. As mentioned earlier, scholars have variously seen Wumingshi's fiction as either romantic or modernist, and his two popular novels, *The Woman in the Tower* and *North Pole Landscape Painting*, show how such different styles were in fact combined within the same works. While both novels are primarily romantic love stories, they contain enough modernist elements to qualify as interesting hybrids.

Equally interesting, *North Pole Landscape Painting* shows how a popular romantic novel could successfully incorporate a nationalist message, calling attention to the anti-Japanese Korean resistance movement. It is not a rousing call to action and Lin's heroism and self-sacrifice throughout the book is implied rather than spelled out. There are no actual battles or fighting in either of these works. Yet the nationalistic message features prominently, showing again how popular literature could blur and incorporate other genres. In terms of capturing a wide readership, this work was probably more significant at the time than any of the pieces coming out of Yan'an or the All-China Resistance Association of Writers and Artists.

Wumingshi's success as a popular writer was followed by an increasingly strong wish to make a unique impact on the literary field and denounce political ideology. His eventual rejection of nationalism and other ideologies culminated in the huge modernist work, *The Nameless Book*, in which he puts forth his thoughts and ideas on morality, religion and the path to individual fulfilment in life.

Compared with Xu Xu and the modernist New Sensationist writers, the representation of modernity is usually less distinct in Wumingshi's writings. That is not to say that modernity does not play a prominent role. In all of Wumingshi's novels, the protagonists are indeed modern, well educated and culturally accomplished. Like, say, Cheng Xiaoqing 程小青, he wants to educate his readers. Lin's extended homage to Marie Curie in *North Pole Landscape Painting* is a case in point. The protagonists speak several languages, master musical instruments, and know about history and international events. They are interested in culture and art. But they are not symbols of modernity as is the case in Xu Xu's stories. They are not *flâneurs* or dandies strolling about the city at night and they are not confounded by mystical *femmes fatales* or their own subconscious fantasies. Instead, they are fighters or intellectuals who are weary of the world and its troubles. Their outlook is quite different and, therefore, their romantic adventures are equally different. The rationality and worldly outlook of the male protagonists are never challenged.

The levels of narration play an interesting role in this regard. In both *The Woman in the Tower* and *North Pole Landscape Painting*, the first-level narrators encounter the protagonists under mysterious circumstances. Juekong is playing music in the middle of the night much as Lin is howling on a snowy mountain peak. Here these two second-level narrators are configured as otherworldly and exotic in a way that resembles the unreal characters in New Sensationist fiction or the supernatural female characters in the works by Xu Xu. Yet when the mysterious strangers become narrators themselves, they align themselves with progress instead – fighting for freedom, playing music, practicing medicine. In both cases, it is their tragedies in love that launch them into another life of mystery and solitude. Luo Shengti becomes a monk as Juekong, and Lin disappears without trace. Thereby they retreat from modern life, but it is not an escape from modernity. Unlike the flower spirits and taxi dancers of New Sensationist fiction, Lin's and Luo's retreats are simply the conclusions that prove the depth of their grief.

Wumingshi developed a distinctively ebullient narrative style that culminates in *The Nameless Book*, which contains peaks of emotion created by the narrative style. This is one of the main hallmarks of Wumingshi's fiction. Certainly, he was far more interested in narrative voice than Xu Xu, who puts more emphasis on maintaining plot progress. Wumingshi's narrative innovation also characterises his more avant-garde works, particularly *The Nameless Book*, which deliberately attacks prevalent modes of artistic expression and the role of art in society.

The latter volumes of *The Nameless Book* could not be published in mainland China. Consequently, they had no impact on the current literary field. And by the time they appeared in Hong Kong, their intended effect was perhaps no longer relevant: their status as protest ceased to be applicable since the context of production had become entirely different. Yet there is no gainsaying that when the first volumes of *The Nameless Book* were published in the late 1940s they manifested a direct attack on current cultural and social trends. Thus, they may be said to represent one of the last attempts to oppose the politicisation of art before the far greater regulation of cultural production was imposed by the Communist government.

Notes

1. Geng Chuanming, *Duxing ren zong: Wumingshi zhuan*, p. 86.
2. Wang Yingguo and Zhao Jiangbin, *Wumingshi chuanqi*, p. 4.
3. Geng Chuanming, *Duxing ren zong: Wumingshi zhuan*, p. 58.
4. Hockx, 'Theory as Practice', p. 232.
5. Li Wei, *Shenmi de Wumingshi*, p. 58.
6. Wang Yingguo and Zhao Jiangbin, *Wumingshi chuanqi*, p. 4.
7. Wang Yingguo and Zhao Jiangbin, *Wumingshi chuanqi*, p. 22.
8. Wang Yingguo and Zhao Jiangbin, *Wumingshi chuanqi*, p. 34.
9. Wang Yingguo and Zhao Jiangbin, *Wumingshi chuanqi*, p. 42.
10. Also written as Yi Pom-seok or Lee Bum Suk, but Lee Beom-seok is still the more common form. After the liberation of Korea in 1945, Lee became the first prime minister of South Korea, serving from 1 August 1948 until 21 April 1950.
11. Wang Yingguo and Zhao Jiangbin, *Wumingshi chuanqi*, p. 59.
12. Li Wei, *Shenmi de Wumingshi*, p. 79.
13. Wumingshi 無名氏, *Yi bai wan nian yiqian* 一百萬年以前 (*A Million Years Ago*) (Hong Kong: Xinwen tiandi she, 1977).
14. Wang Yingguo and Zhao Jiangbin, *Wumingshi chuanqi*, p. 90.
15. Chen Qingsheng 陳青生, *Nianlun: Sishi niandai houbanqi de Shanghai wenxue* 年輪: 四十年代後半期的上海文學 (*Growth Rings: Shanghai Literature of the late 1940s*) (Shanghai: Shanghai renmin chubanshe 上海人民出版社, 2002), p. 132.
16. Geng Chuanming, *Duxing ren zong: Wumingshi zhuan*, p. 150.
17. Mr Anonymous, *The Scourge of the Sea* concerns his own experiences and recounts trying to hide his manuscripts from officials searching his house. Another work is Pu Ning, *Red in Tooth and Claw*.
18. Wang Ling 汪凌, 'Wentan de dubuwu: Wumingshi lun', 文坛的独步舞: 無名氏論

('A Solitary Dancer in the Literary Field: on Wumingshi'), in Chen Sihe 陳思和 et al. (eds), *Wuming shidai de wenxue piping* 無名時代的文學批評 (*Literary Criticism in Non-name Period* (English title on cover)) (Guilin: Guangxi shifan daxue chubanshe 廣西師範大學出版社, 2004), p. 29.

19. Wang Yingguo and Zhao Jiangbin, *Wumingshi chuanqi*, p. 328.
20. Wang Yingguo and Zhao Jiangbin, *Wumingshi chuanqi*, p. 334.
21. Wang Yingguo and Zhao Jiangbin, *Wumingshi chuanqi*, pp. 36–7.
22. Wang Yingguo and Zhao Jiangbin, *Wumingshi chuanqi*.
23. Wumingshi 無名氏, 'Luxiya zhi lian', 露西亞之戀 ('Love of Russia'), in *Zhongguo xiandai wenxue buyi shuxi*, p. 525.
24. Wumingshi, 'Luxiya zhi lian', p. 541.
25. Wumingshi 無名氏, 'Hong mo', 紅魔 ('Red Demons'), in *Zhongguo xiandai wenxue buyi shuxi*, p. 546.
26. Wumingshi, 'Hong mo', pp. 547–8.
27. Wumingshi 無名氏, 'Haibian de gushi', 海邊的故事 ('A Story from the Seaside'), in *Zhongguo xiandai wenxue buyi shuxi*.
28. See Chapter 1, above, for examples.
29. Interestingly, the three biographies of Wumingshi barely mention his early short stories, if at all. The longest treatment, a few paragraphs, is found in Wang Yingguo and Zhao Jiangbin, *Wumingshi chuanqi*, pp. 36–7.
30. Li Wei, *Shenmi de Wumingshi*, p. 79.
31. Zhu Xi and Chen Xingwu, *Zhongguo xiandai langman zhuyi xiaoshuo moshi*, p. 272.
32. Bu Shaofu 卜少夫, quoted in *Zhongguo xiandai wenxue buyi shuxi*, p. 497.
33. Wumingshi 無名氏, Postscript to *Tali de nüren* 塔裡的女人 (*The Woman in the Tower*), 6th edn (Shanghai: Shanghai wenyi chubanshe, 2001), pp. 136–7.
34. Geng Chuanming, *Duxing ren zong: Wumingshi zhuan*, p. 59.
35. Wang Yingguo and Zhao Jiangbin, *Wumingshi chuanqi*, p. 62.
36. Wumingshi 無名氏, *Beiji fengqing hua* 北極風情畫 (*North Pole Landscape Painting*) (Shanghai: Wuming shuwu, 1944), p. 25.
37. Wumingshi, *Beiji fengqing hua*, p. 10.
38. Wumingshi, *Beiji fengqing hua*, pp. 87–8.
39. Wumingshi, *Beiji fengqing hua*, pp. 53–4.
40. Wumingshi, *Beiji fengqing hua*, p. 165.
41. Wumingshi, *Beiji fengqing hua*, pp. 100–4.
42. Wumingshi, *Beiji fengqing hua*, p. 106.
43. Geng Chuanming, *Duxing ren zong: Wumingshi zhuan*, p. 67.
44. Geng Chuanming, *Duxing ren zong: Wumingshi zhuan*, p. 67.
45. Wumingshi 無名氏, *Tali de nüren* 塔裡的女人 (*The Woman in the Tower*) (Hong Kong: Xinwen tiandishe, 1979), p. 4.
46. Wumingshi, *Tali de nüren*, p. 33.
47. Wumingshi, *Tali de nüren*, p. 180.
48. Kirk A. Denton, *The Problematic of Self in Modern Chinese Literature: Hu Feng and Lu Ling* (Stanford, CA: Stanford University Press, 1998), pp. 164–5.
49. Li Wei, *Shenmi de Wumingshi*, p. 124.

50. Wang Yingguo and Zhao Jiangbin, *Wumingshi chuanqi*, pp. 5–16.

51. Wumingshi 無名氏, *Yeshou, yeshou, yeshou* 野獸,野獸,野獸 (*Beast, Beast, Beast*) (Shanghai: Wuming shuwu, 1946), p. 1.

52. Based on summary in Wang Yingguo and Zhao Jiangbin, *Wumingshi chuanqi*, pp. 206–20.

53. Wumingshi 無名氏, *Jinse de she ye* 金色的蛇夜 (*Golden Snake Nights*) (Shanghai: Shanghai wenyi chubanshe, 2001), vol. 1, p. 190.

54. Geng Chuanming, *Duxing ren zong: Wumingshi zhuan*, p. 198.

55. Wang Yingguo and Zhao Jiangbin, *Wumingshi chuanqi*, pp. 10–13; Geng Chuanming, *Duxing ren zong: Wumingshi zhuan*, pp. 150–1.

Chapter 6

Opposition, Imitation, Adaptation and Diffusion in Popular Chinese Literature

This study has followed a trajectory of fiction in late Republican China by comparing the popular wartime literature by Xu Xu 徐訏 and Wumingshi 無名氏 with the works of two 1930s Shanghai modernists, Shi Zhecun 施蟄存 and Mu Shiying 穆時英. As New Sensationist writers, Shi and Mu consciously set out to challenge the literary establishment and the precepts of good writing that guided the literary field of the time. By combining genres and styles from both the modern and the traditional, they were intent on undermining the notions of rationalism, progress and modernity as immutable and stable constructions. In their rejection of such constructs, they directly attacked the standards of progressive literature set out by the New Culture Movement before them.

By the early 1940s, the Shanghai modernist writers were no longer active, but their narrative style had left an impact that is rarely recognised today. The highly popular work of several writers, notably Xu Xu and Wumingshi, echoed the styles and tropes of Shi's and Mu's short stories. Due to the changes in historical and cultural context, the latter had ceased to function as modernist or avant-garde stances of protest. Rather, the narrative styles of the past avant-garde were adopted and adapted into the realm of popular writing, demonstrating a process of diffusion as previously challenging ways of writing became widely accepted. Wumingshi, however, did eventually shift to more experimental literature as well as attacking the prevalence of nationalism and ideology, and his novels of the late 1940s were among the last modernist pieces that were written before the founding of the People's Republic in 1949.

While both Xu Xu and Wumingshi would have been worthy of extended research projects on their own, they have been considered together in this study to achieve two aims: first, to show that the trend of modernist writing initiated by the New Sensationist authors had a lasting legacy in the wider development of Chinese literature; and, second, to show how such a trend was variously positioned in the literary field – at first a bold stand against the New Culture Movement's principles of good literature, and later a gradual absorption into mainstream popular culture.

The Japanese surrendered in August 1945, but the civil war between the Nationalist government and the Communists continued to keep ideology at the forefront of cultural production. Artists and writers were mobilised, particularly in the Communist-controlled areas.[1] Popular literature, however, continued to be frowned upon as not relevant to the state of the nation. By the time of the founding of the People's Republic, the four writers considered in this study had all departed from mainland China's new literary field. Mu Shiying had been killed; Shi Zhecun stopped creative writing entirely and had turned to classical studies, much like Shen Congwen 沈從文, Qian Zhongshu 錢鐘書 and several others;[2] Xu Xu moved to Hong Kong in 1950, where he continued writing and gained some fame as a popular writer; and Wumingshi settled in Hangzhou and continued writing on his magnum opus in secret.[3]

Comparison

While the four authors have many points in common with regard to both plot structure and narrative style, the differences are equally striking. All four are considered Shanghai authors, but the role played by the city in their stories is dissimilar. Most of Shi Zhecun's and Mu Shiying's works are set in Shanghai and it often looms large in the life of the protagonists, whereas it usually plays a minor role, if any, in Xu Xu's and Wumingshi's works, which are frequently set abroad. Looking beyond the settings, Xu's plot developments often bear a surface resemblance to Shi Zhecun's. In Xu's writing, we repeatedly find educated urbanites confronting mystical and alluring women in a manner that clearly echoes Shi Zhecun's works, such as 'An Evening of Spring Rain' ('*Meiyu zhi xi*' 梅雨之夕). Xu Xu's novella *Ghostly Love* (*Gui lian* 鬼戀) from 1937 is a modern recasting of a classical *zhiguai* 志怪 tale much like Shi Zhecun's gothic short story 'Yaksha' ('*Yecha*' 夜叉) or numerous similar pieces. On occasion, Wumingshi also made use of New Sensationist story elements. His two romantic novels, *North Pole Landscape Painting* (*Beiji fengqing hua* 北極風情畫) and *The Woman in the Tower* (*Tali de nüren* 塔裡的女人), both contain first-level narrative frameworks that blur the boundaries between the real and the imagined. The references to dreams and nervous distress and the nightly pursuits of wonderful music or enigmatic beings clearly echo themes found in much New Sensationist fiction. But most of Wumingshi's stories are different: his writings about Korean soldiers and his melodramatic love stories have little in common with works of the 1930s. Thus, the differences between the four authors tend to equal or out-weigh the similarities. None of Shi Zhecun's extremes of madness and delusion are to be found in the later authors' works. Nor do the later authors ever manage to achieve the depth of character found in Shi's short stories, such as the troubled relationships between husbands and wives found in *Exemplary Conduct of Virtuous Women* (*Shan nüren xing pin* 善女人行品).

With regard to narrative style, Shi Zhecun used interior monologue in streams-of-consciousness and indirect discourse to present incoherent and unreliable narrative voices. He experimented with different types of internal and external focalisation, such as limiting the narration to the protagonist's thoughts as story events take place or switching between incompatible narrative modes. Similarly, Mu Shiying used various techniques to interrupt textual flows and dismiss standard conventions of prose text. In Mu's short stories, urban space is often represented in a montage-like style with narrative sweeps across neon lights, skyscrapers, night clubs and coffee bars. The typographical setup in some works arranges the written characters in novel ways across the page to achieve jarring effects. In both authors' works, narrative style often plays a more important role than the sequence of events at the story level. Some of their most interesting short stories are simply experiments in narrative voice that convey a scene or a setting rather than a plot with a well-defined beginning and end.

In a manner that clearly builds upon such narrative techniques, Wumingshi developed his own highly distinctive style characterised by a relentless stream of metaphors intended to convey the moods of the protagonists or the dramatic nature of their situation. In some of his early short stories, the narrative techniques resemble the camera-like effect used by Mu Shiying, and the resulting confusion and chaos are identical. In yet other works his overflowing narrative style takes other forms and is applied far more extensively to convey pathos, drama, vistas of history and high emotion. The narrative style thus becomes a part of the textual flow, producing an impression very different from Mu Shiying's fragmented staccato narration. Xu Xu, on the other hand, rarely attempts to break new ground in narrative style. His use of first-person narrators and techniques, as *in medias res*, is vaguely reminiscent of New Sensationist methods, but the narrative language is mostly simple and unadorned in the period covered by this study. Apart from a few interesting exceptions from the mid-1930s and late 1940s, he rarely experimented with unreliable narrators, changing narrative voices or other such techniques. Xu's narrators tend to retell the plot as a straightforward exposition instead of using, say, Shi Zhecun's extended streams-of-consciousness in which events are filtered unmediated through the narrator's mind as they take place. Compared with Wumingshi, Xu Xu is generally more concerned with the unfolding of plot events than with narrative experimentation.

The representation of modernity and tradition also varies between the four authors. There are clear similarities between Mu Shiying and Shi Zhecun. Both make intertextual references to traditional literature, particularly the *Water Margin* (*Shuihu zhuan* 水滸傳), in their writings.[4] The use of references to Chinese tradition is a consistent thread throughout Shi's authorship, from the early short stories in *Spring Festival Lamp* (*Shangyuan deng* 上元燈) to 'Master Huangxin' (*'Huangxin dashi'* 黃心大師) from 1937. These references to cultural tradition do not merely demonstrate a preoccupation with the past or a nostalgic desire for the bygone days of old. In Shi's stories, it is never the past in a simple sense that is referred to, but always the past refracted through literature, myth or tradition. It is a culturally mediated and imagined past that is held up against a modern, urban, rational present. In both Shi's and Mu's renditions, the heroic virtues of the *Water Margin* are polluted with sadism, jealousy and violence.

On occasion, such as in 'The Haunted House' ('*Xiongzhai*' 凶宅), Shi Zhecun weaves an amalgam of popular and elitist genres into a single piece, including horror, reportage, love story and detective thriller. Such works relate to these genres as meta-literature. They disrupt the way in which such genres usually work within self-contained fictional universes. His works freely mix the present and the traditional (not the historical), thereby calling attention to the distinct borders normally prevailing between genres.

In contrast, the 'ghostly' women in Xu Xu's short stories, as in *Ghostly Love* or in 'The Flower Spirit of the Gambling Den' ('*Duku li de hua hun*' 賭窟裏的 花魂), simply use tradition and legend to represent themselves as exotic. It is part of a playfully sophisticated façade that confronts the narrator with a challenge to be overcome. This limits the intertextual basis in Xu's works since the references to tradition operate as specific story elements that play their own role within the unfolding plot. In these instances, Xu's supernatural women tend to fit into a more general pattern of exoticism and otherworldly beauty. Alongside foreign nationality and glamorous careers as covert agents, tradition simply adds a layer of mystery to their otherwise exotic attraction. The relation to tradition is quite different in Wumingshi's works, which contain practically no references to Chinese legend and myth. The male protagonists deliver numerous expositions on aspects of Western culture in displays of learning and wit, but Chinese culture rarely plays a part. Again, the first-level narratives in his two romantic novels are something of an exception. The role of Huashan Mountain does indeed represent something primordial, majestic and ultimately Chinese. It is the retreat of Buddhist monks or loners who are seeking a space beyond their personal tragedies in love. As such, the mountain becomes the diametric opposite of the protagonist's previously international and extroverted life. On the whole, however, Chinese history and tradition play a marginal role in Wumingshi's works.

The authors' use of cultural tradition naturally relates directly to how their works represent modernity and progress. The New Sensationist writers fundamentally set out to question the notion of modernity. In Shi Zhecun's short stories, tradition, myth and fantasies of desire invariably challenge the modern rationalism of the narrators. In the collision between modernity and its unknown other, modernity loses every time. Modern life is thereby not aligned with progress, but with degeneration, madness and neurasthenic illusions. In 'An Evening of Spring Rain', a fleeting urban encounter is overlaid with a layer of voyeuristic desire that blends fantasy and reality. Modernity becomes the basis of sexual frustration and insecurity where individualism, rationality and reality fall apart. Mu Shiying is equally direct in his attack upon modern life, such as in 'Black Peony' ('*Hei mudan*' 黑牡丹). It is a pressure that bears down upon the characters as rushed, mechanical, impersonal, corrupt and unfeeling. The dance halls are places of male lust and a dehumanising race to keep up with the times. The characters are in a constant state of fatigue or frustration. In Mu's short stories set in Shanghai, modernity can be titillating and thrilling, but always entirely divorced from anything that might be seen as positive or related to progress. On the contrary, it is something the characters seek to escape.

Xu juxtaposes tradition with modernity in much the same manner. The cosmopolitan protagonist is faced with mysterious women who are aligned with timeless traditions, but the results in Xu's fiction are fundamentally different. In his writings the rational outlook of the male protagonist eventually wins out. The women's secrets are eventually revealed and this translates into a vindication of the narrator's modern scientific scepticism. The challenge posed to rationality is finally overcome and he either wins the woman or unravels her secrets. Wumingshi is again something of an exception among the four authors. He does not juxtapose modernity and tradition and, consequently, the modern outlook of the male protagonists is never questioned or challenged. Only in *The Nameless Book* (*Wumingshu* 無名書) do we see Wumingshi taking a stand on the issue. In his attack upon the validity and usefulness of nationalism and ideology, he directly attacks the primacy of politics in the contemporary literary field. But this extends beyond the New Sensationists' nihilistic attack on modernity as progress. Instead, he presents his own view of enlightenment and progress for the nation. Interestingly, this puts him closer to the mould of the New Culture generation of writers, engaging with progress and writing for the didactic benefit of others.

This is perhaps the most fundamental difference between the two generations of authors. The New Sensationists generally attempt to undermine any cohesive notion of modernity linked to progress and national development. Instead, the notion of progress falls apart as an unstable construction that contains its diametric opposite: neurasthenic distress, sexual insecurity and irrationality. Xu Xu and Wumingshi, on the other hand, rarely undermine the notion of progress in their works. Xu Xu playfully juxtaposes tradition and modernity, but the results are quite different as the cosmopolitan outlook is rarely challenged. Instead, it is reaffirmed as the protagonists self-assuredly navigate between various foreign and enticing women who court them.

As this quick overview shows, the differences between the four authors tend to outweigh the things they have in common. It shows that the four authors cannot reasonably be lumped together in a single 'school' or 'group' in Chinese literature. The differences between their styles of writing and subject matter are too great for any such categorisation to be meaningful. This is why overarching labels, such as 'Shanghai School' ('*haipai*' 海派), are too broad in attempting to see such diverse authors as part of a single trend. Mu Shiying and Shi Zhecun might be considered part of a group with some justification, but any attempt to group Xu Xu and Wumingshi together as 'late romanticists' or 'late modernists' is more difficult to defend. Such categorisations over-generalise and gloss over the many fundamental differences between their writings.

The comparison between the works of the earlier writers and the later ones does, however, reveal the strong influence and inspiration flowing from one period to the next. Elements of both plot and narrative style from New

Sensationist writings are found in the works of Xu Xu and Wumingshi. It is clear that the New Sensationists had a greater impact on the literary field and the development of Chinese literature than has hitherto been recognised.

Opposition, imitation, diffusion and the avant-garde

By the early 1930s, the cultural field in China had become more firmly institutionalised, expanding rapidly with an increasingly popular fiction press, a variety of cultural and intellectual journals, and the largely accepted canonisation of the New Literature writers as the founding fathers of modern Chinese fiction and poetry. This formation of a literary establishment enabled a new iconoclastic generation of writers to appear that challenged the establishment's precepts in art. The literary field of the 1930s was characterised by the rejection of tradition, the privileging of realism and a turn towards leftist politics. All three of these aspects fit within the overarching idea that the author should engage with modernity with didactic intent. It was exactly these principles that the New Sensationist writers decided to challenge in their writings, so they are worth exploring a bit further.

With regard to realism, the New Sensationist authors used various modernist narrative styles that deliberately rejected any attempt at verisimilitude. In fact, their works frequently highlight their own status as artifice or fiction – their inherent fictionality – by self-referentially combining different literary genres and popular stereotypes. This is the case with some of Shi Zhecun's writings that present a unique hybrid amalgam of cultural signifiers taken from popular fiction, Chinese legend and tradition, and foreign literature. Intertextual references are layered one upon the other as paraphrase and pastiche. By playing upon and juxtaposing such a diverse range of cultural signifiers, the New Sensationists highlight the work of art as an artificial construct. Narrative coherence falls apart. Mu Shiying deliberately challenged realism with his distinctly jarring narrative style in a different way. Such writing was a deliberate affront to conventional modes of narrative representation.

On the other hand, some of Shi's short stories such as 'Water Shield Soup' ('*Chun geng*' 蓴羹) are far more gentle and might be termed psychological realism with their explorations of how couples relate to each other in daily life. Read today, such pieces hardly seem challenging at all, but in the context of the literary field at the time, they challenged the notion that literature should take a political stand and refrain from focusing on petty bourgeois concerns. As the literary debates of the time show, the New Sensationists refused to take sides in ideological debates. This stance of independence can be seen in their fiction as well. There are no heroes of progress or victims of class oppression. Political events on the national stage are absent and there is nothing resembling didactic intent. Instead, the characters are challenged by their own imagined problems, sexual frustration and the crushing pressures of modern life.

However, this sense of protest is absent from most of the writings of Xu Xu and Wumingshi. Xu Xu used tradition playfully to add layers of exoticism to his glamorous characters. Modernity and rationality are never seriously questioned. The departures from realism are of a similar nature. Xu's works are full of extreme characters and settings that are as far from the realistic as one can imagine. The parallel repetitions of events in works like *The Gypsy's Seduction* (*Jibusai de youhuo* 吉布賽的誘惑, 1939) also detract from any sense of realism. The backgrounds in such works are rarely developed and mostly serve as abstract settings for the characters' evolving relationships – even the political utopia found on the pirate island in *The Absurd English Channel* (*Huangmiu de Ying-Fa haixia* 荒謬的英法海峽). Yet these departures from realism seem simply a consequence of Xu's romanticist approach, not a deliberate wish to challenge the ideals of how art should relate to the real. Wumingshi presents a more direct challenge to realism with his distinct narrative style. Yet the purpose of this mode of narration is mostly aimed at conveying strong emotions and mood in his works. It does not undermine the coherence of the narrative voice in the same nihilistic manner seen in the writings by Mu and Shi.

In Xu Xu's and Wumingshi's work of the 1940s, politics and ideology are also conspicuously absent. Like the New Sensationists, they refused to take sides in current debates (though they did so years later). In Xu's novels, political events play a negligible role and form a distant backdrop to justify his plots of drama and action. The female spies and agents embody the characters' glamour, not the author's political leanings. Of the four authors studied here, Wumingshi's writings are the most engaged in contemporary events. The Japanese figure several times as sources of evil, but usually in an abstract sense in which the specifics of nationality fade away against timeless notions of freedom and liberty. Even though particular political developments are mostly quite remote from the main plot events, the protagonists – frequently Korean – are often soldiers, ardent patriots and men who fight for their nation. Compared with Xu's philosophical and cosmopolitan protagonists, the men in Wumingshi's fiction are often more traditionally masculine, and they show how nationalism and the state of war were absorbed into popular romantic literature. Nationalistic sentiment is a strong part of Wumingshi's male ideal – at least until he turned directly against such pursuits in *The Nameless Book*. Yet even this work demonstrates the author's refusal to take sides in current ideological debates. By this point in his authorship, a non-partisan stance is raised to the level of a virtue on the step towards final enlightenment.

This diversity among the authors shows how they assumed different positions within the literary field. Where the New Sensationists oppose the New Literature established writers and their principles of gaining symbolic capital, Xu Xu and Wumingshi set out to broaden the scope of popular literature. Some of Xu Xu's short stories from the late 1940s reveal a modernist direction that he was to explore further after moving to Hong Kong. Wumingshi later claimed that his two romantic novels challenged the New Culture Movement's hegemony in art. But apart from *The Nameless Book*, there is little sense of anti-art or attack upon current literary values in their writing from this period.

The works of Xu Xu and Wumingshi fit into an altered dynamic between elite and popular writing in the 1940s. The New Culture Movement literary elite was scattered and no longer commanded the same influence as before. Nationalism and politics had become the overriding concerns of the age, so realism and tradition were being re-evaluated in an attempt to create mass appeal. Literary precepts of the past were questioned and were losing their value. Consequently, Xu Xu and Wumingshi were freer to make use of Chinese tradition and depart from a realist narrative style. It was less contentious. This is clear when reading the works themselves. There is little of the nihilistic aggression or opaque narrative experimentation found in Shi Zhecun's and Mu Shiying's works. Xu Xu's novels explore Freudian themes and juxtapose the modern and the mythical, but they are mostly melodramatic love stories that rely on a full array of popular contemporary stereotypes, including pirates, prostitutes, corrupt officials, female assassins and passionate lovers. They are a part of popular literature, rather than an intertextual play upon it. Similarly, some of Wumingshi's novels that use modernist narrative techniques are still principally escapist melodrama and dramatic tales of passionate love and jealousy. The echoes of themes and tropes from the New Sensationist avant-garde lend their works an air of worldliness and raise them above mere potboiler entertainment. But they rarely approached the literary field in anything resembling the confrontational manner of the New Sensationists. Their works were mostly seen as playful entertainment, not as challenges to the cultural establishment.

This study has traced a few patterns of imitation and popular adaptation in Chinese literature during the Second Sino-Japanese War. With regard to the comparative method utilised here, it touches upon the surface of a larger field in which popular literature is situated within the wider context of modern Chinese literary history. Many interesting popular writers of the 1940s remain poorly studied, including Zhou Lengjia 周楞伽 (1911–1992), Yu Qie 予且, Tan Weihan 譚惟翰 (1913–1994), Wang Xiaoyi 王小逸 (1895–1962) and others. How their works fit into the overall trends of the time remains to be explored further.

One of the points of this study has been to show the value of a comparative approach in looking at some of these writers. Notions of cultural protest and opposition are important when drawing such comparisons, and, accordingly, neither popular nor avant-garde art can be studied in a cultural vacuum. The late Republican era was an age preoccupied with factions, cliques and cultural debates. The war altered previously fixed boundaries and positions. In this shifting cultural milieu, it is increasingly necessary to follow the structures of opposition, adaptation, imitation and diffusion that developed. The enormously popular works of Xu Xu and Wumingshi written during the 1940s built upon themes and styles established by the modernist writers of the 1930s, and this in turn shows how similar techniques and themes take on different meanings and significance in a rapidly changing cultural setting.

Notes

1. Chang-tai Hung, *War and Popular Culture*, pp. 221ff.
2. McDougall and Louie, *The Literature of China in the Twentieth Century*, pp. 232 and 212.
3. Wang Yingguo and Zhao Jiangbin, *Wumingshi chuanqi*, pp. 185–6.
4. Several short stories in Mu Shiying's 穆時英 first short-story collection, *Nanbeiji* 南北極 (*North Pole, South Pole*) from 1932, feature characters who see themselves as righteous rebels in the vein of *Shuihu zhuan* 水滸傳. See Rosenmeier, 'The Subversion of Modernity and Socialism in Mu Shiying's Early Fiction', pp. 6–7.

Bibliography

Alber, Charles J., *Enduring the Revolution: Ding Ling and the Politics of Literature in Guomindang China*, Westport, CT: Praeger, 2002.

Anderson, Marston, *The Limits of Realism: Chinese Fiction in the Revolutionary Period*, Berkeley, CA: University of California Press, 1990.

Ba Jin 巴金 et al., 'Wenyijie tongren wei tuanjie yuwu yu yanlun ziyou xuanyan', 文藝界同人為團結禦侮與言論自由宣言 ('A Manifesto of Fellows in Literature and Art, United against Foreign Aggression and in Defence of Free Speech'), *Wenxue* 文學, 7(4) (1936): 744

Bieg, Lutz, 'Shi Zhecun und seine Erzählung Große Lehrerin Huangxin, oder die bewußte Rückwendung zur Tradition', in Helwig Schmidt-Glintzer (ed.), *Das Andere China: Festschrift für Wolfgang Bauer zum 65. Geburtstag*, Wiesbaden: Harrassowitz Verlag, 1995.

Bourdieu, Pierre, *The Field of Cultural Production: Essays on Art and Literature*, ed. Randal Johnson, Cambridge: Polity Press, 1993.

Bourdieu, Pierre, *The Rules of Art: Genesis and Structure of the Literary Field*, trans. Susan Emanuel, Cambridge: Polity Press, 1996.

Bu Shaofu 卜少夫 (ed.), *Wumingshi yanjiu* 無名氏研究 (*Wumingshi Research*), Hong Kong: Xinwen tiandi she新聞天地社, 1981.

Bu Shaofu卜少夫, 'Mu Shiying zhi si', 穆時英之死 ('Mu Shiying's Death'), in Mu Shiying 穆時英, *Mu Shiying quanji* 穆時英全集 (*The Complete Works of Mu Shiying*), ed. Yan Jiayan 嚴家炎 and Li Jin 李今, Beijing: Shiyue wenyi, 2008.

Chan, Sylvia, 'Realism or Socialist Realism? The "Proletarian" Episode in Modern Chinese Literature, 1927–1932', *Australian Journal of Chinese Affairs*, 9 (1983): 55–74.

Chen Naixin 陳乃欣, 'Xu Xu er san shi', 徐訏二三事 ('A Few Things about Xu Xu'), in Chen Naixin 陳乃欣 et al. (eds), *Xu Xu er san shi* 徐訏二三事 (*A Few Things about Xu Xu*), Taipei: Erya chubanshe 爾雅出版社, 1980.

Chen Qingsheng 陳青生, *Kangzhan shiqi de Shanghai wenxue* 抗戰時期的上海文學 (*Shanghai Literature during the Sino-Japanese War*), Shanghai: Shanghai renmin chubanshe上海人民出版社, 1995.

Chen Qingsheng 陳青生, *Nianlun: Sishi niandai houbanqi de Shanghai wenxue* 年輪: 四十年代後半期的上海文學 (*Growth Rings: Shanghai Literature of the late 1940s*), Shanghai: Shanghai renmin chubanshe 上海人民出版社, 2002.

Chen Sihe 陳思和, 'Shilun Wumingshi de *Wumingshu*', 試論無名氏的《無名書》('On

The Nameless Book by Wumingshi'), in Chen Sihe 陳思和 (ed.), *Zhongguo dangdai wenxue guanjianci: Shi jiang* 中國當代文學關鍵詞: 十講 (*Keywords on Modern Chinese Literature: Ten Talks*), Shanghai: Fudan daxue chubanshe 復旦大學出版社, 2002.

Chen Xuanbo 陳旋波, *Shi yu guang: 20 shiji Zhongguo wenxueshi geju zhong de Xu Xu* 時與光: 20世紀中國文學史格局中的徐訏 (*Time and Light: Xu Xu in the Landscape of 20th-century Chinese Literary History*), Nanchang: Baihuazhou wenyi chubanshe 百花洲文藝出版社, 2004.

Cheng Xiaoqing 程小青, 'The Ghost in the Villa', in *Stories for Saturday: Twentieth-Century Chinese Popular Fiction*, trans. Timothy C. Wong, Honolulu, HI: University of Hawai'i Press, 2003.

Davies, Gloria, *Lu Xun's Revolution: Writing in a Time of Violence*, Cambridge, MA: Harvard University Press, 2013

Denton, Kirk A. (ed.), *Modern Chinese Literary Thought: Writings on Literature 1893–1945*, Stanford, CA: Stanford University Press, 1996.

Denton, Kirk A., *The Problematic of Self in Modern Chinese Literature: Hu Feng and Lu Ling*. Stanford, CA: Stanford University Press, 1998.

Dikötter, Frank, *Sex, Culture and Modernity in China*, London: Hurst, 1995.

Doleželová-Velingerová, Milena (ed.), *A Selective Guide to Chinese Literature, 1900–1949, Vol. 1: The Novel*, Leiden: Brill, 1988.

Dooling, Amy D., *Women's Literary Feminism in Twentieth-century China*, New York: Palgrave Macmillan, 2005.

Fan Boqun 范伯群 (ed.), *Zhongguo jinxiandai tongsu wenxue shi* 中國近現代通俗文學史 (*A History of Late Qing and Republican Popular Literature*), Nanjing: Jiangsu jiaoyu chubanshe, 2000.

Fan Boqun 范伯群 and Kong Qingdong 孔慶東, *Tongsu wenxue shiwu jiang* 通俗文學十五講 (*Fifteen Talks on Popular Literature*), Beijing: Beijing daxue chubanshe 北京大學出版社, 2003.

Fan Boqun 范伯群, Tang Zhesheng 湯哲聲 and Kong Qingdong 孔慶東, *20 shiji Zhongguo tongsu wenxue shi* 20世紀中國通俗文學史 (*A History of Chinese Popular Literature in the 20th Century*), Beijing: Gaodeng jiaoyu chubanshe 高等教育出版社, 2006.

Feng, Liping, 'Democracy and Elitism: The May Fourth Ideal of Literature', *Modern China*, 22(2) (1996): 170–96.

Feuerwerker, Yi-tsi Mei, *Ding Ling's Fiction: Ideology and Narrative in Modern Chinese Literature*, Cambridge, MA: Harvard University Press, 1982.

FitzGerald, Carolyn, *Fragmenting Modernisms: Chinese Wartime Literature, Art, and Film, 1937–49*, Leiden: Brill, 2013.

Fu, Poshek, *Passivity, Resistance, and Collaboration: Intellectual Choices in Occupied Shanghai, 1937–1945*, Stanford, CA: Stanford University Press, 1993.

Geng Chuanming 耿傳名, *Duxing ren zong: Wumingshi zhuan* 獨行人蹤: 無名氏傳 (*Traces of a Solitary Walker: A Biography of Wumingshi*), Nanjing: Jiangsu wenyi chubanshe 江蘇文藝出版社, 2001.

Gimpel, Denise, *Lost Voices of Modernity: A Chinese Popular Fiction Magazine in Context*, Honolulu, HI: University of Hawai'i Press, 2001.

Green, Frederik H., 'A Chinese Romantic's Journey through Time and Space:

Cosmopolitanism, Nationalism and Nostalgia in the Work of Xu Xu (1908–1980)', PhD disssertation, Yale University, 2009.

Green, Frederik H., 'The Making of a Chinese Romantic: Cosmopolitan Nationalism and Lyrical Exoticism in Xu Xu's Early Travel Writings', *Modern Chinese Literature and Culture*, 23(2) (2011): 64–99.

Green, Frederik H., 'Rescuing Love from the Nation: Love, Nation, and Self in Xu Xu's Alternative Wartime Fiction and Drama', *Frontiers of Literary Studies in China*, 8(1) (2014): 126–53.

Gui Wenya 桂文亞, 'Xu Xu lai Tai xiaozhu', 徐訏來臺小住 ('Xu Xu Visits Taiwan'), in Chen Naixin 陳乃欣 et al. (eds), *Xu Xu er san shi* 徐訏二三事 (*A Few Things about Xu Xu*), Taipei: Erya chubanshe 爾雅出版社, 1980.

Gunn, Edward, *Unwelcome Muse: Chinese Literature in Shanghai and Peking 1937–1945*, New York: Columbia University Press, 1980.

Hockx, Michel (ed.), 'Introduction', in *The Literary Field of Twentieth-century China*, Richmond: Curzon Press, 1999.

Hockx, Michel, *Questions of Style: Literary Societies and Literary Journals in Modern China, 1911–1937*, Leiden: Brill, 2003.

Hockx, Michel, 'Theory as Practice: Modern Chinese Literature and Bourdieu', in Michel Hockx and Ivo Smits (eds), *Reading East Asian Writing: The Limits of Literary Theory*, London: RoutledgeCurzon, 2003.

Holm, David, *Art and Ideology in Revolutionary China*, Oxford: Oxford University Press, 1991.

Hsia, C. T., *A History of Modern Chinese Fiction*, New Haven, CT: Yale University Press, 1971.

Hsia, Tsi-an, *The Gate of Darkness: Studies on the Leftist Literary Movement in China*, Seattle, WA: Washington University Press, 1971.

Hsu Yu (Xu Xu), *Bird Talk* 鳥語, trans. Lin Yutang, Hong Kong: Nantian shuye, 1971?.

Huang, Nicole, *Women, War, and Domesticity: Shanghai Literature and Popular Culture of the 1940s*, Leiden: Brill, 2005.

Huang Wei 黃炜, 'Guicai Xu Xu', 鬼才徐訏 ('The Literary Genius Xu Xu'), *Xin wenxue shiliao* 新文學史料, 4 (1996): 119–26.

Hung, Chang-tai, *War and Popular Culture: Resistance in Modern China, 1937–1945*, Berkeley, CA: University of California Press, 1994.

Huters, Theodore, 'In Search of Qian Zhongshu', *Modern Chinese Literature and Culture*, 11(1) (1999): 193–9.

Huters, Theodore, *Qian Zhongshu*, Boston, MA: Twayne, 1982.

Idema, Wilt and Lloyd Haft, *A Guide to Chinese Literature*, Ann Arbor, MI: Center for Chinese Studies, University of Michigan, 1997.

Jiang Shuxian 蔣淑嫻 and Yin Jian 殷鉴, *Zhongguo xiandai wenxue shi* 中國現代文學史 (*History of Modern Chinese Literature*), Beijing: Kexue chubanshe 科學出版社, 2002.

Jin Yi 靳以, *Zhongshen* 眾神 (*The Gods*), Hong Kong: Xinyi chubanshe 新藝出版社, 1958.

Kinkley, Jeffrey C., *Chinese Justice, the Fiction: Law and Literature in Modern China*, Stanford, CA: Stanford University Press, 2000.

Kodansha Encyclopedia of Japan, 9 vols., Tokyo: Kodansha, 1983.

Kong Fanjin 孔范今 and Pan Xueqing 潘學清 (eds), *Zhongguo xiandai wenxue buyi shuxi* 中國現代文學補遺書系 (*Supplemental Series to Modern Chinese Literature*), Jinan: Mingtian chubanshe 明天出版社, 1991.

Kong Qingdong 孔慶東, 'Guotongqu de tongsu xiaoshuo', 國統區的通俗小說 ('Popular Fiction in the Hinterland'), *Fuling shi zhuanxuebao* 涪陵師專學報, 16(1) (2000): 2–16.

Kubin, Wolfgang (ed.), *Die Chinesische Literatur im 20. Jahrhundert*, Geschichte der chinesischen Literatur, vol. 7, Munich: K. G. Saur, 2005.

Lao She 老舍, *Maocheng ji* 貓城記 (*Cat City*), Hong Kong: Huitong shudian 會通書店, 1976.

Laughlin, Charles A., *Chinese Reportage: The Aesthetics of Historical Experience*, Durham, NC: Duke University Press, 2002.

Laughlin, Charles A., 'The All-China Resistance Association of Writers and Artists', in Michel Hockx and Kirk A. Denton (eds), *Literary Societies of Republican China*, Lanham, MD: Lexington Books, 2008, p. 379.

Lee, Gregory B., *Troubadours, Trumpeters, Troubled Makers: Lyricism, Nationalism, and Hybridity in China and its Others*, London: Hurst, 1996.

Lee, Leo Ou-fan, 'Literary Trends: The Road to Revolution 1927–1949', in John K. Fairbank and Albert Feuerwerker (eds), *The Cambridge History of China*, vol. 13, Cambridge: Cambridge University Press, 1986.

Lee, Leo Ou-fan, *Shanghai Modern: The Flowering of a New Urban Culture in China, 1930–1945*, Cambridge, MA: Harvard University Press, 1999.

Li Huibin 李惠彬, 'Lüe tan Shi Zhecun xiaoshuo chuangzuo de yishu jilei yu zhunbei', 略談施蟄存小說創作的藝術積累與準備 ('A Brief Talk on the Artistic Accumulation and Preparation for Shi Zhecun's Creative Work'), *Zhongguo xiandai wenxue yanjiu congkan* 中國現代文學研究叢刊, 1 (1994): 286–90.

Li Junguo 李俊國, *Zhongguo xiandai dushi xiaoshuo yanjiu* 中國現代都市小說研究 (*A Study of Modern Chinese Urban Fiction*), Beijing: Zhongguo shehui kexue chubanshe 中國社會科學出版社, 2004.

Li Oufan 李歐梵 (Leo Ou-fan Lee), *Xiandaixing de zhuiqiu: Li Oufan wenhua pinglun jingxuan ji* 現代性的追求: 李歐梵文化評論精選集 (*Pursuit of the Modern: Selected Cultural Critiques by Li Oufan*), Taipei: Maitian chuban gufen youxian gongsi 麥田出版股份有限公司, 1996.

Li Wei 李偉, *Shenmi de Wumingshi* 神秘的無名氏 (*The Mysterious Wumingshi*), Shanghai: Shanghai shudian chubanshe 上海書店出版社, 1998.

Li Yeping 李掖平 (ed.), *Xiandai Zhongguo wenxue zuopin daodu 1900–1949* 現代中國文學作品導讀 1900–1949 (*A Guide to Reading Modern Chinese Literary Works, 1900–1949*), Jinan: Shandong huabao chubanshe 山東畫報出版社, 2002.

Link, Perry, *Mandarin Ducks and Butterflies: Popular Fiction in Early Twentieth-Century Chinese Cities*, Berkeley, CA: University of California Press, 1981.

Liu Guangyu 劉光宇, 'Cong Wumingshi xiaoshuo de rensheng zhexue mingti kan 40 niandai Zhongguo xiandai zhuyi xiaoshuo zhuti de bianxin', 從無名氏小說的人生哲學命題看 40 年代中國現代主意小說主題的變新 ('A Look at Changes in the Themes of 1940s Modernist Fiction from the Perspective of Wumingshi's Position on the

Philosophy of Life in his Fiction'), *Shandong shida xuebao (shehui kexue bao)* 山東師大學報(社會科學報), 4 (1995): 91–4.

Liu Hua 劉華, 'Luanshi qiju zhong de zhexue ganwu: Xu Xu xiaoshuo pian lun', 亂世棲居中的哲學感悟: 徐訏小說片論 ('Philosophic Understanding Gained from Living in Troubled Times: On Xu Xu's Fiction'), *Jinzhou shifan xueyuan xuebao* 錦州示範學院學報, 21(3) (1999): 67–72.

Liu Jianmei, *Revolution Plus Love: Literary History, Women's Bodies, and Thematic Repetition in Twentieth-Century Chinese Fiction*, Honolulu, HI: University of Hawai'i Press, 2003.

Liu Ts'un yan (ed.), *Chinese Middlebrow Fiction from the Ch'ing and Early Republican Eras*, Hong Kong: Chinese University Press, 1984.

Lou Shiyi 樓適夷, 'Shi Zhecun de xin ganjue zhuyi: Du "Zai Bali daxi yuan" yu "Modao" zhi hou', 施蟄存的新感覺主義: 讀《在巴黎大戲院》與《魔道》之後 ('The New Sensationism of Shi Zhecun: On Reading "In the Paris Cinema" and "Demon's Way"'), in Ying Guojing 應國靖 (ed.), *Zhongguo xiandai zuojia xuanji: Shi Zhecun* 中國現代作家選集: 施蟄存 (*Selections of Modern Chinese Authors: Shi Zhecun*), Hong Kong: Sanlian shudian youxian gongsi 三聯書店有限公司, 1988.

Louie, Kam (ed.), *Eileen Chang: Romancing Languages, Cultures, and Genres*, Hong Kong: Hong Kong University Press, 2012.

Lü Qingfu 呂清夫, 'Xu Xu de huihua yinyuan', 徐訏的繪畫姻緣 ('Xu Xu's Affair with Painting'), in Chen Naixin 陳乃欣 et al. (eds), *Xu Xu er san shi* 徐訏二三事 (*A Few Things about Xu Xu*), Taipei: Erya chubanshe 爾雅出版社, 1980.

Lu Xun 魯迅, *Lu Xun quanji* 魯迅全集 (*The Complete Works of Lu Xun*), Beijing: Renmin wenxue chubanshe, 1981.

Ma Yixin 馬以鑫, *Zhongguo xiandai wenxue jieshou shi* 中國現代文學接受史 (*A History of the Reception of Modern Chinese Literature*), Shanghai: Huadong shifan daxue chubanshe 華東師範大學出版社, 1998.

Malssen, Hubertus van, 'Redefining Xia: Reality and Fiction in Wang Dulu's Crane-Iron Series, 1938–1944', PhD dissertation, Manchester University, 2013.

Mao Dun 茅盾, 'Literature and Art for the Masses and the Use of Traditional Forms', trans. Yu-shih Chen, in Kirk A. Denton (ed.), *Modern Chinese Literary Thought: Writings on Literature, 1893–1945*, Stanford, CA: Stanford University Press, 1996.

McClellan, T. M., 'Change and Continuity in the Fiction of Zhang Henshui (1895–1967): From Oneiric Romanticism to Nightmare Realism', *Modern Chinese Literature*, 10 (1998): 113–34.

McClellan, T. M., *Zhang Henshui and Popular Chinese Fiction, 1919–1949*, Lewiston, NY: Edwin Mellen, 2005.

McDougall, Bonnie S. and Kam Louie, *The Literature of China in the Twentieth Century*, London: Hurst, 1997.

Mr Anonymous (Wumingshi 無名氏), *The Scourge of the Sea: A True Account of My Experiences in the Hsia-sa Village Concentration Camp*, trans. unknown, Taipei: Kuang Lu, 1985.

Mu Shiying (穆時英), 'Five in a Nightclub', trans. Randolph Trumbull, *Renditions*, 37 (1992): 5–22.

Mu Shiying 穆時英, 'Bei dangzuo xiaoqianpin de nanzi', 被當做消遣品的男子 ('The Man Who Was Made a Plaything'), in Yue Qi 樂齊 (ed.), *Zhongguo xin ganjue pai shengshou: Mu Shiying xiaoshuo quanji* 中國新感覺派聖手: 穆時英小說全集 (*The Chinese Master of New Sensationism: The Complete Fiction of Mu Shiying*), Beijing: Zhongguo wenlian chuban gongsi 中國文聯出版公司, 1996, pp. 151–76.

Mu Shiying 穆時英, 'Hei mudan', 黑牡丹 ('Black Peony'), in Yue Qi 樂齊 (ed.), *Zhongguo xin ganjue pai shengshou: Mu Shiying xiaoshuo quanji* 中國新感覺派聖手: 穆時英小說全集 (*The Chinese Master of New Sensationism: The Complete Fiction of Mu Shiying*), Beijing: Zhongguo wenlian chuban gongsi 中國文聯出版公司, 1996, pp. 260–9.

Mu Shiying 穆時英, 'Shanghai de hubuwu', 上海的狐步舞 ('Shanghai Foxtrot'), in Yue Qi 樂齊 (ed.), *Zhongguo xin ganjue pai shengshou: Mu Shiying xiaoshuo quanji* 中國新感覺派聖手: 穆時英小說全集 (*The Chinese Master of New Sensationism: The Complete Fiction of Mu Shiying*), Beijing: Zhongguo wenlian chuban gongsi 中國文聯出版公司, 1996.

Mu Shiying 穆時英, 'Ye', 夜 ('Night'), in Yue Qi 樂齊(ed.), *Zhongguo xin ganjue pai shengshou: Mu Shiying xiaoshuo quanji* 中國新感覺派聖手: 穆時英小說全集 (*The Chinese Master of New Sensationism: The Complete Fiction of Mu Shiying*), Beijing: Zhongguo wenlian chuban gongsi 中國文聯出版公司, 1996, pp. 241–48.

Ng Mau-sang, 'Popular Fiction and the Culture of Everyday Life: A Cultural Analysis of Qin Shou'ou's *Qiuhaitang*', *Modern China*, 20(2) (1994): 131–56.

Ng Mau-sang, 'A Common People's Literature', *East Asian History*, 9 (1995): 20.

Ning, Pu (Wumingshi 無名氏), *Red in Tooth and Claw: Twenty-Six Years in Communist Chinese Prisons*, trans. Tung Chung-hsuan, New York: Grove Press, 1994.

Otsuka, Yutaka, 'Japan's Involvement with Higher Education in Manchuria: Some Historical Lessons from an Imposed Educational Cooperation', in Glen Peterson, Ruth Hayhoe and Yongling Lu (eds), *Education, Culture and Identity in Twentieth-century China*, Ann Arbor, MI: University of Michigan Press, 2001.

Ping Jinya 平襟亞 (Qiu Weng 秋翁), 'Kongfuzi de kumen', 孔夫子的苦悶 ('Confucius' Concern'), *Wanxiang* 萬象, 1(1) (1941): 54–7.

Pu Songling 蒲松齡, *Strange Tales from the Liaozhai Studio*, trans. Zhang Qingnian et al., 4 vols, Beijing: People's China Publishing House, 1997.

Qian Liqun, 'An Overview of Chinese Theories of Fiction from the 1940s', trans. Steven P. Day, *Modern Chinese Literature*, 9 (1995): 59–78.

Qian Suoqiao, *Liberal Cosmopolitan: Lin Yutang and Middling Chinese Modernity*, Leiden: Brill, 2011.

Qin Xianci 秦賢次, '*Jianghu xing* jin *Feng xiaoxiao*', 江湖行盡風蕭蕭 ('*Characters in Society* and *The Rustling Wind*'), in Chen Naixin 陳乃欣 et al. (eds), *Xu Xu er san shi* 徐訏二三事 (*A Few Things about Xu Xu*), Taipei: Erya chubanshe 爾雅出版社, 1980.

Riep, Steven L., 'Chinese Modernism: The New Sensationists', in Joshua Mostow (ed.), *The Columbia Companion to Modern East Asian Literature*, New York: Columbia University Press, 2003.

Rojas, Carlos, 'Introduction: The Disease of Canonicity', in Carlos Rojas and Eileen

Cheng-yin Chow (eds), *Rethinking Chinese Popular Culture: Cannibalizations of the Canon*, London: Routledge, 2009, p. 1.

Rosenmeier, Christopher, 'Women Stereotypes in Shi Zhecun's Short Stories', *Modern China*, 37(1) (2011): 44–68.

Rosenmeier, Christopher, 'The Subversion of Modernity and Socialism in Mu Shiying's Early Fiction', *Frontiers of Literary Studies in China*, 7(1) (2013): 1–22.

Sang, Deborah Tze-lan, 'The Transgender Body in Wang Dulu's Crouching Tiger, Hidden Dragon', in Larissa Heinrich and Fran Martin (eds), *Modernity Incarnate: Refiguring Chinese Body Politics*, Honolulu, HI: University of Hawaii Press, 2006, pp. 98–112.

Schaefer, William, 'Kumarajiva's Foreign Tongue: Shi Zhecun's Modernist Historical Fiction', *Modern Chinese Literature*, 10(1/2) (1998): 25–69.

Schaefer, William, 'Relics of Iconoclasm: Modernism, Shi Zhecun, and Shanghai's Margins', PhD dissertation, University of Chicago, 2000.

Shennü 神女 (*The Goddess*), director Wu Yonggang 吳永剛, Shanghai: Lianhua yingye gongsi 聯華影業公司, 1934.

Shi Zhecun 施蟄存, 'Bomu de wunü', 薄暮的舞女 ('The Twilight Taxi Dancer'), in *Shi Zhecun wenji: Shi nian chuangzuo ji* 施蟄存文集: 十年創作集 (*The Works of Shi Zhecun: Ten Years of Creative Writing*), Shanghai: Huadong shifan daxue chubanshe 華東師範大學出版社, 1996.

Shi Zhecun 施蟄存, 'Chun geng', 蓴羹 ('Water Shield Soup'), in *Shi Zhecun wenji: Shi nian chuangzuo ji* 施蟄存文集: 十年創作集 (*The Works of Shi Zhecun: Ten Years of Creative Writing*), Shanghai: Huadong shifan daxue chubanshe 華東師範大學出版社, 1996.

Shi Zhecun 施蟄存, 'Hongzhi fashi de chujia', 宏智法師的出家 ('How Master Hongzhi Became a Monk'), in *Shi Zhecun wenji: Shi nian chuangzuo ji* 施蟄存文集: 十年創作集 (*The Works of Shi Zhecun: Ten Years of Creative Writing*), Shanghai: Huadong shifan daxue chubanshe 華東師範大學出版社, 1996, pp. 101–7.

Shi Zhecun 施蟄存, 'Jiangjun de tou', 將軍的頭 ('The General's Head'), in *Shi Zhecun wenji: Shi nian chuangzuo ji* 施蟄存文集: 十年創作集 (*The Works of Shi Zhecun: Ten Years of Creative Writing*), Shanghai: Huadong shifan daxue chubanshe 華東師範大學出版社, 1996, pp. 111–243.

Shi Zhecun 施蟄存, 'Jiumoluoshi', 鳩摩羅什 ('Kumarajiva'), in *Shi Zhecun wenji: Shi nian chuangzuo ji* 施蟄存文集: 十年創作集 (*The Works of Shi Zhecun: Ten Years of Creative Writing*), Shanghai: Huadong shifan daxue chubanshe 華東師範大學出版社, 1996, pp. 111–38.

Shi Zhecun 施蟄存, 'Lüshe', 旅舍 ('The Inn'), in *Shi Zhecun wenji: Shi nian chuangzuo ji* 施蟄存文集: 十年創作集 (*The Works of Shi Zhecun: Ten Years of Creative Writing*), Shanghai: Huadong shifan daxue chubanshe 華東師範大學出版社, 1996.

Shi Zhecun 施蟄存, 'Meiyu zhi xi', 梅雨之夕 ('An Evening of Spring Rain'), in *Shi Zhecun wenji: Shi nian chuangzuo ji* 施蟄存文集: 十年創作集 (*The Works of Shi Zhecun: Ten Years of Creative Writing*), Shanghai: Huadong shifan daxue chubanshe 華東師範大學出版社, 1996.

Shi Zhecun 施蟄存, 'Modao', 魔道 ('Sorcery'), in *Shi Zhecun wenji: Shi nian chuangzuo ji* 施蟄存文集: 十年創作集 (*The Works of Shi Zhecun: Ten Years of Creative Writing*), Shanghai: Huadong shifan daxue chubanshe 華東師範大學出版社, 1996.

Shi Zhecun (施蟄存), *One Rainy Evening*, trans. Wang Ying, Paul White and Rosemary Roberts. Beijing: Panda Books, 1994.

Shi Zhecun 施蟄存, '*Shangyuan deng* chuban zixu', 《上元燈》初版自序 ('Preface to the 1st edition of *Spring Festival Lamp*'), in *Shi Zhecun wenji: Shi nian chuangzuo ji* 施蟄存文集: 十年創作集 (*The Works of Shi Zhecun: Ten Years of Creative Writing*), Shanghai: Huadong shifan daxue chubanshe 華東師範大學出版社, 1996.

Shi Zhecun 施蟄存, 'Shangyuan deng', 上元燈 ('Spring Festival Lamp'), in *Shi Zhecun wenji: Shi nian chuangzuo ji* 施蟄存文集: 十年創作集 (*The Works of Shi Zhecun: Ten Years of Creative Writing*), Shanghai: Huadong shifan daxue chubanshe 華東師範大學出版社, 1996, pp. 14–20.

Shi Zhecun 施蟄存, 'Shi Xiu', 石秀, in *Shi Zhecun wenji: Shi nian chuangzuo ji* 施蟄存文集: 十年創作集 (*The Works of Shi Zhecun: Ten Years of Creative Writing*), Shanghai. Huadong shifan daxue chubanshe 華東師範大學出版社, 1996, pp. 172–211.

Shi Zhecun 施蟄存, 'Wu', 霧 ('Fog'), in *Shi Zhecun wenji: Shi nian chuangzuo ji* 施蟄存文集: 十年創作集 (*The Works of Shi Zhecun: Ten Years of Creative Writing*), Shanghai: Huadong shifan daxue chubanshe 華東師範大學出版社, 1996.

Shi Zhecun 施蟄存, 'Xiongzhai', 凶宅 ('The Haunted House'), in *Shi Zhecun wenji: Shi nian chuangzuo ji* 施蟄存文集: 十年創作集 (*The Works of Shi Zhecun: Ten Years of Creative Writing*), Shanghai: Huadong shifan daxue chubanshe 華東師範大學出版社, 1996, pp. 356–79.

Shi Zhecun 施蟄存, 'Yecha', 夜叉 ('Yaksha'), in *Shi Zhecun wenji: Shi nian chuangzuo ji* 施蟄存文集: 十年創作集 (*The Works of Shi Zhecun: Ten Years of Creative Writing*), Shanghai: Huadong shifan daxue chubanshe 華東師範大學出版社, 1996, pp. 327–40.

Shi Zhecun 施蟄存, 'Zatan *Jin Ping Mei*', 雜談金瓶美 ('Rambling on *Jin Ping Mei*'), in Tang Wenyi 唐文一 and Liu Pin 劉屏 (eds), *Wangshi suixiang* 往事隨想 (*Random Thoughts on Past Events*), Chengdu: Sichuan renmin chubanshe 四川人民出版社, 2000.

Shih, Shu-mei, *The Lure of the Modern: Writing Modernism in Semicolonial China, 1917–1937*, Berkeley, CA: University of California Press, 2001.

Shu, Yunzhong, *Buglers on the Home Front: The Wartime Practice of the Qiyue School*, Albany, NY: State University of New York Press, 2000.

Sima Zhongyuan 司馬中原, 'Chuntian de huahuan', 春天的花環 ('Flower Wreaths of Spring'), in Chen Naixin 陳乃欣 et al. (eds), *Xu Xu er san shi* 徐訏二三事 (*A Few Things about Xu Xu*), Taipei: Erya chubanshe 爾雅出版社, 1980, p. 179.

Smith, Norman, *Resisting Manchukuo: Chinese Women Writers and the Japanese Occupation*, Vancouver: UBC Press, 2007.

Song Jianhua 宋劍華, 'Shengcun de tansuo yu yishu de xuanze: Lun Wumingshi yu Xu Xu de xiaoshuo chuangzuo', 生存的探索與藝術的選擇: 論無名氏與徐訏的小說創作 ('Explorations of Existence and Artistic Choice: On the Fiction of Wumingshi and Xu Xu'), *Hebei xuekan* 河北學刊, 3 (1995): 58–63.

Tam, King-Fai, 'The Detective Fiction of Ch'eng Hsiao-ch'ing', *Asia Major*, 5(1) (1992): 113–32.

Tan Chuliang 譚楚良, *Zhongguo xiandaipai wenxue shilun* 中國現代派文學史論 (*On the

History of Chinese Modernist Literature), Shanghai: Xuelin chubanshe 學林出版社, 1997.

Tang Yuan 唐沅 et al. (eds), *Zhongguo xiandai wenque qikan mulu huibian* 中國現代文學期刊目錄彙編 (*Compilation of Tables of Contents of Journals in Modern Chinese Literature*), Tianjin: Tianjin renmin chubanshe 天津人民出版社, 1988.

Tang Zhesheng 湯哲聲, 'Lun 40 niandai de liuxing xiaoshuo: yi Xu Xu, Wumingshi (Bu Naifu), Zhang Ailing, Su Qing de xiaoshuo weili', 論40 年代的流行小說: 以徐訏、無名氏(卜乃夫)、張愛玲、蘇青的小說為例 ('On the Popular Fiction of the 1940s: Using the Fiction of Xu Xu, Wumingshi (Bu Naifu), Zhang Ailing, and Su Qing as Examples'), *Huadong chuanbo gongye xueyuan xuebao* 華東船舶工業學院學報 4(2) (June 2004): 1–6.

Wang, David Der-wei, 'Popular Literature and National Representation: The Gender and Genre Politics of *Begonia*', in Carlos Rojas and Eileen Cheng-yin Chow (eds), *Rethinking Chinese Popular Culture: Cannibalizations of the Canon*, London: Routledge, 2009.

Wang Ling 汪凌, 'Wentan de dubuwu: Wumingshi lun', 文坛的独步舞: 無名氏論 ('A Solitary Dancer in the Literary Field: on Wumingshi'), in Chen Sihe 陳思和 et al. (eds), *Wuming shidai de wenxue piping* 無名時代的文學批評 (*Literary Criticism in Non-name Period* (English title on cover)), Guilin: Guangxi shifan daxue chubanshe 廣西師範大學出版社, 2004.

Wang Qinghua 王慶華, 'Zuowei gushijia de Xu Xu: cong *Gui lian* dao *Feng xiaoxiao*', 作為故事家的徐訏 – 從《鬼戀》到《風蕭蕭》 ('The Storyteller Xu Xu: from *Ghostly Love* to *The Rustling Wind*'), *Nanjing shida xuebao* 南京師大學報, 4 (1994): 99–102.

Wang Wenying 王文英, *Shanghai xiandai wenxueshi* 上海現代文學史 (*The History of Modern Shanghai Literature*), Shanghai: Shanghai renmin chubanshe 上海人民出版社, 1999.

Wang Xiaoping, 'An Alienated Mind Dreaming for Integration: Constrained Cosmopolitanism in Wumingshi's "Modern Literati Novel"', *Journal of Australasian Popular Culture*, 2(3) (2012): 425–38.

Wang Yingguo 汪應果 and Zhao Jiangbin 趙江濱, *Wumingshi chuanqi* 無名氏傳奇 (*The Legend of Wumingshi*), Shanghai: Shanghai wenyi chubanshe 上海文藝出版社, 1998.

Widmer, Ellen, 'The Rhetoric of Retrospection: May Fourth Literary History and the Ming-Qing Woman Writer', in Milena Doleželová-Velingerová and Oldřich Král (eds), *The Appropriation of Cultural Capital: China's May Fourth Project*, Cambridge, MA: Harvard University Press, 2001, pp. 193–225.

Wong, Wang-chi, *Politics and Literature in Shanghai: The Chinese League of Left-wing Writers, 1930–1936*, Manchester: Manchester University Press, 1991.

Wu Daoyi 吳道毅, 'Xu Xu, Wumingshi xiaoshuo chuanqi tezheng lun', 徐訏、無名氏小說傳奇特徵論 ('On the *chuanqi* Characteristics of the Fiction by Xu Xu and Wumingshi'), *Wuhan daxue xuebao* 武漢大學學報, 53(6) (2000): 864–9.

Wu Fuhui 吳福輝, 'Zuowei wenxue (shangpin) shengchan de haipai qikan', 作為文學(商品)生產的海派期刊 ('Shanghai School Journals as Literary (Commodity) Productions'), *Zhongguo xiandai wenxue yanjiu congkan* 中國現代文學研究叢刊, 1 (1994): 1–15.

Wu Fuhui 吳福輝, *Dushi xuanliu zhong de haipai xiaoshuo* 都市旋流中的海派小說 (*Shanghai School Fiction in the Urban Maelstrom*), Changsha: Hunan jiaoyu chubanshe 湖南教育出版社, 1995.

Wu Lichang吳立昌, 'Preface', in Wu Lichang (ed.), *Shi Zhecun: Xinli xiaoshuo*施蟄存: 心理小說 (*Shi Zhecun: Psychological Short Stories*), Shanghai: Shanghai wenyi chubanshe 上海文藝出版社, 1992.

Wu, Yenna, 'Expressing the "Inexpressible": Pain and Suffering in Wumingshi's Hongsha', in Philip F. Williams and Yenna Wu (eds), *Remolding and Resistance Among Writers of the Chinese Prison Camp: Disciplined and Published*, Abingdon: Routledge, 2006, pp. 122–56.

Wu Yiqin 吳義勤 and Wang Suxia 王素霞, *Wo xin panghuang: Xu Xu zhuan* 我心彷徨: 徐訏傳 (*My Wavering Heart: A Biography of Xu Xu*), Shanghai: Shanghai sanlian shudian 上海三聯書店, 2012.

Wumingshi 無名氏, *Beiji fengqing hua*北極風情畫 (*North Pole Landscape Painting*), Shanghai: Wuming shuwu無名書屋, 1944.

Wumingshi 無名氏, 'Haibian de gushi', 海邊的故事 ('A Story from the Seaside'), in Kong Fanjin 孔范今 and Pan Xueqing 潘學清(eds), *Zhongguo xiandai wenxue buyi shuxi* 中國現代文學補遺書系 (*Supplemental Series to Modern Chinese Literature*), vol. 4, Jinan: Mingtian chubanshe 明天出版社, 1991.

Wumingshi 無名氏, 'Hong mo', 紅魔 ('Red Demons'), in Kong Fanjin 孔范今 and Pan Xueqing 潘學清 (eds), *Zhongguo xiandai wenxue buyi shuxi* 中國現代文學補遺書系 (*Supplemental Series to Modern Chinese Literature*), vol. 4, Jinan: Mingtian chubanshe 明天出版社, 1991.

Wumingshi 無名氏, 'Luxiya zhi lian', 露西亞之戀 ('Love of Russia'), in Kong Fanjin 孔范今 and Pan Xueqing 潘學清(eds), *Zhongguo xiandai wenxue buyi shuxi* 中國現代文學補遺書系 (*Supplemental Series to Modern Chinese Literature*), vol. 4, Jinan: Mingtian chubanshe 明天出版社, 1991.

Wumingshi 無名氏, *Jinse de she ye* 金色的蛇夜 (*Golden Snake Nights*), 2 vols, Shanghai: Shanghai wenyi chubanshe上海文藝出版社, 2001.

Wumingshi 無名氏, 'Postscript', in *Tali de nüren* 塔裡的女人 (*The Woman in the Tower*), 6th edn, Shanghai: Shanghai wenyi chubanshe 上海文藝出版社, 2001.

Wumingshi 無名氏, *Tali de nüren* 塔裡的女人 (*The Woman in the Tower*), Hong Kong: Xinwen tiandishe 新聞天地社, 1979.

Wumingshi 無名氏, *Yeshou, yeshou, yeshou*野獸, 野獸, 野獸 (*Beast, Beast, Beast*), Shanghai: Wuming shuwu 無名書屋, 1946.

Wumingshi無名氏, *Yi bai wan nian yiqian* 一百萬年以前 (*A Million Years Ago*), Hong Kong: Xinwen tiandi she 新聞天地社, 1977.

Xin Dai 心岱, 'Taipei guoke', 臺北過客 ('Visiting Taipei'), in Chen Naixin 陳乃欣 et al. (eds), *Xu Xu er san shi* 徐訏二三事 (*A Few Things about Xu Xu*), Taipei: Erya chubanshe 爾雅出版社, 1980, p. 38.

Xu Xu 徐訏, 'Alabohai de nüshen', 阿拉伯海的女神 ('The Spirit of the Arabian Sea'), in Kong Fanjin 孔范今 and Pan Xueqing 潘學清 (eds), *Zhongguo xiandai wenxue buyi shuxi* 中國現代文學補遺書系 (*Supplemental Series to Modern Chinese Literature*), vol. 4, Jinan: Mingtian chubanshe 明天出版社, 1991.

Xu Xu 徐訏, 'Benzhi', 本質 ('Essence'), *Xiandai* 現代, 4(2) (1934): 403–19.

Xu Xu 徐訏, 'Daode yaoqiu yu daode biaozhun', 道德要求與道德標準 ('Moral Demands and Moral Standards'), in Chen Naixin 陳乃欣 et al. (eds), *Xu Xu er san shi* 徐訏二三事 (*A Few Things about Xu Xu*), Taipei: Erya chubanshe 爾雅出版社, 1980.

Xu Xu 徐訏, 'Dukuli de huahun', 賭窟裏的花魂 ('The Flower Spirit of the Gambling Den'), in *Yanquan* 煙圈 (*Smoke Rings*), Shanghai: Yechuang shuwu 夜窗書屋, 1946.

Xu Xu 徐訏, '*Feng xiaoxiao*', 風蕭蕭 ('The Rustling Wind'), in Kong Fanjin 孔范今 and Pan Xueqing 潘學清 (eds), *Zhongguo xiandai wenxue buyi shuxi* 中國現代文學補遺書系 (*Supplemental Series to Modern Chinese Literature*), vol. 6, Jinan: Mingtian chubanshe 明天出版社, 1990.

Xu Xu 徐訏, *Gui lian* 鬼戀 (*Ghostly Love*), in Kong Fanjin 孔范今 and Pan Xueqing 潘學清 (eds), *Zhongguo xiandai wenxue buyi shuxi* 中國現代文學補遺書系 (*Supplemental Series to Modern Chinese Literature*), vol. 4, Jinan: Mingtian chubanshe 明天出版社, 1991.

Xu Xu 徐訏, *Huang-miu de Ying-Fa haixia* 荒謬的英法海峽 (*The Absurd English Channel*), Shanghai: Yechuang shuwu 爺窗書屋, 1946.

Xu Xu 徐訏, *Jibusai de youhuo* 吉布賽的誘惑 (*The Gypsy's Seduction*), Shanghai: Yechuang shuwu 爺窗書屋, 1940.

Xu Xu 徐訏, *Jingshenbing huanzhe de beige*, 精神病患者的悲歌 (*The Lament of the Mental Patient*), in Kong Fanjin 孔范今 and Pan Xueqing 潘學清 (eds), *Zhongguo xiandai wenxue buyi shuxi* 中國現代文學補遺書系 (*Supplemental Series to Modern Chinese Literature*), vol. 4, Jinan: Mingtian chubanshe 明天出版社, 1991.

Xu Xu 徐訏, 'Jinguo', 禁果 ('Forbidden Fruit'), *Xiandai* 現代, 5(3) (1935): 514–24.

Xu Xu 徐訏, 'Qifen yishu de tiancai', 氣氛藝術的天才 ('The Master of the Art of Smelling'), in *Yanquan* 煙圈 (*Smoke Rings*), Shanghai: Yechuang shuwu 夜窗書屋, 1946.

Xu Xu 徐訏, *Xu Xu quanji* 徐訏全集 (*The Complete Works of Xu Xu*), 15 vols., Taipei: Zhengzhong shuju 正中書局, 1973.

Xu Xu 徐訏, 'Yanquan', 煙圈 ('Smoke Rings'), in *Yanquan* 煙圈 (*Smoke Rings*), Shanghai: Yechuang shuwu 夜窗書屋, 1946.

Xu Xu 徐訏, 'Youtai de huixing', 猶太的彗星 ('The Jewish Comet'), in *Yanquan* 煙圈 (*Smoke Rings*), Shanghai: Yechuang shuwu 夜窗書屋, 1946.

Yan Jiayan 嚴家炎, *Lun xiandai xiaoshuo yu wenyi sichao* 論現代小說與文藝思潮 (*On Modern Fiction and Trends in Literary Thought*), Hunan: Hunan renmin chubanshe 湖南人民出版社, 1987.

Yan Jiayan 嚴家炎, 'Lun xinganjuepai xiaoshuo', 論新感覺派小說 ('On New Sensationist Fiction'), in Yan Jiayan et al. (eds), *Zhongguo xiandai wenxue lunwen ji* 中國現代文學論文集 (*Essays on Modern Chinese Literature*), Beijing: Beijing daxue chubanshe 北京大學出版社, 1986.

Yan Jiayan 嚴家炎, *Zhongguo xiandai xiaoshuo liupai shi* 中國現代小說流派史 (*A History of Schools in Modern Chinese Fiction*), Beijing: Renmin wenxue chubanshe 人民文學出版社, 1989.

Yang Yi 楊義, *Jingpai haipai zonglun (tu zhi ben)* 京派海派总论 (图志本) (*An Overview of Beijing and Shanghai Schools*, illustrated edition), Beijing: Zhongguo shehui kexue chubanshe 中國社會科學出版社, 2003.

Yang Yi 楊義, 'Lun haipai xiaoshuo', 論海派小說 ('On Shanghai School Fiction'), *Zhongguo xiandai wenxue yanjiu congkan* 中國現代文學研究叢刊, 2 (1991): 167–81.

Yeh, Michelle, 'Chinese Literature from 1937 to the Present', in Kang-I Sun Chang and Stephen Owen (eds), *The Cambridge History of Chinese Literature*, vol. 2, Cambridge: Cambridge University Press, 2010.

Yu Qie 予且, *Qianshui guniang* 淺水姑娘 (*Miss Stranded*), ed. Wu Fuhui 吳福輝, Beijing: Huaxia chubanshe 華夏出版社, 2011.

Zhang Ailing 張愛玲, *Love in a Fallen City*, trans. Karen S. Kingsbury, New York: New York Review Books, 2007.

Zhang Henshui 張恨水, *Shanghai Express*, trans. William A. Lyell, Honolulu, HI: University of Hawai'i Press, 1997.

Zhang, Yingjin, *The City in Modern Chinese Literature and Film: Configuration of Space, Time, and Gender*, Stanford, CA: Stanford University Press, 1996.

Zhao Jiangbin 趙江濱, 'Yixiang "xiandai" de zuji: Wumingshi wenxue chuangzuo jianlun', 移向 '現代' 的足跡: 無名氏文學創作簡論 ('Moving Towards the "Modern": Comments on Wumingshi's Creative Writing'), *Shijie huawen wenxue luntan* 世界華文文學論壇, 4 (1999): 30–5.

Zhao Zhi 趙智, 'Lun Wumingshi de zongjiao qinghuai', 論無名氏的宗教情懷 ('On Wumingshi's Religious Feelings'), *Peixun yu yanjiu: Hubei jiaoyu xueyuan xuebao* 培訓與研究: 湖北教育學院學報, 21(3) (2004): 8–11.

Zhongguo wenxue da cidian 中國文學大辭典 (*Encyclopaedia of Chinese Literature*), 8 vols., Tianjin: Tianjin renmin chubanshe 天津人民出版社, 1991.

Zhongguo xiandai zuojia da cidian 中國現代作家大辭典 (*Encyclopaedia of Modern Chinese Authors*), Beijing: Xin shijie chubanshe 新世界出版社, 1992.

Zhou Zuoren 周作人, 'Humane Literature', in *Modern Chinese Literary Thought: Writings on Literature, 1893–1945*, ed. Kirk A. Denton, trans. Ernst Wolff, Stanford, CA: Stanford University Press, 1996.

Zhu Xi 朱曦 and Chen Xingwu 陳興蕪, *Zhongguo xiandai langman zhuyi xiaoshuo moshi* 中國現代浪漫主義小說模式 (*Modes of Modern Chinese Romantic Fiction*), Chongqing: Chongqing chubanshe 重慶出版社, 2002.

Index

Page numbers followed by 'n' indicate a note.